Dyslexia Matters

A Celebratory Contributed Volume to Honour Professor T.R. Miles

Edited by Gerald Hales, PhD
Chartered Psychologist and Research Fellow,
Institute of Educational Technology
The Open University

Whurr Publishers Ltd
London

© 1994 Whurr Publishers Ltd except for Chapter 10 © Michael Thomson
First published 1994 by
Whurr Publishers Ltd
19b Compton Terrace, London N1 2UN, England

Reprinted 1995

British Library Cataloguing in Publication Data
A catalogue record for this book is available from the
British Library.

ISBN 1-897635-11-7

Photoset by Stephen Cary
Printed and bound in the UK by Athenaeum Press Ltd,
Gateshead, Tyne & Wear

Foreword

It has given me great joy over the very many years I have had the good fortune to be associated with Professor Emeritus T. R. Miles. Tim has always been my friend and mentor, and provided support and encouragement when the going was tough and when the struggle to make dyslexia a recognised and respected concept seemed to take a long time. Tim saw his first case of dyslexia in 1949 and was able, as Professor of Psychology at the University of Wales, Bangor, to approach this with an unbiased and uninhibited mind. This was the first of many many other cases who have been seen with understanding and compassion.

In the 1960s Tim served on the Invalid Children's Aid Association Committee which was responsible for setting up the Word Blind Centre at Coram's Fields in London, and also hosting the eight founder Dyslexia Associations who launched the British Dyslexia Association.

Tim and his wife Elaine were responsible for the formation of the Dyslexia Unit at the University of Wales in Bangor. This Unit and the one at the University of Aston were the first attempts to make dyslexia academically respectable. Many teachers have taken their MEd at Bangor with a special input on dyslexia, thereby benefiting untold numbers of children. Tim is an active Vice President of the British Dyslexia Association and he has always been willing to visit local associations and share his knowledge with them.

His many publications, some written with Elaine, have provided a fund of help and information.

On travels Tim has provided a strong arm when needed and relaxation with music. Together with Elaine he has shared many joys and celebrations and provided comfort during the vicissitudes of life. Conferences, meetings and parties have always seemed brighter for his presence and I hope there will be many years of like occasions.

I am delighted and very privileged to be asked to take part in this tribute to Tim and I wish him many more years to continue doing all the things he does so well. I recently saw a quote in the magazine of

Maryland Associates for Dyslexia Adults and Youth Inc. which I am sure they will not mind me using as it is so applicable to Tim:

History occurs because men and women stir themselves to change their communities.

Marion Welchman, MBE
(the mother from Bath)

Tim Miles retired as Head of Psychology Department at the University College of North Wales, Bangor, in 1987. Because it was he who in 1963 founded the Department and was its first Psychology Chair, his retirement marked a milestone of considerable significance and regret for his colleagues. Happily though, we have not yet had to forego his company or active contribution; he and his wife, Elaine, out of their base in the Department's Dyslexia Unit, continue an output of prolific brilliance.

Tim's career has been distinguished and varied from the outset. He obtained First Class Honours in psychology and philosophy at Oxford where in 1946 he also captained the University tennis team. In addition to his valuable work on dyslexia, with which this volume is primarily concerned, his interests have been wide ranging. The titles of some of his books, other than those on dyslexia, give an indication of his diversity: *Religion and the Scientific Outlook* (1959), *Eliminating the Unconscious* (1966), *Religious Experience* (1970), *Conceptual Issues in Operant Psychology* (1978) (with P. Harzem) and *Bilingualism in Caernarfonshire* (1953). He had a much-quoted paper entitled 'On Defining Intelligence' in 1957, and he has also written on gestalt theory (*Encyclopaedia of Philosophy*) and on Gilbert Ryle (*Oxford Companion to the Mind*). The interest in gestalt theory was partly stimulated by the fact that Elaine and he were responsible for translating Albert Michotte's *La Perception de la Causalité* into English. More recently they have translated Michotte's *Les Complements Amodaux*. Tim has even published an experimental paper on skill in sport.

Those of us who have had the privilege of working with Tim in Bangor will always think of him with fondness. He is a man of famous generosity and principle and, above all, of humanity. Whoever one is, one can rely on a reception from Tim that will be open-hearted and courteous; his international reputation as a scholar affects him not one whit. There is no pomposity in a man who can fairly boast, as he does, of having played for the UCNW staff against students in no less than six sports – tennis, golf, cricket, squash, table tennis and hockey!

His knowledge of dyslexia is encyclopaedic; his colleagues in that field will attest to his stature. For those of us not involved in dyslexia, however, his contribution has been no less significant. In particular, he has done a great deal to clarify some of psychology's knottier issues. His incisive approach to conceptual analysis is one that is needed more than ever in our discipline. It is something to celebrate, then, that there is promise of still more to come from Tim; nothing is ended; all his responsiveness and curiosity are in full flow

Fergus Lowe
Professor of Psychology and Head of Department
University College of North Wales

Preface

It is an obvious statement that the majority of history is made by a minority of people. Indeed, some of the greatest developments in human history have come about because one person became so convinced that the rest of the world was wrong that the idea was pursued long after the accepted wisdom of the day suggested it should be forgotten.

The story of dyslexia is not that of a one-man crusade against all the odds, but it would not be unfair to describe it as a few-people crusade against very many of the odds. Among those few people, the name of Tim Miles must be 'writ large'. Without his efforts to introduce the idea as an academically respectable concept, his research to discover the details of how to proceed, his writings to disseminate all the knowledge he has gained, and his constant help, advice and encouragement of countless individuals, organisations and dyslexic people, the story of our learning would have been much diminished.

Dyslexia is an invisible handicap. It is not alone in that, for there are many invisible difficulties, and in many cases sufferers and their families and supporters have had to work very hard to obtain things like official recognition, help, treatment and funding. However, dyslexia is fairly unusual in that the professionals have also had to struggle to obtain those things! Many respected academics, practitioners and professional people have spent many years being told that they were chasing rainbows, investigating something that did not exist and was the figment of the imagination of the pushy parents of dim children.

This arose because for a long time people would use as evidence for this point of view the fact that there was nothing to see in dyslexia except the symptoms. At long last, that situation is beginning to change. We are now learning more and more about the differing constructions in the brains of dyslexic people, and how the construction and migration of neurons affects development. We stand on the threshold of exciting times indeed: we know *what* happens to the dyslexic person; we are now beginning to unravel *how* it happens, and slowly but surely we shall move forward towards an understanding of *why* it happens.

That, though, is for the future. This book is about the present and is compiled especially to honour the name and work of Tim Miles, who contributed so fulsomely to the past. Tim graduated with a first class honours degree from Magdalen College, Oxford, in the 1940s – in fact, he was a student in the first year of there ever being a psychology degree at Oxford. Although he did well, there was a little time for relaxation: a little known fact about Tim was that he was captain of the University tennis team and played at Wimbledon in 1946 and 1948!

Tim took up his first appointment at The University College of North Wales, Bangor, in 1949. In his early years he also did voluntary work in North Wales Child Guidance Clinics and trained as an educational psychologist. It was after this that he founded the psychology laboratory and set up an honours degree course. In 1963 he was invited to set up a Word Blind Centre in London; this was quite a year in Tim's life, for in this same year he graduated PhD and was appointed as Professor of Psychology at Bangor.

Tim did stalwart work in many areas in the cause of dyslexia, setting up the unit at Bangor and serving on the Kershaw Committee in the 1970s and the working party of the Department of Education and Science in the 1980s. He was appointed a member of the Council of the Royal Institute of Philosophy in the 1970s, has given an invited lecture at the Royal Institution and is a scientific member of the Rodin Remediation Academy. He retired from the University in 1987 and was appointed Professor Emeritus.

This book, then, is to honour Tim and all his work; but it is not *about* Tim. It is about dyslexia and dyslexic people, although many of the contributors mention Tim, his work and the effects of that work. I suspect that many of them could not avoid doing so. Tim would not want a eulogy, but something far more practical and useful. The idea of the book was the brainchild of Ved Varma. He was in contact with Tim and carried out some of the early spadework to ensure its viability. He and I discussed the project on a number of occasions, and eventually I was invited to become the Editor. I was honoured to be asked, and acknowledge here how much easier it was because of Ved's early preparation.

So, you have in your hand *Dyslexia Matters*. This is an intentionally ambiguous title, and you are welcome to take it more than one way. It contains a number of chapters, all written by eminent and highly experienced professionals in the field, aimed at everyone who has contact with dyslexia. The main works are split into five sections. Part I commences with a foray into thought-provoking territory in P. Aaron's chapter, which discusses the idea that there are many different kinds of reading disabilities and developmental dyslexia is only one of them. Gordon Stanley then reminds us that reading is a complex skill and involves many separate processes: he discusses in particular visual deficit models. Finally in this first section, Drake Duane reports on neurobiological patterns, detailing some of the many correlations between dyslexic symptoms and brain and neurological construction and function.

Part II narrows the focus, considering the specific nature of dyslexia. Here Rod Nicolson and Angela Fawcett first present the results of a study they have recently completed which they believe is the most wide-ranging analysis of the skills of dyslexic children yet performed. Then Nick Ellis reviews some of the work concerning cognitive psychological descriptions of dyslexia, a programme of research started by Tim Miles 17 years ago. Finally, Che Kan Leong looks deeply into symbol processing in less skilled readers.

In Part III we examine matters surrounding the identification of dyslexia. Peter Gardner presents a model for diagnosing dyslexia in the classroom; Tim himself considers the whole rationale for diagnosis; and Martin Turner argues the case for a psychometric approach to dyslexia, stating that skilled cognitive performances can and should be measured. Part IV delves into the complexities of the educational management of the dyslexic child. Here, Michael Thomson looks at some of the practical and theoretical issues arising from the ways in which dyslexic children respond to specialised teaching; Steve Chinn considers the educational, social, parental and political factors which affect the design of provision for dyslexic children; and the section closes with a chapter by Jean Augur, arguing that very early training in some activities help to build firm foundations for later training. Jean sadly died in the summer of 1993, but the fruits of what she achieved live on in many ways, and we are particularly proud to have this final contribution from her.

The last section looks outward, considering some of the matters not usually regarded as part of the mainstream provision for dyslexic people. So, here, Colin Wilsher considers some unconventional treatments, claiming that there is no particular merit in being deemed conventional and no slur in being labelled unconventional. In this section I have contributed a chapter myself, presenting some data and some thoughts about the effects of being dyslexic on wider aspects of the individual's personality and place in society. Finally, Margaret Hubicki offers some fascinating and highly practical advice in the field of dyslexic people learning musical skills.

In particular, we hope that the labourers 'at the coal-face' – the teachers, befrienders, parents and supporters – will find in this volume information to support their work, explanations to clarify what they see happening, and hope that research and development still continue apace.

That last item is what I would like to think you will get from this volume – hope. Hope that, as we move towards the new millenium, we can see a development of future provision for dyslexic people. In the work involved in turning this project into a reality I owe a debt of thanks to many people. These range from Ved Varma, whose idea it was, through Colin Whurr who advised me on many things, my secretary Wendy Morgan who particularly helped me to communicate with everyone, to my wife Margaret who put up with me while I was doing it. I must record my particular gratitude, of course, to all the authors who contributed, sticking (mostly!) to some very tight deadlines that I foisted on them. Finally, to Tim himself; the entire book is really one big 'thank you', of course, but you will notice that in his still busy life he has written a chapter himself. The real thanks are due to him for everything he has done, and I hope that this book contributes to enabling the work to be taken forward into the future.

Dr Gerald Hales
Milton Keynes, December 1993

Contributors

Professor P.G. Aaron, Department of Educational Psychology, Indiana State University, USA

Dr Steve Chinn, Mark College, Mark, Somerset, UK

Professor Drake Duane, Scottsdale, Arizona, USA

Nick Ellis, Department of Psychology, University College of North Wales, Bangor, UK

Dr A. Fawcett, Department of Psychology, University of Sheffield, UK

Peter Gardner, Chartered Educational, Legal and Counselling Psychologist, Bristol, UK

Dr Gerald Hales, Institute of Educational Technology, The Open University, Milton Keynes, UK

Margaret Hubicki, Musician, London, UK

Professor C.K. Leong, Department for the Education of Exceptional Children, College of Education, University of Saskatchewan, Canada

Professor Tim Miles, Dyslexia Unit, University College of North Wales, Bangor, UK

Roderick Nicolson, Department of Psychology, University of Sheffield, UK

Professor Gordon Stanley, Department of Psychology, The University of Melbourne, Australia

Dr M. Thomson, East Court School, Ramsgate, UK

Martin Turner, Dyslexia Institute, Staines, UK

Dr Colin Wilsher, Bushey, UK

Contents

Part I
The Theoretical
Constructs of Dyslexia

Chapter 1
Differential diagnosis of reading disabilities

P.G. AARON

Introduction

This chapter describes a diagnostic procedure which is based on the assumption that there are different kinds of reading disabilities, and that developmental dyslexia is but one of them. The belief that there are different forms of reading disabilities arises from the observation that reading skill is made up of several components and that weakness in each one of these would result in a different form of reading disability.

A component can be defined as an elementary information processing system that operates upon internal representations of objects and symbols (Sternberg, 1985). To be considered a component, the process should be demonstrably independent of other processes. An additional constraint placed on this definition is the level of theorising chosen by the researcher, often dictated by practical considerations. Because of this subjectivity, some researchers have identified the components of reading at a comparatively general level (e.g. Leong, 1988), whereas others have preferred a fine grained analysis (e.g. Frederiksen, 1982) of reading. The diagnostic procedure described in this chapter defines components at a general level and considers reading to be made up of two components: *word recognition* and *comprehension*. The first component, word recognition, refers to the ability to pronounce the written word either overtly or covertly and is largely determined by the phonological skills of the reader. In the present context word recognition, therefore, refers to an ability to translate graphemes into phonemes. In other words, it is the ability to decode the written word. Comprehension, the second component, is a higher level information-processing ability and is used here as a generic term to include both reading and listening comprehension. Evidence for the componential nature of reading comes from four sources: experimental psychology, developmental psychology, neuropsychology and genetic studies of dyslexia.

Experimental psychology

In an experimental investigation, Jackson and McClelland (1979) studied undergraduate students and found that comprehension ability and reaction time in a letter-matching task accounted for nearly all of the variance seen in reading achievement. Investigations by Hunt, Lunneborg and Lewis (1975) and by Palmer et al. (1985) also found that comprehension and speed of decoding the printed word are the two most important components of reading. More recently, Levy and Carr (1990), after discussing the nature of the reading process, concluded that comprehension and word recognition are dissociable processes and, therefore, can be considered to be components of reading.

Developmental psychology

Findings of developmental psychology are in agreement with the two-component view of the reading process. Frith and Snowling (1983) found that children with dyslexia comprehend much better than they can read aloud, whereas some autistic children with hyperlexic symptoms decode print with considerable facility but do not comprehend well what they read. Indeed, studies of hyperlexic children show that printed words could be recognised and read aloud without being understood (e.g. Healy, 1982; Aaron, Franz and Manges, 1990).

Neuropsychology

Neuropsychological studies of 'deep dyslexia' and 'surface dyslexia' also indicate that comprehension and word recognition can be independently affected (e.g. Marshall and Newcombe, 1973). The reading deficits seen in cases of 'deep dyslexia' indicate that word decoding skills can be impaired leaving comprehension relatively intact, whereas cases of 'surface dyslexia' indicate that words can be recognised without being correctly comprehended.

Genetic studies

Studies of developmental dyslexia also support the view that word pronunciation skill is independent of comprehension skill. In a study of twins with reading disabilities, DeFries, Fulker and LaBuda (1987) found significant heritability for word recognition, spelling, and WISC-R digit span (Wechsler Intelligence Scale for Children – Wechsler, 1976) but not for reading comprehension. After investigating monozygotic and dizygotic twins with reading disabilities, Olson and his associates (cited in Pennington and Smith, 1988) found that non-word reading skill is highly heritable whereas comprehension is not. Commenting on these studies, Pennington and Smith (1988) conclude that, in dyslexia, single-word reading, spelling and digit span, but not comprehension, are genetically influenced.

The choice of the two-component model is influenced by this empirical evidence as well as by pragmatic considerations. The pragmatic considerations include the fact that the two-component model of reading requires relatively simple diagnostic procedures which can be carried out quickly and easily without the need for elaborate test instruments. More importantly, the diagnostic procedure leads directly to remedial instructional strategies. In other words, the diagnostic procedure is 'outcome based', a phrase that has gained much popular-ity recently in the USA. It follows then that poor readers with a weakness in word recognition skills will do best when they receive remedial instruction that focuses on improving phonological skills; remedial instruction of children with weak comprehension ability will attempt to improve this ability; children who are weak in both these areas will receive comprehensive remedial instruction. In this respect, the procedure presented in this chapter differs radically from the procedure that is used presently in the USA to diagnose learning disability.

The term 'learning disability' is used in the USA to cover a broad spectrum of learning problems, with reading disability constituting the core. More than 75% of the children identified as having learning disability experience difficulty in acquiring reading skills (Kavale, 1988) and an equal percentage of children identified as having learning disability receive remedial instruction in reading (Sartain, 1976). For these reasons, statements about learning disability are equally applicable to reading disabilities.

The conventional diagnostic procedure that is used for identifying learning disability is based on the extent of the discrepancy found between a child's potential for reading and his or her actual reading achievement. This diagnostic procedure runs into two problems: one is the determination of the extent of discrepancy that marks reading disability and the other is the method adopted for estimating the child's reading potential.

Determination of the extent of the discrepancy that serves as a marker for reading disability is actually not a psychological decision but a fiscal one, based on the amount of monies allocated to a school district in any given year. Because of this, the number of children identified as having reading disability can vary from year to year. As a matter of fact, in 1968, nearly 120 000 American children were identified as having learning disability; by the year 1986, this number exceeded 1.7 million. The method used for estimating the reading potential is to administer an intelligence test to the child and then projecting his or her reading potential from the IQ obtained from the test. This practice is based on two assumptions:

1. The relationship between IQ and reading achievement is unidirectional (i.e. IQ determines reading ability and not vice versa).
2. The correlation between IQ and reading achievement is sufficiently high to predict the latter from the former.

Both these assumptions are, however, unwarranted. For example, the observation that poor readers read less than good readers and, as a result, fail to develop sufficient language and vocabulary skills which, in turn, can lower the verbal IQ is well documented (Stanovich, 1986; van den Bos, 1989). This phenomenon labelled as the *Matthew Effect* (Gospel according to St Matthew, 25: 29) indicates that the IQ–reading relationship is not unidirectional but can be reciprocal. As for the second assumption, the correlation coefficients obtained between IQ and reading achievement scores generally fall in the vicinity of 0.4. Interpreted statistically, this means that IQ can account for only about 16% of the variance seen in reading achievement scores.

Perhaps the most serious drawback in using IQ tests for identifying reading disability is that such a procedure is not outcome-based. In other words, the IQ–reading achievement discrepancy may be able to detect a reading disability but it gives us no hint regarding the cause of the reading problem nor does it lead to decisions regarding remedial instructions. The procedure described in the following pages overcomes these problems to some degree.

The diagnostic procedure described in this chapter is based on the following propositions:

1. Reading ability is composed of two independent components – decoding and language comprehension.
2. Reading ability is, ultimately, the ability to comprehend written language.
3. Apart from decoding and the differences attributable to modalities effects, reading comprehension and listening comprehension are mediated by the same cognitive mechanisms and, therefore, are highly correlated.
4. The best available predictor of reading comprehension is, therefore, listening comprehension.
5. Development of decoding and comprehension skills can be arrested independently of each other, resulting in three kinds of poor readers:
   (a) those with deficient decoding but adequate comprehension skills;
   (b) those with poor comprehension but adequate decoding skills;
   (c) those with deficiencies in both components.

There is empirical evidence to support the proposition that poor readers can be classified into three categories. The first group of individuals, marked by adequate listening comprehension skills but poor decoding skills, is referred to by labels such as 'dyslexics' and 'children with specific reading disability'.

In the present context, developmental dyslexia is defined as deficient reading comprehension in the presence of adequate listening comprehension, problems in reading comprehension arising from weak word-recognition skill. Defining dyslexia in these operational terms also mitigates the fact that a satisfactory definition of dyslexia has always eluded experts in the field of reading disability (see Miles and Miles, 1990, for a discussion of this issue). In a recent study yet unpublished, Aaron and Boyd surveyed 79 children from grades 2 to 5 and found 16 children who had average or above average listening comprehension scores (standard score 95 and above on Wechsler Individual Achievement Test – 1992) but had word recognition scores (on Woodcock Reading Mastery Tests – Woodcock, 1987) one or more standard deviation lower than their listening comprehension scores.

The existence of the second group – those with adequate word recognition skills but poor comprehension – is also fairly well documented. Carr et al. (1990) report that nearly 25% of poor readers fall in this category. In a British study, Oakhill and Garnham (1988) found that nearly 10% of children in early primary grades have this form of reading problem. Children with hyperlexia represent an extreme condition of this form of reading disability. The third form of reading disability which arises out of deficits in both word recognition and comprehension skills is, perhaps, the most prevalent category of reading problem. Individuals who can be placed in this category invariably have IQs in the low–average or borderline range. A good deal of confusion exists in the dyslexia research literature because of failing to identify children belonging to this group and separating them from children with dyslexia. The focus of the present chapter will be developmental dyslexia because this book is mainly about this form of reading disability.

Evidence supporting the componential nature of reading was presented at the beginning of this chapter. The proposition that comprehension is a generic process which includes both listening and reading comprehension is supported by the findings of numerous studies which report correlation coefficients significantly higher than the ones obtained in studies that compared IQ and reading achievement. A typical finding is that of a study by Palmer et al. (1985) in which a coefficient of 0.82 was obtained between reading comprehension and listening; this comprehension led the investigators to conclude that reading comprehension can be predicted almost perfectly by a listening measure (see Aaron and Joshi (1992) for a review of related studies).

The syndrome of developmental dyslexia

The phonological weakness seen in individuals with dyslexia manifests itself in several symptoms, hence it is best to consider dyslexia as a syndrome. The following description of the dyslexia syndrome is based on the proposition that the difficulty experienced by individuals with dyslexia in recognising words can be traced to phonological weaknesses. Some researchers have, however, proposed that a different type of dyslexia, arising from problems related to visual processes, also exists. Evidence for this view, however, is scanty (e.g. Aaron, 1993; for a dispassionate discussion of this issue, see Miles and Miles, 1990). The symptoms that constitute the syndrome of developmental dyslexia are described in the following sections.

Poor word recognition (decoding) skill

The most obvious deficit seen in people with dyslexia is poor word-recognition skills. Even though the written word could be recognised by extracting its meaning and without resorting to phonological transformation, such a strategy appears to develop as a result of extensive reading. It can, therefore, be assumed that, not having a sizeable vocabulary, beginning readers tend to rely on the decoding strategy for recognising printed words. Furthermore, in order to extract the meaning of a sentence, the string of words in the sentence has to be kept in a temporary memory store. Phonological memory appears to be well suited for this purpose. The phonological memory of individuals with developmental dyslexia is almost always poor, as indicated by low digit span, a condition that can impede reading comprehension.

The traditional means of assessing decoding skill is by administering a list of 'pronounceable non-words'. Standardised tests of reading such as Woodcock Reading Mastery Tests (Woodcock, 1987) contain such lists of 'non-words'. A non-standardised list of 'non-words' based on developmental trends of the acquisition of grapheme–phoneme relational skills is presented in the Appendix to this chapter.

Slow reading speed

A number of studies show that the speed with which words are recognised is a major variable that contributes to individual differences in reading skills. Even though some poor readers may be able to recognise some written words without resorting to phonological recoding, these children are held back when they encounter unfamiliar words and words that lack meaning. Slow reading is not limited to children; college students with dyslexia are also slow readers (Aaron and Phillips, 1986).

Even though requiring subjects to read a passage and computing the time it takes to read would appear to be a straightforward method for assessing reading speed, this procedure runs into a peculiar problem, i.e. even young children who are proficient in reading, pause and ponder over words they have not encountered before. Consequently, two or three unfamiliar words in a passage can have a disproportionately large depressing effect on the reading speed and thus confound the results. For this reason, the use of a list of highly familiar function words and a list of matched content words is recommended. A list of function words and a list of content words matched for word frequency and length is presented in the Appendix to this chapter. Children (and adults) with dyslexia, when compared to skilled readers, take a longer time to read both lists. The difference between the time taken to read the two lists also has diagnostic value, with function words invariably taking longer time to read. This time difference is much larger for individuals with dyslexia than it is for skilled readers. This is one of the most robust findings I have come across in my study of dyslexic subjects.

Yet another way of evaluating the effect of reading speed on comprehension is to assess reading comprehension by administering two kinds of tests, one a timed test and the other an untimed test, and noting the difference in performance. Tests such as the Stanford Diagnostic Reading Test (Karlsen, Madden and Gardner, 1984) are designed to be administered as timed tests; this test also comes in two equivalent forms. It is, therefore, possible to administer one form of the test as a timed test and the other as an untimed test. Dyslexic students frequently reach almost normal levels of comprehension under the untimed condition whereas under time constraints they perform poorly. Runyon (1991) found that college students identified as having reading disability performed much worse than students from a control group on the comprehension part of the timed Nelson–Denny reading test (Brown, Bennett and Hanna, 1981). When the test was administered without time restrictions, however, there was no significant difference between the two groups in reading comprehension. Contrary to these observations, poor readers belonging to the other two categories of reading disability do not show substantial improvement in comprehension when the time restrictions are removed.

Errors in oral reading

Oral reading is routinely employed by teachers as a means of assessing the reading skills of children as well as for improving the reading skills of young children. Although poor readers tend to make more errors than skilled readers, it is the type of oral reading errors that distinguishes dyslexic readers from the other types of poor readers. Substitution errors committed by dyslexic readers indicate that they depend on context for recognising words, which often does not radically alter the meaning of the sentence. Thus, a dyslexic child may read the sentence 'This is the house that Jack built' as 'This is the home that Jack built'. In contrast, poor readers with comprehension deficit often produce words that alter the meaning of the sentence; occasionally, they also produce neologisms. Sometimes, dyslexic readers use minimal cues involving the first two letters of a word and guess the word. They, however, seldom generate neologisms.

Individuals with dyslexia also tend to omit many function words and word suffixes; they also frequently substitute one function word for another. For instance, the article 'a' may be substituted for 'the' and the preposition 'on' for 'above'. When evaluating these errors, the most important criterion to be kept in mind is whether the gross meaning of the sentence or phrase is preserved or not.

Poor spelling

Many studies of developmental dyslexia suggest that poor spelling is a concomitant of reading disability. This should come as no surprise because spelling-to-sound relational rules are used both in reading and spelling. Being weak in phonological skills, dyslexic readers commit an unusually large number of spelling errors.

Traditionally, the ability to spell was thought to be a visual process involving memorisation of the sequence of letters in words. On the basis of her own research and that of others, Treiman (1993), however, has shown that spelling is more an attempt to represent a word's sound than it is an attempt to recall the string of letters in a word. Consequently, the correlation between spelling and phonological skills involved in the decoding of printed words is impressively high (Ehri, 1983; Bruck and Waters, 1988; Rohl and Tunmer, 1988). Sometimes it is claimed that there are adults who are poor spellers but good readers. A study by Joshi and Aaron (1991), however, shows that these so-called 'poor spellers but good readers' indeed have subtle phonological deficits.

Children's mastery of spelling skills appears to proceed in stages that correspond to the development of grapheme–phoneme relational skills. Treiman (1993) has identified four stages of spelling development:

1. Precommunicative stage in which there is little evidence of correspondence between phonemes and graphemes.
2. Semiphonetic stage (e.g. mail – 'ml'; carpet – 'crpt').
3. Phonetic stage (e.g. city – 'sity'; blue – 'bloo').
4. The correct spelling stage.

I have gone into some detail about the acquisition of spelling skills because there have been attempts to classify dyslexia into subtypes on the basis of spelling errors. Perhaps the best known work in this regard is the one by Boder (1973), who classified spelling errors into three categories: *dyseidetic* (e.g. girl – 'gal'; blue – 'bloo'), *dysphonetic* (e.g. girl – 'gril'; stop – 'spot') and *mixed*. Sometimes, *dyseidetic* and *dysphonetic* subtypes are considered equivalent to 'visual dyslexia' and 'auditory dyslexia', respectively. If, indeed, there are two different kinds of dyslexic subjects, they will require different forms of remedial instruction. For this reason, the issue of subtypes is not a trivial one. However, the developmental trends seen in the acquisition of spelling skills discussed above challenge the validity of classifying dyslexic subjects into subtypes on the basis of spelling errors. It appears that the different kinds of spelling errors, instead of representing different subtypes of dyslexia, represent two substages of spelling development. Evidence for this interpretation of spelling errors was obtained by Phillips, Taylor and Aaron (1985). Indeed, dysphonetic spelling errors are seldom seen in the writings of college students with dyslexia. In addition, clinical observations of Miles and Miles (1990) show that mild cases of dyslexia may display spelling errors that are phonologically acceptable, whereas severe cases commit phonologically deviant errors. The important point to remember is not to interpret the reading problem of children who commit phonologically acceptable spelling errors as evidence of adequate phonological skills but as a manifestation of weak visual memory. Phonologically acceptable spelling errors indicate that the subject has reached Treiman's (1993) stage (3) of spelling acquisition but not stage (4).

Diagnostic testing involves asking the subject to read a list of words which is appropriate for his or her grade level and during a subsequent session asking the subject to write down only those words he or she had correctly read earlier. This ensures that the words are not misspelled because of the subject's lack of familiarity with the word, but are genuine instances of spelling errors. Many standardised tests of spelling fail to take this precautionary measure.

Errors of syntax in written language

Errors of function-word usage and word suffixes are often seen in the writings of dyslexic subjects. Even though there may be a considerable amount of intersubject variation in this regard, errors of written syntax mirror those seen in the oral reading of these individuals. Some of these errors are due to confusion between homophones ('were' for where; 'one' for won) and thus reflect a subtle phonological weakness. Experimental studies also show that, when a printed word is read, the root morpheme is stripped of its suffix and is processed as a separate unit (Gibson and Guinet, 1971). It would be reasonable to expect that, lacking semantic content, suffixes are handled by the phonological mechanisms. This would explain the large number of suffix omissions and substitutions seen in the oral reading and writing of the dyslexic subject.

Excessive reliance on context for word recognition

A distinction should be maintained between using context for comprehension and depending on context for word recognition. It is in the latter sense that 'context dependency' is used here. A substantial number of studies show that subjects with weak word recognition skills depend more on context for recognising written words than good readers do (e.g. Allington and Fleming, 1978; Mitchell, 1982). The extent to which a reader depends on context could be determined by asking him or her to read aloud a passage and at a later time asking him or her to read a selection of words taken from the passage and arranged in the form of a list. The number of words incorrectly read from the word list but correctly read when they were embedded in the passage provides a measure of context dependency.

Adequate listening comprehension

Even though an ability to listen and comprehend spoken language well cannot be considered a symptom of a problem, it is very useful for differentiating developmental dyslexia from the other two types of reading disabilities. As noted earlier in this chapter, reading comprehension and listening comprehension are highly correlated and developmental dyslexia is indicated by poor reading comprehension in the presence of adequate listening comprehension. It should, however, be noted that poor reading comprehension of dyslexic subjects is not a primary deficit but is secondary to word-recognition problems.

Very few standardised tests of listening comprehension are available. As far as my knowledge goes, the only standardised test that is published in the USA is a subtest from the Wechsler's Individual Achievement Test. It is, however, possible to use the alternative form of any standardised reading comprehension test as an informal test of listening comprehension. Using Form G of the Woodcock subtest as a test of reading comprehension and Form H of the same test as a test of listening comprehension has produced satisfactory results (Aaron and Joshi, 1992).

The differential diagnostic procedure

Diagnosis involves two testing procedures: formal assessment and informal assessment. The formal procedure uses standardised tests and the informal procedure locally developed tests as well as clinical observations.

The formal diagnostic procedure is based on the expectation that, because reading comprehension and listening comprehension are highly correlated and reading is made up of two components, comprehension and decoding, once the contribution of listening comprehension to reading is factored out, the remaining deficit could be attributed to decoding. This view is advocated by investigators who subscribe to the componential view of reading. For instance, according to Gough and Tunmer (1986), reading (R) equals the product of decoding (D) and comprehension (C), i.e. $R = D \times C$. It follows that if $D = 0$, then $R = 0$, and if $C = 0$, then R is also 0. When this proposition is translated into pragmatic terms, it follows that the reading difficulty of a subject who has good listening comprehension but lower reading comprehension can be attributed to poor word recognition skill. Conversely, the reading problems of children who have poor listening comprehension skill originate from comprehension deficits.

Formal assessment

Reading comprehension can be assessed with the aid of any well-standardised diagnostic reading test. In the Porter School Psychology Clinic at Indiana State University, we use two tests: an untimed test and a timed test. These are the Woodcock Reading Mastery Tests and the Stanford Diagnostic Reading Test, respectively. These two tests use different methods for assessing comprehension; the Woodcock test is in a cloze format whereas the Stanford test requires the subject to read a passage and then answer a set of questions. As noted earlier, the difference in performance between a timed test and an untimed test could yield useful diagnostic information. In addition to the test of comprehension the Woodcock test also has tests of vocabulary and word attack. We assess listening comprehension in two ways:

1. By administering the Woodcock subtest of reading comprehension, Form H, as a test of listening comprehension.
2. By using the listening comprehension subtest from the Wechsler Individual Achievement Test – this test has been standardised on a nation-wide sample.

In a pilot study, we administered the Woodcock Reading comprehension subtest and the Wechsler Listening comprehension subtest to 87 children from grades 2, 3, 4 and 5 and obtained the correlation coefficients 0.45, 0.49, 0.67 and 0.55, respectively for these grades.

The raw scores obtained from these tests can be converted into standard scores. The next step in the diagnostic procedure is to compare the reading comprehension score of the student with his or her listening comprehension score, both obtained from the alternative forms of the Woodcock test. The raw scores obtained in these tests are converted into standard scores for the purpose of comparison. The logic involved in this comparison is that, if the student has a listening comprehension score that is average or better and a reading comprehension score which is lower, his or her reading difficulty is due to poor decoding skill. In contrast, if the student has below-average scores in both forms of comprehension, the deficit is not limited to the written language but includes spoken language as well. The listening comprehension score from the Wechsler Achievement subtest is used to confirm or disconfirm the findings of the Woodcock subtest.

How large must the discrepancy between the two comprehension scores be to be considered indicative of genuine difference? At a very basic level, if there is no overlap between the confidence limits set up by +1.96 standard error of measurement, then it can be inferred that a difference between these two scores exists and that such a difference is not due to errors of measurement. For instance, a college student obtains a standard score of 93 on reading comprehension and a score of 110 on listening comprehension. When the 95% confidence range is computed by adding and subtracting 1.96 standard error of measurement to each of these standard scores, we obtain a range of 87–101 for reading comprehension and a range of 104–112 for listening comprehension. Given that there is no overlap between these two estimates, we can conclude with 95% confidence that a true difference exists between reading comprehension and listening comprehension, and that the source of this discrepancy is poor decoding skills. The student's performance on tests of word recognition, and on other formal and informal tests, can be checked to see if this inference is correct.

Additional confirmational information can be obtained by examining the student's performance on the Stanford Diagnostic Reading test, which, it may be recalled, is a timed test. A substantially lower score on the Stanford test as compared to the one obtained on the Woodcock Reading comprehension test (which is an untimed test) is an indication of slow reading speed.

The IQ test is often useful as a backup tool. The test that has been most frequently used for assessment purposes is the WISC-R (WISC III, now) or Wechsler Adult Intelligence Scale (WAIS – Wechsler, 1983). One of the robust findings that has emerged from our clinical studies is that the Digit span of dyslexic individuals, regardless their age, is always well below average. Individuals with other forms of reading disabilities may also perform poorly on the Digit span test; however, dyslexic individuals get above-average scores on many of the subtests of the Performance Scale. This is particularly true of the Block design subtest. Poor readers who are not dyslexic do not show this discrepant profile. Thus, an average or above-average Performance IQ, along with a low Digit span score, is an additional marker for developmental dyslexia.

In general, as Miles and Miles (1990) point out, dyslexic individuals perform poorly on the WISC-R subtests which have significant loadings on 'speed of information processing'. These include the subtests, of Digit span, Arithmetic, Coding and Information. Dyslexic individuals generally perform poorly on the verbal part of the Wechsler Scales. This could be partly due to their tendency to process information rather slowly, or it could be a manifestation of the Matthew Effect, which is the cumulative product of limited reading experience. Again, as Miles and Miles (1990) have cautioned, it is a wise policy to examine the subtest scores individually and to treat the overall score with caution.

Informal assessment

Informal assessment provides supporting evidence for the initial diagnosis made on the basis of the results of formal testing. This form of assessment would include information obtained during interview, observations made during a testing session and clinical impressions, as well as the results obtained by administering certain non-standardised tests. The informal tests described in this chapter are suggestive; items from tests such as the Bangor Dyslexia Test (Miles, 1982) can be added or substituted. Informal tests evaluate the subject for all the symptoms of dyslexia described earlier, with the exception of comprehension. The subject's performances on all these tests are audio-taped and subsequently analysed. Teachers and clinicians can develop their own local norms in order to correctly interpret students' performance on these tests.

Decoding skills

The best way to assess decoding skill is to require the student to read a list of words with which he or she is unfamiliar. Familiar words would not serve the purpose because they could be read as sight words, without resorting to decoding. For this reason, decoding skill is almost always assessed by using a list of pronounceable non-words. A list of non-words which we use in the Porter School Psychology clinic is presented in the Appendix to this chapter. This list of non-words is constructed on the basis of the sequential progression of the acquisition of grapheme–phoneme relational rules by children.

Reading speed

As noted earlier, dyslexic subjects are typically slow readers. The lists of function and content words that can be used for assessing reading rate are shown in the Appendix to this chapter. These two lists are matched for syllables and the frequency with which they appear in children's textbooks (Carroll, Davies and Richman, 1971). Not only are dyslexic readers slow in reading the list of function words, but they also show a marked discrepancy in the speeds with which they read the two lists, with function words being read at a much slower rate than content words. Dyslexic children from primary grades also misread many more function words than content words.

Oral reading

Information about errors in oral reading can be obtained by selecting a passage from a textbook appropriate for the grade the child is in. It is preferable to select a passage which the child has not encountered before.

Spelling

Poor spelling is assessed by first requiring the child to read aloud a list of words and subsequently dictating only those words that the child had successfully read earlier. It is good practice for the examiner to read to the child the target word first, then read aloud a sentence in which the word is embedded, read the word aloud again, and then to require the child to write it down. The quality of the written spelling invariably provides hints about the level of the child's mastery of phoneme–grapheme skills; the percentage of errors committed yields a quantitative measure.

Errors of syntax

Errors of syntax in written language are noted by asking the subject to write a paragraph or two on a topic specified by the examiner. The product is evaluated both for quality of writing and for errors of syntax and errors involving the use of grammar words.

Context dependency

Context dependency is assessed by asking the subject to read aloud a long list of words taken from the passage used for evaluating errors in oral reading (see above). The words on the list that are misread by the subject are noted and then his or her reading of the passage is examined to see how many of the words missed in the list are read correctly in context. The percentage of words read correctly in context but missed in the list provides a measure of context dependency.

Many parents with children in the first grade become aware, for the first time, that their child may have a reading problem. The parents may be referred by the teacher to the psychologist. A diagnostic reading test is out of question because the child is just beginning to learn to read. In such cases, assessment must focus on skills that are prerequisites for learning to read. One such skill is phonological awareness. A combination of a phonological awareness test and an IQ test could be used to differentiate dyslexia from other reading problems. Items that can be used in developing a phonological awareness test can be taken from an experimental list developed by Stanovich, Cunningham and Cramer (1984). If the child is found to be deficient in phonological awareness, the same test can also be used as an instructional tool for developing phonological awareness in the child. At the initial stage, the instruction is entirely oral–aural. After the child has demonstrated an awareness of phonemes, graphemes are introduced and, subsequently, the relationship between graphemes and phonemes is taught. Detailed information about phonological awareness training and transferring such awareness to the reading task is presented in Aaron (1989) and in Aaron and Joshi (1992).

A diagnosis of developmental dyslexia implies a weakness in phonological processing and, therefore, leads to instructional methods that focus on improving this skill. A remedial method that has received much publicity is the Orton–Gillingham Approach (Gillingham and Stillman, 1979). There is, however, insufficient research data to indicate how effective this approach is. In contrast, the Spaldings' Writing Road to Reading Method (Spalding and Spalding, 1986) has a good track record as indicated by research findings. The 'Spalding method' has many similarities to the Orton–Gillingham Approach. In fact, Romalda Spalding spent three years with Samuel Orton practising his remedial method. However, unlike the Orton–Gillingham Approach, the 'Spalding method' introduces letter sounds first and not letter names. Furthermore, writing is emphasised from the very beginning. For these reasons, the 'Spalding method' is likely to be preferred by remedial instructors.

Miles and Miles (1990) note that methods similar to the Orton–Gillingham Approach are available in the UK. In particular, they recommend the Bangor Dyslexia Teaching System (Miles, 1992) and the booklets published in 1985 by the Kingston Polytechnic.

In the USA in recent years, teaching of reading with heavy emphasis on phonics and drill-work has come under severe criticism. The critics, instead, promote the 'whole language' approach which emphasises meaning and literature. Although I believe that mastery of word recognition skills is essential for extracting meaning from the printed page and that reading has to be taught explicitly and not incidentally, it has to be kept in mind that motivation is, perhaps, the most important element in learning to read and that excessive drill and monotonous repetition can be counter-productive when it comes to the acquisition of reading skills. For this reason, instruction in word recognition skill using the phonics approach should, as far as possible, be in a game-like format and dispensed in small doses, not exceeding 15 or 20 minutes every day

Appendix

List of non-words

1	gare	10.	chape	19.	gend	28.	cilly
2	duncle	11.	skar	20.	cend	29.	cept
3.	ract	12.	kute	21.	grone	30.	colp
4.	gar	13.	gite	22.	chind	31.	kar
5.	bace	14.	fedge	23.	gen	32.	pare
6.	recide	15.	git	24.	pice	33.	sute
7.	kaces	16.	bage	25.	tite	34.	kare
8.	gade	17.	ling	26.	cad	35.	par
9.	skare	18.	gog	27.	dit	36.	sut

List of function words

1.	let	11.	also
2.	has	12.	must
3.	ago	13	even
4.	off	14.	such
5.	why	15.	once
6.	any	16.	soon
7.	yet	17.	ever
8.	nor	18.	upon
9.	will	19.	else
10.	much	20.	thus

List of content words

1.	cat	11.	book
2.	run	12.	feet
3.	men	13.	back
4.	boy	14.	room
5.	say	15.	name
6.	dog	16.	page
7.	she	17.	work
8.	man	18.	come
9.	bird	19.	look
10.	gold	20.	time

Chapter 2
Visual deficit models of dyslexia

GORDON STANLEY

Introduction

Reading is a complex skill and involves several distinct processes (Mitchell, 1982). Given this complexity it is not surprising to find many candidates for accounting for specific reading disability or dyslexia. As reading involves looking at print, it is important to consider whether there are any visual factors which contribute directly to reading problems. Surveys suggest that common visual problems are not disproportionately represented in a group of people with dyslexia (Helveston et al., 1985; Lennerstrand and Ygge, 1992), but this leaves open the question as to whether or not there are specific visual deficits which are not picked up by routine visual screening.

Since Vellutino (1979) visual deficit theories have been less popular than those which directly involve aspects of language processing. In a number of studies (e.g. Stanley, 1977; Ellis and Miles, 1981; Legein and Bouma, 1981), which addressed the different stages of processing written text, results indicated that differences between people with dyslexia and normals became more significant at the level of verbal encoding of the visual information than in the visual analysis stage itself.

Nevertheless, one good reason for considering the case for visual deficits in relation to specific reading disability (dyslexia) is that many dyslexic children report symptoms which appear to be 'visual' in nature, despite having normal visual acuity. Symptoms reported commonly include: blurred print, moving print, diplopia (double vision), losing place, omitting words and a resultant fatigue and aversion to reading. Although these symptoms may arise simply as a response to the linguistic difficulty the children experience in decoding print, it is also possible that they are indicative of a specific visual deficit. In this chapter we will consider some of the recent research supporting the idea of a visual deficit.

In recent years three classes of research involving visual factors have emerged in the literature:

1. A number of studies have been conducted within the framework of the transient deficit theory formulated by Lovegrove, Martin and Slaghuis (1986).
2. There have been a series of experiments examining the role of reference eye stability centred around the work of Stein.
3. There have been a number of studies addressing the scotopic sensitivity theory of Irlen.

The transient deficit theory

The transient deficit theory of reading disability has been developed from the sustained and transient approach to visual information processing (Breitmeyer and Ganz, 1976). Reading proceeds by a series of eye movements and fixations as one scans a line of print. Information from the text is transmitted slowly during an eye fixation by the action of the sustained subsystem. The initiation and cessation of the eye movement to the next point of fixation in the text is driven by the transient system which is responsible for fast transmission of information.

Local structural detail about the stimulus is transmitted by the slower sustained system, whereas global characteristics, movement and positional information are transmitted by the faster transient system. The processes are mutually inhibitory and therein lies their importance for reading according to Breitmeyer (1989). Transient or sustained inhibition is considered to be of particular value in reading as the onset of transient activity with the initiation of an eye movement to a new fixation point terminates the continuing sustained activity from the previous fixation. This inhibitory activity acts to separate the information encoded in a sequence of fixations and prevents spatial overlay of words and letters.

Lovegrove, Martin and Slaghuis (1986) reviewed the outcomes of a series of experiments conducted in their laboratories which were interpreted to support the notion that reading disability is associated with a transient system deficit. Disabled readers were reported to be less sensitive on some measures of pattern contrast sensitivity at low spatial frequencies and to have more difficulty in detecting visual flicker than do controls (Lovegrove et al., 1980a; Lovegrove, Heddle and Slaghuis, 1980; Martin and Lovegrove, 1984). Other research claims that reading-disabled children have slower rates of visual search and have more difficulty in visual perceptual grouping tasks than do controls (Williams and Bologna, 1985; Williams, Brannan and Lartigue, 1987; Brannan and Williams, 1988). They also appear to have longer separation times before they can correctly report which of two temporally asynchronous patterns appeared first (May, Williams and Dunlap, 1987) and make larger errors when asked to specify the spatial location of a flashed pattern (Solman and May, 1990).

In each of the studies reported the results were interpreted in the framework of a transient deficit hypothesis. Although the cumulative evidence from a large number of psychophysical experiments provides impressive support for the transient deficit model (Lovegrove, Martin and Slaghuis, 1986; Lovegrove and Slaghuis, 1989) not all researchers have accepted the claim. For example, Smith, Early and Grogan (1986), who attempted to test the transient deficit model, did not get positive results. They used a 6 Hz flicker masking of five horizontally presented sinusoidal gratings ranging from 0.5 to 8 cycles/degree (cpd) and made measurements of the reaction times of 20 dyslexic and 20 control children to the offsets of different spatial frequency gratings. They found between groups no significant differences related to spatial frequency as predicted from a defective transient system model. Instead they found a longer reaction time (some 25 ms) for dyslexic children irrespective of stimulus conditions.

Georgeson (1985) criticised the subjective and variable criterion used by the Lovegrove group in their most commonly reported measure of visual persistence. Using a similar procedure he found the measure to be unreliable with a group of adult subjects. In an attempt to counter this criticism, Lovegrove and Slaghuis (1989) presented the results of three occasions of testing to provide what they considered to be good evidence for test–re-test reliability. The correlations across occasions of testing averaged about 0.5 which, although statistically significant, can hardly be considered impressive.

Perhaps more interesting evidence for the possibility of a visual deficit in line with the transient deficit model comes from additional research using physiological measures. To appreciate this work it is necessary to know that, in the most recent understanding of primate visual system physiology, the magnocellular pathway mediates the transient system and the parvocellular pathway the sustained system.

Livingstone et al. (1991) have investigated both physiological and anatomical evidence for a magnocellular defect in dyslexic subjects. Their subjects were a group of five adults with a history of developmental dyslexia, who were compared with seven adults with normal reading history. Averaged visually evoked potentials were recorded in response to the contrast reversal of a checkerboard pattern binocularly presented at both low and high contrasts. Dyslexic subjects showed diminished visually evoked potentials in response to rapid low-contrast stimuli but normal responses to slow or high-contrast stimuli.

These differences were interpreted as evidence for a defect in the magnocellular pathway at visual area 1 of the cortex or earlier. If the mean plots from their studies are inspected, it can be seen that although there were differences in the earliest components of the visually evoked potentials in line with their interpretation, the largest differences were at the later stages which they claimed were 'uninterpretable'. Whilst this is the case in terms of their model, it may mean that the most significant result was overlooked because it does not represent evidence in support of their position.

On the assumption that the defect posited in the model of Livingstone et al. (1991) occurs earlier in the visual pathway than the cortex, they examined the lateral geniculate nuclei in post-mortem specimens from five dyslexic brains and five control brains and found abnormalities in the magnocellular, but not the parvocellular, layers. The control sample had had sufficient testing during life to enable exclusion of developmental dyslexia and the dyslexic sample had been diagnosed dyslexic in life and had willed their brains for investigation. The magnocellular layers were more disorganised in the dyslexic brains and the cell bodies appeared smaller. Smaller cell bodies are likely to have thinner axons, which should have slower conduction velocities. Thus, this anatomical evidence appears supportive of the specific transient deficit model.

Earlier anatomical studies with the same post-mortem specimens had found anomalous asymmetry of the language area known as the planum temporale. This, together with the more recent finding with repect to the visual system, suggests that in these mature dyslexic brains there were both visual and language deficits coexisting. It is possible to speculate that an earlier abnormal sensory defect may lead to abnormal development of the language area. Nevertheless, taken by themselves, these anatomical results do not allow definitive support for a causative role for a specific transient deficit in the visual system of dyslexics.

Lehmkuhle et al. (1993) measured visually evoked potentials with scalp electrodes in 8 dyslexic and 13 control children aged 8–11 years. Potentials were obtained for low (0.5 cpd) and high (4.5 cpd) spatial frequency targets which were surrounded by either steady-state background or a uniform 12 Hz flickering field. Flicker would be expected to dampen the amplitude and increase the latency of a transient potential in response to a low-spatial-frequency target but not to a high-spatial-frequency target.

The results showed that when the stimulus was a low-frequency target the latencies of the early components of the evoked potentials were longer in the reading-disabled sample than in the controls. No differences between the groups occurred when the target was a high-frequency stimulus. For normal readers the flickering background increased the latency and reduced the amplitude of the early components of the evoked response but in the dyslexic subjects only the amplitude was altered. In line with expectation, flicker had no effect in the high-spatial-frequency condition for either group.

These results are consistent with the idea of a sluggish response of the magnocellular (transient) system in dyslexic children. The investigators conclude their study with the speculation that 'a defect in the magnocellular pathway creates a timing disorder that precludes the rapid and smooth integration of detailed information necessary for efficient reading' (Lehmkuhle et al., 1993, p. 995).

At this stage there does appear to be a converging body of evidence to support the transient deficit model. It appears that such a deficit may occur alongside phonological deficits and the possible causal path is not established.

Reference-eye instability

Although visual information is bilaterally represented in both eyes, most people have a stable reference (dominant) eye. The reference eye helps resolve fine positional location where there may be some potential conflict between the eyes in situations of imperfect convergence. Often assessing the reference eye involves pointing at a target or testing the sighting eye, which can confound hand preference with eye preference. For this reason measures of sensory dominance are often used in which stress is placed on the visual system and one eye dominates in the resolution.

One of the measures most commonly used to assess reference-eye stability is that developed by Dunlop and Dunlop (1976). Their test was based on determining which eye provides the reference for movement when two eyes are made to move in different directions while they attempt to maintain the fusion of stereoscopic slides of a house and trees presented in a device that enables the separation of the slides for each eye. Clearly the test is only meaningful for those who have normal binocular vision in the central field. Using this test Stein and Fowler (1984) found unstable reference eyes in 63% of a sample of dyslexic subjects and only one instance in a control group of normal readers matched for age and intelligence.

In a subsequent study Stein et al. (1986) found unstable reference eyes using the Dunlop test in 30% of 753 primary school children aged between 7 and 11 years. The results on reference eye were compared with reading performance for 451 of the sample. The reading of children with a stable reference eye was on average 6.3 months in advance of those with an unstable reference eye. Among those with more than 18 months reading lag, nearly half had an unstable reference eye compared to 24% of those whose reading was above age expectation. This result suggests that, although there may be some relationship between reference-eye instability and reading failure, the relationship is not strongly causal.

In a study using a procedure to assess reference instability without stressing the system, Stanley, Howell and Marks (1988) reported a positive relationship between eye stability and reading. However, this work again only provided weak evidence for any causal model implicating a visual instability or vergence deficit. Newman et al. (1985), Aasved

(1987) and Lennerstrand and Ygge (1992) reported studies in which there was no greater incidence of reference-eye instability among poor readers than among average readers.

Although there are now a large number of studies devoted to examining the relationship between visual instability in terms of fine positional location and visual instability in terms of reading, the results are somewhat inconclusive and certainly not supportive of a strong causal direction.

The scotopic sensitivity syndrome

Irlen (1983) introduced the idea of a 'scotopic sensitivity syndrome' to describe her therapy for those with reading disability affected by a visual defect that could be alleviated by the use of coloured filters or lenses. Early papers by practitioners of the Irlen technique did not attempt to relate the therapeutic claims in any direct way to known visual physiology beyond a reference to retinal or post-retinal processes. The term 'scotopic sensitivity syndrome' introduced by Irlen (1983) was somewhat confusing because the defect appears to be related to difficulties associated with photopic sensitivity, and reading is most frequently carried out at photopic levels of illumination. Although there are spectral differences in acuity at low luminances, at high luminances any spectral composition should lead to the same limiting acuity values for normal eyes (Pirenne, 1962).

In recent years much progress has been made in our understanding of the chromatic code of the visual system (Boynton, 1979; Alpern, 1981; Dain, 1984). There are a number of possibilities for consideration when seeking to understand the basis of the presumed beneficial effects of colour for those with specific reading disability (dyslexia). Differences between dyslexic and normal people could occur at one or more levels within the visual information-processing system. The effects of the coloured lenses or filters could then compensate at the level(s) where differences occur.

Differences could occur at the pre-retinal level through differences in the absorption of light in the ocular media. There is no evidence either for such differences having functional significance or for dyslexic subjects having other than normal variation in ocular media.

At the retinal level there are three cone mechanisms responsible for the transduction of colour. Traditional colour vision tests are able to detect differences due to abormality of cone function. However, dyslexic subjects are no more likely to manifest traditional colour defects than average or above average readers (Helveston et al., 1985).

Output signals from the different cone mechanisms combine antagonistically to produce narrow-band responses at all post-retinal levels of the visual pathway. At the ganglion cell and geniculate levels of the primate visual system a distinction is made between the parvo- (P) and magnocellular streams of processing (Livingstone and Hubel, 1987). The parvocellular system involves sustained processing such as detailed analysis of form and narrow-band opponent responses are associated with it. The magnocellular system involves transient processing and is suppressed by diffuse red backgrounds (Livingstone and Hubel, 1983).

Assuming that there is a transient deficit in dyslexic subjects, Breit-meyer (1989) has provided a theoretical prediction from that account to indicate the circumstances under which coloured filters may have a beneficial effect for those with dyslexia. He predicted that they would 'tend to avoid lenses that pass red or long wavelengths of the spectrum, because such lenses would exacerbate the transient channel deficit and presumably also the attendant retinal smear and visual instabilities' (p. 537). This hypothesis provides a link between colour preference and an influential theory of visual deficit in those with dyslexia that is related to contemporary visual physiology.

Empirical evaluation of Breitmeyer's prediction

The filters prescribed by Irlen practitioners are selected from a range of up to 150 broad-band filters with different densities. These filters differ in both their spectral and luminance characteristics. As the system has been commercialised and patient data cannot be readily accessed by researchers, it is necessary to rely on published data sources to evaluate the Breitmeyer prediction.

Wilkins (1991) reports results from his laboratory which studied 20 volunteers with a history of reading difficulty selected by the Irlen Insti-tute as having benefited from Irlen lenses. A comparison was made between Irlen lenses, neutral-density lenses having the same luminance transmission and untinted lenses that corrected any residual refractive error. For a few subjects acuity and muscle balance were significantly improved when Irlen lenses were worn, and for all there was a modest improvement in visual search and fewer illusions were reported in a pattern of stripes. Given that the subjects were selected on the basis that their Irlen lenses were beneficial, the relative advantages over the substitute lenses were rather disappointing.

The most relevant finding in the light of Breitmeyer's (1989) predic-tion was that all the chosen tints transmitted in the range 650–700 nm and many had peak absorption in the range 500–550 nm, appearing rose or yellow in colour. In a second study reported by Wilkins (1991) children with moderate learning difficulties were required to mix red, green and blue lights to provide a colour that minimised the illusory effects of a repetitive striped pattern. Consistently a mixture deficient in green was selected.

Stanley (1991) reported a study in which 20 adults attending an adult literacy course chose a yellow filter more frequently than other colours. In that study the correlation between the extent of effective energy absorption of the filter and the proportion of times that the filter was chosen was high ($r = 0.86$) suggesting that the subjects may have been simply maximising the amount of light transmitted.

Although the data may appear to run against the Breitmeyer hypothesis, there are studies which suggest that sometimes blue is preferred. In a case study involving two patients reported by Hannell et al. (1989) both boys chose blue filters in line with the prediction. Solman et al. (1991) also report another source in which 35 out of 44 prescribed lenses were blue.

As so often the case in this field what appears to be a nice clear-cut prediction is ambiguously supported by the data.

Research evaluating Irlen lenses

There is a growing literature on the use of Irlen lenses and coloured filters, though many of the studies reported still do not meet rigorous standards of design to enable clear conclusions to be drawn (Stanley, 1991). Researchers have used various approaches ranging from the use of a selected array of overlay transparencies to the full range of Irlen lenses.

The Irlen claim is that the lenses are only effective with those who manifest the 'scotopic sensitivity syndrome'. This syndrome is operationally defined by reference to performance on the Irlen Differential Perceptual Schedule. As many earlier studies did not select their dyslexic sample on this basis, it could be claimed that their results are not strictly relevant to the evaluation of the Irlen lens treatment. In this section we will review some recent studies which have met this requirement.

O'Connor et al. (1990) studied the effect of coloured transparencies on reading performance. A sample of 105 children from grades 2 to 6 who were reading at least 18 months below grade level were drawn from a total population of 600. All were average to above IQ. Of this group 52 had been assessed by optometrists and 10 had corrective lenses and 15 low-powered stress lenses. The children were screened for scotopic sensitivity using the Irlen Differential Perceptual Schedule and for colour vision using the Ishihara Tests. After the Irlen Differential Perceptual Schedule a reading assessment was made and children who 'displayed definite scotopic signs *and* displayed marked improvement in reading performance with a particular colored transparency overlay were classified as scotopic' (p. 399). Those without scotopic signs were classified non-scotopic and none of these showed any positive effects of the transparencies on reading.

The scotopic children were randomly assigned to one of four treatment groups. Children in group A were given their initially preferred colour, those in group B and D were given a clear transparency and those in group C were given a non-preferred colour. The non-scotopic children in group E were given clear transparencies and those in group F were given a randomly selected transparency. With the exception of group D each group was pre-tested on two reading tests and post-tested a week later, each child having been asked to use his or her assigned filter over white paper for all reading activities for the week. They were each told that 'We think this might make reading a little easier for you'. Every child in group A improved in reading rate and comprehension and only one did not improve in accuracy. Members of the other groups showed a mixture of outcomes ranging from improvement similar to those in group A to no change and regression.

Although much has been made of this study as a well-controlled and double-blind trial, unfortunately the design does not control adequately for the placebo response which may have produced the first colour preference. The study only demonstrates that those who initially indicated that the coloured filter improved their reading of text showed consistent gain when given that filter. Others were given their non-preferred or no coloured filter and then told it would have the same effect. The responses in these groups were inconsistent, ranging from improvement to deterioration. It is difficult to explain the improvement which occurred for some individuals in these latter groups if the original effect had no placebo component.

Robinson and Conway (1990) followed up 44 reading-disabled children who had been fitted with Irlen lenses at 6 and 12 months after fitting. Improvements occurred in the children's perception of their own ability as well as in reading comprehension and accuracy, but not in reading rate. Clearly there were positive subjective responses, but in the absence of a control group it was not possible to rule out a placebo response, as the authors acknowledged.

Winter (1987) studied 15 children aged 7–11 years who had been fitted with Irlen lenses by an authorised practitioner. Thirteen of them had refractive corrections incorporated into their Irlen lenses. In this study the children read without glasses for 10 minutes, after which in 4 minutes they had to locate as many examples of the letter 'b' as they could find in pages of random letters arranged in lines and paragraphs. The children were assigned to four groups and four conditions of presentation: with Irlen lenses, without lenses, with plain lenses and with grey lenses. Each group received each condition, but in a different order. Winter reported no difference in performance between conditions. He also reported that school records on standardised tests for the children did not reveal 'any beneficial effect of Irlen lenses upon academic performance of those identified as Scotopic Sensitive' (p. 5).

Cotton and Evans (1989) studied 60 children of normal intelligence who had been referred to a special education centre as a result of reporting reading difficulties. They were tested individually over two sessions 6 weeks apart. On the first occasion they were administered the Irlen Differential Perceptual Schedule, a reading test, personality measures and tests of stereoscopic vision. On the second occasion those with mild to severe symptoms of scotopic sensitivity as defined by the Irlen Differential Perceptual Schedule were fitted with Irlen lenses by a franchised practitioner. After this they were tested on an equivalent form of the reading test used on the first occasion. They also read in random order four parallel forms of another test under four conditions: with the prescribed lenses, with coloured lenses chosen at random, with clear plastic lenses and with no lenses.

Of the 60 children, 38 (21 boys, 17 girls) were diagnosed as scotopic sensitive and 22 (16 boys, 6 girls) not sensitive. The mean age and reading rate, comprehension and accuracy were not statistically different for the two groups. The scotopic-sensitive differed from the non-sensitive on a number of personality variables. The scotopic-sensitive were higher on external control, neuroticism and anxiety, and lower on self-esteem than the non-sensitive. The scotopic-sensitive appeared to have less strong depth perception, but were not different in the performance of a simple eye–hand coordination task like star tracing. There were no beneficial effects of the prescribed lenses relative to any of the other conditions for those diagnosed as scotopic sensitive for reading or any of the perceptual and eye–hand coordination tests. When Cotton and Evans looked at individual data for the prescribed lenses they reported some individual gains of up to 29 and 42 months on the Neale Reading test, but these were offset by some individual deteriorations as large as 23 months.

Cotton and Evans (1989) report that in terms of subjective assessments of the amount of distortion, 81% indicated less distortion using Irlen lenses as compared with 38% for random or plain tints and 19% for no lenses. However, when performance was assessed, no differences were manifest. There was no significant correlation between the Irlen Differential Perceptual Schedule diagnostic measure and reading deficit or between the measure and reading improvement. They conclude their paper by suggesting that the effect of the lenses may be both motivational and attributional. The motivational effect they see as deriving from the interest and expectations of the parent, teacher and practitioner, and the attributional effect as deriving from allowing a reattribution of failure away from the individual and towards a physical problem to be solved by prescription.

The evidence from these studies using subjects selected according to the Irlen profile does not provide compelling scientific support for the Irlen therapy. Howell and Stanley (1988) raised the issue as to whether or not the visual characteristics associated with scotopic sensitivity were unique. Scheiman, Blaskey and Ciner (1990) report that 95%

of 39 subjects identified as candidates for Irlen filters had significant and readily identifiable vision anomalies which could be treated by conventional optometric means.

We conclude that although there is some cumulative evidence of a transient deficit commonly occurring in dyslexic children, this deficit does not play a strong causal role.

Chapter 3
Neurobiological patterns in dyslexia

DRAKE D. DUANE

Introduction

In his book, *Dyslexia: The Pattern of Difficulties,* Tim Miles wisely observed that dyslexia occurs not as an isolated phenomenon but rather as a cohesive pattern of historical events and clinical manifestations which distinguish this condition as a selective form of academic under-achievement (Miles, 1993). Such clinical patterns are noteworthy for they correspond with, and are the direct product of, neurobiological patterns within the central nervous system of the dyslexic individual. The following review attempts to correlate clinical manifestations with central nervous system mechanisms so as to serve as a brief status report on the neurobiological issues in reading disorders.

Clinical/biological patterns

Familial occurrence

It was already clear by the time of World War I that students who demonstrated difficulties in acquiring the skill to read commonly had siblings, parents, grandparents or aunts and uncles who had had similar difficulties in learning to read as children and commonly as adults remained uncertain in the accuracy of their spelling (Hinshelwood, 1917).

Two parallel but not specifically related projects within the USA bear on this question. One, 'the decade of the brain', is concerned with a wide spectrum of neurological disorders in which government spending in neurological disease is focused on explaining neurobiological mechanisms in the last decade of the twentieth century. Among those disorders are developmental disorders and among the developmental disorders is the phenomenon of dyslexia. Several specifically funded dyslexia research institutes have been created in the USA, some of which have been expanded to include the broader problem of learning disorders (Alexander, Gray and Lyon, 1993). The other project is the 'human genome project', in which considerable government expense is focused on identifying the specific chromosomes and genetic sites at which are located a spectrum of health problems, among which is dyslexia.

Three separate programmes of investigation conclude that an important aetiology in disorders of reading is a specific genetic mechanism dominantly inherited (Lubs et al., 1991), concordant in 70% of monozygotic twins and 43% of dizygotic twins (DeFries, 1991), in which the specific genetic site may be located on chromosome 6, as the previous speculation on chromosome 15 has been abandoned (Smith et al., 1983, 1990). Intriguing is the observation that a key factor in gaining skill at reading is itself heritable, namely phonological awareness (DeFries, 1991).

It should be recalled, however, that it was Geschwind and Galaburda (1985) who reminded us that familial occurrence may not represent in each instance a genetic mechanism because the specific aetiology for the phenomenon under investigation may relate to some other factor tied to genes which leads to a common end result; thus, the necessity of investigating the spectrum of behaviours and biological traits of the individuals afflicted with the condition under investigation, in this instance dyslexia. For example, if high male occurrence of reading disability is observed, this may not represent specific interaction of sex chromosomes but rather reflect an effect of testosterone, secreted *in utero* by the male fetus, influencing brain development (Galaburda, 1990).

Our own work suggests that when attention-deficit disorder, a condition characterised by impulsivity, distractibility and in childhood motoric restlessness, is combined with reading disability, both conditions are much more prevalent in other family members versus controls. Further, there is a much higher probability that reading disability will occur in other family members of index cases which also demonstrate specific reading disorder. Thus, there may be two genes, one for reading, the other for attention, which may co-occur (Duane et al., 1993). In an analysis of twin data, Gilger, Pennington and DeFries (1992) observed a probable separate genetic effect to account for the occurrence of each of these phenomena.

Gender

Beginning with the initial description of reading disability in a male, the literature until recently has emphasised an over-representation of males with dyslexia (Morgan, 1896; Orton, 1937). This certainly was true in the landmark Isle of Wight studies (Rutter et al., 1976), in which boys outnumbered girls at a rate of 3.5 to 1. However, a recent survey in the USA, employing an epidemiological sample of students in Connecticut and using a standard formula as employed by the State of Connecticut in identifying students qualifying for Special Education services in reading, suggested an almost equal occurrence of females (Shaywitz et al., 1990). However, employing a statistical formula for the identification of reading disabilities may not separate the specific dyslexia population from a broader population of disabled readers (Stanovich, 1993) who do not fit the *pattern* of dyslexia which the Yale investigators themselves admitted in a subsequent report that with such statistical criteria students may fall in or out of the category of 'dyslexia' within one grade year (Shaywitz et al., 1992).

The work in familial dyslexia, whether it be the twin studies in Colorado (DeFries et al., 1987) or the dominantly inherited penetrant form in three generations (Lubs et al., 1991), suggests only a slight increment in the occurrence of familial reading disorders in males. Furthermore, studies of referral populations in the USA are often biased in male referral by the greater occurrence of attention and behaviour problems in males versus females. Nevertheless, clinical experience teaches that random surveys of patients seen as adults for unrelated neurological symptoms reflect a much higher frequency of recalled underachievement in reading and spelling (and demonstrated during clinical examination) in males than females (Duane, personal observation). Thus, the pattern for dyslexia is that *persistent* reading disability at the decoding level is more prevalent among males than females.

Early speech and oral language development

Orton (1937) observed unexpectedly high rates of stuttering and delays in speech milestones in his sample of dyslexic subjects. The Isle of Wight survey demonstrated an antecedent speech milestone anomaly as common in those with specific reading retardation (Rutter et al., 1976). When one also observes the ability to rhyme and phonologically segment as predictive of reading skills (Snowling, 1981; Bradley and Bryant, 1983) and a difficulty in acquiring skill in a second language (Dinklage, 1971) as characteristic of dyslexic subjects, one is compelled to consider disorders of reading as developmental written language disorders, strongly correlated with oral language mechanisms.

Temporal processing

Tallal and co-workers have suggested that developmental language disorders, both spoken and written, correlate with an inability to perceive two speech sounds presented in close temporal order (150 ms or less) as separate (Tallal, Miller and Fitch, 1993). A similar temporal processing deficit may also affect visual processing, manifest as a slowed visually evoked potential latency in dyslexic subjects when the large cell (magnocellular) segment of the visual system is sampled (Livingstone et al., 1991). Post-mortem anatomical correlates in dyslexic subjects have been observed in both the medial and lateral geniculate nuclei which relay auditory and visual stimuli respectively. Thus, the structure and functioning of the perceptual system may characteristically differ in those with developmental language disorders.

The work of Livingstone and her associates offers no specific scientific support for the recently promoted notion of 'scotopic sensitivity' in which colour lenses are claimed to provide improved visual perception and related improved reading decoding (Silver, 1993), but theoretically hue may influence contrast sensitivity and it was manipulation of contrast sensitivity which allowed Livingstone and her co-workers to elucidate these differences in dyslexic subjects, recently reconfirmed in a separate investigation (Lehmkuhle et al., 1993).

A problem in the identification of specific dyslexic subjects are those students whose developmental visual motor problems are accompanied by mild problems in decoding script but in whom there are also major problems in reading comprehension, even when full-scale or verbal IQ scores are well within the normal range. A recent study of adults in mid to late life with this developmental so-called right hemisyndrome (left-body motor signs on quantitative neurological examination, academic underachievement in arithmetic and geometry, and poor visual memory) demonstrated persistent low performance in reading comprehension (Duane, 1993b). These mid and later-life adults are not dyslexic although some had histories of early school problems which included reading. Their adult achievements were marked by high verbal performance, as asserted by advanced degrees in law, education, social work and communications.

Lateralisation

The diversity of opinion on manual, ocular and pedal lateralisation in specific disorders of reading is wide. Studies of familial dyslexic subjects discussed above do not show, as had been asserted by Orton, a higher rate of left-handedness in twins or families with three generations of reading disability. However, employing the Edinburgh Laterality Questionnaire (Oldfield, 1971), my associates and I have observed higher rates of weak right-handedness among a spectrum of developmental disorders including reading (Duane, 1991). The majority of those with reading disability are right-handed, but the degree of their right-handedness as measured by the Oldfield Questionnaire is associated with a much higher rate of laterality quotients less than +75. An index of handedness within an individual is but one of several biological traits which create a pattern characteristic for that individual's central nervous system organisation. Adult levels of laterality in our work seem to be established somewhere between the ages of 8 and 10 years (Duane, personal observations).

Co-morbidity

In the definition of medical disorders, the co-occurrence of conditions presents information which may give insights into the biology of the disorder. The same is true for reading disorder. There are at least four which have been suggested. These include: disorders of attention, disorders of wakefulness or alertness, emotional disturbance and subtle aberrations in the autoimmune system, if not of affected individuals then of their mothers.

Attention deficit–hyperactivity disorder

This noxious condition is probable heterogeneous in origin and is manifest by impaired attention, impulsivity and motoric hyperactivity in childhood, and in adulthood may persist with disorganisation, poor focus and inability to complete tasks. Although the most frequent academic underachievement, if one exists, in those with attention deficit–hyperactivity disorder is in arithmetic, reading disorders may co-occur with disorders of attention. On the other hand, one in three dyslexic subjects demonstrates impaired attention. The genetic origin for attention deficit disorder is distinct from that of reading disability (Gilger, Pennington and DeFries, 1992). When problems of attention co-occur with reading disorder, it lowers the educational level finally achieved by the affected individual and increases the risk of emotional disturbance.

Alertness

While at Mayo Clinic, I observed adult patients with narcolepsy, a disorder characterised by daytime hypersomnia, who would themselves occasionally describe their offspring as experiencing school-based difficulties in attention and/or academic studies. Consequently, an assessment of daytime wakefulness using pupillometry, because pupil size decreases with drowsiness, demonstrated that upwards of 45% of those with attention problems and/or reading problems were non-alert (Duane and Berman, 1992).

The medical management of narcolepsy includes the employment of the stimulants methylphenidate and d-amphetamine, the same medications also at times helpful in treating attention disorders. The importance for educational remediation is that such sleepy students, when alert, profit more from educational therapy.

Emotional disorder

The Isle of Wight study suggested an increased rate of psychiatric diagnosis in the population with specific reading retardation. This threefold increment was marked by especially high levels of conduct disorder, followed in frequency by depression. Although many factors may influence the risk for mood disorder, not the least of which is the frustration of academic underachievement, our own investigations suggest that the risk for depression may be genetic, as family members of those with attention deficit–hyperactivity disorder and/or reading disability have a threefold greater frequency of relatives with a known history of depression (Duane et al., 1993).

Autoimmunity

Two studies suggest a curious association between the autoimmune antibody, anti-nuclear antibody, and reading disability. In the first, two-thirds of mothers of dyslexic children were documented to have elevated titres of this serological antibody which posed no ill effect upon the mother (Pennington et al., 1987). The second demonstrated high rates of learning problems, as well as left-handedness, in the children of mothers with the disease systemic lupus erythematosus, which is characterised by enormously high titres of the anti-nuclear antibody (Lahita, 1988). At one point, there was concern that there might be a causal, perhaps epigenetic, aetiological relationship between the presence of the antibody in mothers and the development of dyslexia in their offspring. However, the inability of the antibody to cross the placental barrier reassures that it does not injure the fetal nervous system *in utero*. The occurrence of this antibody, although perplexing, may represent a related biological trait somehow linked to that which produces disorders of reading and/or of attention. Our preliminary data do not suggest an increased frequency of this antibody in the serum of children diagnosed with reading disorder and/or attention deficit disorder (Duane, personal observation).

Biological substrate

Pathological anatomy

A series of investigations led by Albert Galaburda at the Beth Israel Hospital in Boston, Director of the Orton Neuroanatomic Research Laboratory at that facility, has demonstrated a characteristic anatomical pattern in dyslexic subjects of all ages, both at the gross and light microscopic levels. The former, the temporal plane in the superior temporal regions, usually asymmetrical in approximately 70% of the general population and symmetrical in no more than 15%, has been shown to be uniformly symmetrical among those with dyslexia. This finding has been consistent in all ten post-mortem specimens.

Two types of microscopic cortical anomaly have been identified; the first, referred to as 'focal cortical dysgenesis', consists of ectopic neurons located in the clear zone at the surface of the cortex and just below that dysmorphic arrays of neurons irregularly placed rather than neatly layered as is characteristic in the normal human cortex. This type of anatomical malformation must result from factors which took place during the migration period of neurons during brain development *in utero*. The second observation has been found more frequently among the females in this study and has been referred to as 'fibromyelin plaque' formation. The anomaly consists of tiny cortical scars that may be the consequence of circulatory insufficiency, which might occur on either an immune or a traumatic basis (Galaburda et al., 1985; Galaburda, Rosen and Sherman, 1989). Although originally thought to represent the result of epigenetic or acquired factors, recent work in animals suggests that the dysmorphic cortical anomaly may occur from genetic mechanisms (Nowakowski, 1988).

Magnetic resonance imaging

Without employing X-rays but using the pulsation of a magnetic field, two- and even three-dimensional imaging of the nervous system is generated by a system referred to as magnetic resonance imaging (MRI). When that system is employed to make quantitative comparisons of volume, as well as shape of regions of the nervous system, the term 'morphometrics' has been applied. Such analysis has established that some developmental disorders are associated with specific differences in regional cortical volume. An example is a developmental disorder known as auditory verbal agnosia, in which case symmetrical underdevelopment or hypoplasia of the posterior temporal region has been observed (Filipek et al., 1987). In autism, the previous description of cerebellar hypoplasia has not been confirmed; rather more recent data suggest a generalised megencephaly in autistic persons (P. Filipek, 1992, personal communication).

Employing MRI techniques, the anatomical finding of cerebral symmetry at post-mortem examination has been confirmed (Rumsey et al., 1986). Most recently, anomalous anatomy of the sylvian fissure, which is the deep groove separating the frontal from the temporal lobe, has been shown to have atypical length and shape in dyslexic subjects and their relatives, as well as supernumerary ridges referred to as Heschl's gyri (Leonard et al., 1993). We recently employed this sagittal slicing technique of the Sylvian fissure to determine that a boy who demonstrated reading and attention problems probably had the reading disorder on a constitutional structural basis, while at the same time experiencing attention problems, induced presumably by a head injury at age six, which magnified the child's reading disorder.

That asymmetries may be observed in other developmental conditions is suggested by the observation that, in attention deficit disorder, there is an asymmetry of the caudate nucleus, a region within the deep structures known as the basal ganglia, which distinguishes that population from controls (Hynd et al., 1993).

Electroencephalography

The focal cortical dysgenesis anomaly described originally by Galaburda and Kemper (1979) in a dyslexic subject was first reported in the medical literature in association with patients suffering with epilepsy. Interestingly, the boy described in that original paper, who died at the age of 19, had experienced at the age of 16 a single nocturnal convulsion in his sleep. It may be that the cortical anomaly is associated with a risk of electrical instability to the extent that occasional seizure may result. Schachter at the Beth Israel Hospital Epilepsy Clinic in Boston has suggested that children with various learning disorders may present to a neurologist for the first time with a late childhood or early adolescent onset single seizure (S. Schachter, personal communication, 1992). Our recent experience confirms that observation, suggesting that there may be co-morbidity between the cortical anomaly and clinical seizure and perhaps minor abnormalities in the electroencephalogram (EEG) as well. However, the only EEG pattern which holds diagnostic specificity is that associated with the rare phenomenon of reading epilepsy, in which during reading an actual seizure discharge occurs. Routinely in all subjects whom we evaluate for learning disorders the EEG includes reading and arithmetic.

Computer-assisted electroencephalography and evoked potentials

It has been suggested that subtle differences in brain physiology recorded by computer-assisted EEG techniques (Duffy et al., 1980) segregate individuals with dyslexia from controls. Our own experience has been that such techniques reveal an asymmetrical alpha pattern, greater in the right occipital pole than in the left, in three groups of individuals: those with left-handedness, some with weak right-handedness and others with either of the above traits but demonstrating reading disability (Duane, personal observations).

An additional physiological investigation employing electroencephalography is one in which brain potentials are evoked following sound or light while the individual under study attempts to focus attention. Using the odd-ball paradigm, the $N100/P300$ potential is generated.

We have recently shown that delays in brain processing time are charac-teristic of a wide spectrum of developmental disorders, whether they manifest as problems of oral language, written language and/or atten-tion (Duane, 1993a). It is not clear whether such latency prolongation is related to the aforementioned temporal discrimination deficit described by Tallal et al. (1993).

Cerebral blood flow

Cerebral activity is associated with an increment in the use of oxygen and glucose as measures of metabolic activity. This metabolic increment may be assessed through measures of cerebral blood flow dependent upon rates of exchange of blood gases, one of which has been intro-duced and is radioactively labelled, or by a more complex technique referred to as positron emission tomography, also known as PET scan-ning. Both techniques have been employed by the study group at Bow-man Gray Medical Center in Winston-Salem, North Carolina and involve adults who as children have been diagnosed dyslexic by the late widow of Samuel T. Orton, Mrs June L. Orton. These investigators have shown a posterior shift in cortical activity from the posterosuperior temporal region into the parietal zone (Flowers, Wood and Naylor, 1991). While employing PET, this same group has shown that the usual pattern of simultaneous activation between the left basal ganglia region known as the caudate nucleus and the surface of the left temporal lobe does not occur or is 'uncoupled' in dyslexic adults (Hagman et al., 1992).

Intriguingly, PET studies have been employed in adults learning to read a new list of nouns. In the course of learning, widespread activa-tion of discrete regions within each hemisphere occurs during active learning, although once the list has been mastered, the words no longer initiate cortical activation. The process is renewed when a new or novel list is presented (Posner, 1993).

Dyslexia provides an excellent example of how research into brain func-tion correlates with clinical complex behaviour, in this instance difficul-ty in the acquisition of skill in reading. A pattern of anatomical variation adjusts brain physiology, making the specific activity of decoding script more laborious than in the usual organisation of the nervous system. The clinical behaviour is associated with anomalous development of oral language in which the crucial underachievement is related to impaired phonological awareness, rendering spelling and the acquisi-tion of a second language at risk. However, despite these seemingly negative characterisations, one should recall that within the dyslexic population, this same curious neuroanatomy and neurophysiology may bring with it unusual aptitude in visuospatial motor function, enabling such individuals to achieve beyond the general population in athletics, science and the arts. These biological limits upon facility in reading appear in most instances not to deny the ability to read but rather to retard its development and render intense education mandatory. Consequently, the phenomenon of dyslexia offers the clinician and the neuroscientist a unique window on the broad question of variability in human aptitude.

Part II
The Specific Nature of Dyslexia

Chapter 4
Dyslexia and skill: theoretical studies

RODERICK I. NICOLSON and ANGELA J. FAWCETT

Introduction

It is a great honour to contribute to this book in celebration of the work of Tim Miles. Tim's enthusiasm, guidance and open-mindedness have been an inspiration to us in our research. In this chapter we present the results of a recently completed study which we believe is the most wide-ranging analysis of the skills of dyslexic children yet performed. Whilst confirming the phonological deficits which Tim and others were instrumental in discovering, we also found equal, and sometimes greater, deficits in other areas of skill. We believe that these results are of significance for the whole dyslexia community, emphasising the dangers of focusing on any single facet of dyslexia and pointing the way towards a deeper understanding of the pattern of difficulties. We conclude with three 'buzzes', each a speculative account of a possible cause of dyslexia, at the cognitive level, the connectionist level and the neural level. It is unlikely that these 'buzzes' are completely correct, and they may indeed be completely wrong, but we offer them in the hope that they may inspire further workers to pursue research in this area.

Specific developmental dyslexia, or dyslexia for short, is formally defined as 'a disorder in children who, despite conventional classroom experience, fail to attain the language skills of reading, writing and spelling commensurate with their intellectual abilities' (from the definition by the World Federation of Neurology, 1968); in other words, children of normal or above normal intelligence who, for some otherwise inexplicable reason, have severe problems learning to read and spell. Dyslexia research has seen more than its share of passion and controversy – not surprisingly, given its close links with that very emotive topic, reading failure; its high incidence in Western populations (around 5% is a typical estimate – Badian, 1984; Jorm et al., 1986); and high financial stakes, given the statutory requirement in many Western countries to provide educational support for children with dyslexia.

Over and above these aspects, however, dyslexia provides a challenging paradox to a wide variety of researchers – why do these articulate, intelligent people show such a problem in one of our most routine skills? These background factors have resulted not only in the continuing high public profile of dyslexia research internationally but also in a wide range of research studies aimed at the better understanding, diagnosis or remediation of dyslexia. Illustrative of the significance attached to dyslexia research is the very high level of funding for dyslexia research from the US NICHD (National Institute of Child Health and Human Development) which rose from US\$2 m in 1982 to around US\$10 m per annum currently.

One of the fascinations of dyslexia for researchers is that, whatever one's interest in human behaviour and performance, dyslexic children will obligingly show interestingly abnormal behaviour in precisely that behaviour. Early pioneers in dyslexia research, Morgan, Hinshelwood, and Orton, believed that visual problems underlay the apparent 'word blindness' and Orton introduced the term 'strephosymbolia' to indicate that, although he believed the problem to be primarily visual, it was not one of blindness *per se*, but one of 'twisted symbols', a difficulty in distinguishing the order of letters. Around 20 years ago, there was a gradual realisation that problems of language must be, at least in part, responsible for the reading deficits (Vellutino, 1979). This general hypothesis has been refined over the years (Miles, 1983; Snowling et al., 1986; Stanovich, 1988) to provide what is arguably the consensus theoretical belief of most dyslexia researchers with a background in psychology, namely that dyslexic children suffer from an early impairment in their phonological skills, and this impairment prevents them from acquiring the word decoding and blending skills necessary for normal acquisition of the skill of reading. By contrast, however, driven in part by the need to identify some underlying neurological abnormality in order to obtain statutory educational support from the NICHD, many American researchers have studied the biological substrate. Again, dyslexia has provided intriguing abnormalities. Large-scale twin and familial studies (e.g. Smith et al., 1983) have established specific abnormalities both of chromosome 15 and, more recently, of chromosome 6 (Lubs et al., 1991). Studies of brain electrical activity in response to different types of stimulus have shown abnormalities for the processing of linguistic stimuli (Duffy et al., 1980; Hynd et al., 1990). Most directly, comparative neuroanatomical studies of dyslexic brains have established:

> a uniform absence of left-right asymmetry in the language area and focal dysgenesis referrable to midgestation . . . possibly having widespread cytoarchitectonic and connectional repercussions . . . Both types of changes in the male brains are associated with increased numbers of neurons and connections and qualitatively different patterns of cellular architecture and connections.
>
> (Galaburda, Rosen and Sherman, 1989, p. 383)

One significant recent development has been the re-establishment of visual deficits, in this case in rapid visual processing, specifically the threshold for the detection of flicker (Lovegrove et al., 1990), and in an interdisciplinary project involving both psychophysics and neuro-anatomical analysis, this deficit has been linked to neuroanatomical abnormalities in the magnocellular pathway linking the eye to the visual cortex via the lateral geniculate nucleus (Livingstone et al., 1991).

It is now clearly established by the ethological approach to investigating animal behaviour that if one studies animals behaving in their natural habitat over a period of days or months, one obtains a much richer and more informative pattern of behaviour than obtainable by means of traditional short bouts of observation in fixed locations. We believe the same principles apply also to the study of dyslexia. Those who have 'round the clock' experience of living with dyslexic children often form a very different view of their skills than do researchers who see them only for a brief testing period. A valuable example of the advantages of experience in developing a positive test for dyslexia is the Bangor Dyslexia Test (Miles, 1992) which probes for problems not only in digit span and handedness but also in knowledge of the months of the year – an orthogonal dimension to that of phonological deficit. Many parents of dyslexic children recall that their children were unusual in their early years – slow to walk, slow to talk, rather clumsy, maybe a bit accident prone. These 'anecdotal' reports were distilled by the late Jean Augur into a set of 21 key points (Augur, 1985). There were many references to lack of phonological skill, as expected from the well-established phonological deficit hypothesis. Equally notable, however, are consistent problems with motor skill. Indeed, motor skill problems accounted for the first five points, together with her point 7 (difficulty carrying out more than one instruction at a time) and her point 21 (excessive tiredness due to amount of concentration and effort required).

More formal analyses of motor skill were performed by Rudel (1985) who concluded that 'There is evidence of early difficulties in newly acquired [motor] skills, but these difficulties are largely outgrown by 9–10 years'. A particularly large study was reported by Haslum (1989), as part of the 'National Cohort' study in which 12 905 children were followed through from birth to 10 years, with a systematic series of tests being conducted at birth and at 5 and 10 years. As part of the testing procedure for the 10-year-old children, selected items of the Bangor Dyslexia Test (Miles, 1982) were administered, allowing dyslexic children to be identified, and thereby allowing analysis of those factors that were highly associated with dyslexia at birth, 5 years and 10 years. In brief, the tests that correlated most highly with dyslexia were: balancing on one leg, walking backwards, sorting matches and a 'graphaesthetic' task (identifying by touch a shape traced on the back of the hand), together with family history, birth history and childhood diseases. A recent series of studies by Wolff, Michel and Ovrut (1990) has shown persistent problems in tapping rhythm for dyslexic children, specifically when asked to tap the hands asynchronously. Perhaps most intriguing in this context are our findings that even adolescent dyslexic children have motor skill deficits on even that most practised motor skill, balance, though these deficits can normally be masked by 'conscious compensation' (Nicolson and Fawcett, 1990).

Faced by the apparent diversity of deficits in dyslexia, it is natural to say to oneself 'They can't all be right can they? What is the deficit *really?* Is the phonological, visual, or motor skill deficit the primary one?'. Our view now is that many theorists who do champion one or other such approach have fallen into the trap of premature specificity, opting for a specific theory before alternative approaches have been thoroughly explored. We should note that we too have been guilty of this in suggesting that the most likely cause was a deficit in the ability to become completely fluent in a skill, our 'Dyslexic Automatisation Deficit' (DAD) hypothesis (Nicolson and Fawcett, 1990). With the benefit of four years' further research exploring the DAD hypothesis, we now feel able to give a balanced view of the actual capabilities of dyslexic children, and in this chapter we attempt to describe the data any adequate theory must explain.

The research programme

One of the dilemmas in psychological research is whether to opt for a 'case study' approach, in which a single individual is studied from all angles, and a comprehensive picture of performance built up capable of providing a richly detailed analysis; or for a 'group' approach, in which, say, a group of dyslexic children is compared with a group of control, non-dyslexic children matched for, say, IQ, socioeconomic status and reading ability. This between-groups approach yields comparative statistically quantifiable data of strengths and weaknesses, and permits a limited degree of generalisation of the results to other similar groups of dyslexic children, but it only gives one facet of performance, providing at best a partial view of the issue. By contrast, the case study approach gives a rounded picture, but little indication of the comparative nature of the data or the possibilities of generalisation to other dyslexic children. In an attempt to combine the strengths of both approaches, we constructed a comprehensive battery of tests of skill, suitable for a case study, but then administered the whole battery to groups of dyslexic and non-dyslexic children, reasoning that this approach was the only way to gain a rounded picture that was statistically reliable and could legitimately support generalisation to other groups. Furthermore, in order to investigate the effects of age on skill, we felt it necessary to undertake a pseudo-longitudinal study, examining skill at age 8, 12 and 16 years, in the hope that analysis of changes with age would give an indication of the way that skills develop in dyslexic and control children.

Participants

In brief, we wanted to study 'pure' dyslexia, uncontaminated by factors such as low IQ, economic disadvantage and so on. Consequently, we used the standard exclusionary criterion of 'children of normal or above normal IQ' (operationalised as IQ of 90 or more on the Wechsler Intelligence Scale for Children – WISC-R; Wechsler, 1976), without known primary emotional or behavioural or socioeconomic problems, whose reading age was at least 18 months behind their chronological age. We recruited three groups of dyslexic children, mean ages 16, 12 and 8 years, together with three groups of normal children matched for age and IQ. This gave us six groups, D16, D12 and D8 and C16, C12 and C8, for the three age groups of dyslexic and control children respectively. This three-age-group design allows performance to be compared with children of the same age (D16 vs C16; D12 vs C12; D8 vs C8), children of around the same reading age (D16 vs C12; D12 vs C8) and children of around half the age (D16 vs C8).

Skill tests

Next we designed a variety of tests intended to tap performance on primitive cognitive and motor skills. Wherever possible these were implemented on the Apple Macintosh computer using digitised sound for instructions and stimuli and using automatic event recording and data analysis techniques in order to standardise testing techniques and to facilitate replication by other researchers. Five generic types of test were used, as may be seen in Figure 4.1. The psychometric tests used the WISC-R scales, with spelling age and reading age based on the Schonell tests of single-word reading and spelling (Schonell and Schonell, 1942–1955). The motor skill tests included the balance tasks and tests of bead threading and pegboard peg moving. The working memory tests included non-word repetition (repeating nonsense words of two, three, four and five syllables, based on Gathercole and Baddeley, 1990), the mean Memory Span for words of one, two and three syllables, and articulation rate (the mean time to repeat five times 'bus', 'monkey' and 'butterfly'), which is included in this category because memory span and articulation rate are known to co-vary (Baddeley et al., 1975). Tests of information-processing speed included *tests of speed* of naming of pictures, colours, digits and letters (all presented unpaced), together with simple reaction and selective-choice reaction time to pure tones, visual search (locating a distinctive 'spotty dog' on each of several crowded pages in a child's puzzle book), and tachisto-scopic word recognition on a graded series of words presented for gradually decreasing times. The tests of phonological skill included dis-crimination ability for phonologically confusable stimuli (Bishop, 1985), segmentation ability (Rosner and Simon, 1971) and 'rhyming' ability for phonemes at the beginning, middle and end of words (a simplified version of the tests used in Bradley and Bryant, 1983). The computer-based versions of the tests are available in the COMB set (Nicolson, 1992).

Results

Detailed presentations of results and procedures for the different types of skill are given in Fawcett and Nicolson (1994a,b,c). For this chapter, in order to facilitate comparison between tests, the results for each test

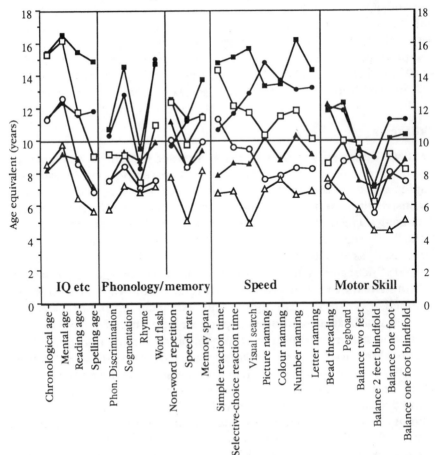

Figure 4.1 Normalised results of the test. ■ C16; ● C12; ▲ C8; □ D16; ○ D12; △ D8

were converted to the age-equivalent scores using the normalising procedures in the COMB set, taking the data from our control groups, together with control data from other studies where possible. It should be noted that this is a somewhat inaccurate transformation of results, owing to difficulties extrapolating from relatively small numbers of participants to develop the age norms. All the observations we make here are supported by our analyses of the original data, presented in the papers cited above. The normalised results are shown in Figure 4.1. Looking just at the three control groups (filled symbols), there are the expected differences on the psychometric tests; with age there is better phonological discrimination and segmentation, roughly equivalent rhyming performance, better performance on the memory, and especially articulation rate, faster processing, better performance on the single task balance, but roughly equivalent fine motor skill (beads and pegs). Whenever there is a difference, the oldest controls perform the best and the youngest controls the worst. In other words, the results for control groups are largely as one would expect, with some of the skills still developing in the teens, and some (such as the rhyming test) already at ceiling (at least on the tests used).

Now consider the performance of the dyslexic groups. The psychometric data are largely as expected, because the pairs of groups were matched for IQ and age. As expected, reading age lags further and further behind chronological age, with an even greater deficit for spelling age. Phonological skills show marked deficits, with the D8 group showing the expected lag, and surprisingly poor performance for the D16 group, in that it is hardly better than the C8 group. In all these phonological skills the dyslexic children performed significantly worse than their reading age controls. Note also the severe deficits of the D8 group in the memory and articulation skills, but in this case the three dyslexic groups show a heartening developmental trend, with the abysmal performance of the D8 group making way to merely poor performance of the D12s and near adequate performance of the D16s. A similar pattern of performance is shown for the tests of processing speed (with the exception of the simple reactions, where the dyslexic children perform at normal standards). In contrast to the other tests, the D16s consistently outscore the C8s on these tests of memory and processing speed. Most notable overall is the extraordinarily poor performance of all three dyslexic groups on the motor skill tasks, in particular bead threading and blindfold balance. Indeed, the D8 group are performing at only 4-year-old level on the balance tasks and, as our norms only go down to 4 years, this is very poor performance indeed.

It is perhaps worth emphasising that in almost all tests of naming speed, phonological skill, motor skill, and also non-word repetition and articulation rate, the dyslexic children performed significantly worse than their reading age controls. Furthermore, it may also be seen that the performance of the oldest dyslexic children is by no means better overall than that of the youngest controls, despite the advantage of around 8 years' experience.

Before attempting a theoretical interpretation of these results, it is important to attempt to characterise them, so as to provide a set of requirements for theorists wishing to develop their own accounts of the data

Breadth of deficit.

Deficits were observed in *all* the primitive skills tested – phonological, speed, memory and motor skill. There is no support here for any of the theories that attempt to tie dyslexia to one specific modality or type of process. Although we have not presented the results of statistical comparisons here, in general the dyslexic children were performing at or around the level of their reading age controls for speed of information processing and for phonological skill, and below reading age for motor skill (Fawcett and Nicolson, 1994a,b,c).

Changes with age

The most striking aspect of our data is the range of very profound deficits suffered by the youngest dyslexic children. Figure 4.1 does not really capture these particularly well, because our age norms go back to only 4 years, and performance worse than that of a 4 year old is allocated a notional 3.5 year label. Consequently it is not possible to get a mean of less than 3.5. Furthermore, many of the youngest dyslexic children have a performance well below the 4-year-old age norm, especially for phonological skill and motor skill. Following this very poor start, the dyslexic children actually make pretty good progress in speed of processing and in memory, possibly even catching up a bit. By contrast, there remain deficits in phonological skill and especially in balance, as shown by the performance of the D16 group. This pattern of results suggests that the learning processes are essentially intact, but that skill acquisition is greatly hampered by the initial very poor performance. This interpretation is strengthened by the results of experiments which investigated acquisition of skill directly, by undertaking a long-term training study in which the blending of two simple reactions (a finger press to a tone and a foot press to a flash) into a choice reaction was studied (Nicolson and Fawcett, 1994b). Here we found that, although each individual simple reaction was at normal speed, the dyslexic group were very much slower than the controls when the two simple reactions were first combined as a choice reaction, but then showed reasonably normal improvement in the skill with practice. Even so, at the end of 25 sessions' practice (some 5000 trials) the dyslexic group were significantly slower than the controls (and more error-prone).

Specific difficulties

Whilst it is clear that there are problems in all primitive skills, it is also important to identify which types of skill show the greatest deficits, because this may give some clue as to the most likely cause(s). As noted above, phonological skill and motor skill appear to be least susceptible to improvement, with information-processing speed and memory showing the greatest improvement. It is also important to consider, within each modality, which type of skill is most affected.

Consider first speed of reaction. Here we find that simple reactions are essentially normal, but that problems arise as soon as a decision is required (selective choice reaction). This is an intriguing result (Nicolson and Fawcett, 1994a) because we designed the simple reaction and selective choice reaction tasks so that the subject has to make an identical response in each case (press the button as soon as you hear the high tone). The only difference is that for the selective choice reaction, there is also an equal likelihood that a low tone will be presented, which the subject must ignore. One possibility is that it is the need for choice that causes the deficit. Another is that for simple reactions it is possible to speed one's reaction by very great concentration, and by priming oneself to press the button at the very first sign of a stimulus (compare conscious compensation), whereas this does not work when a choice must be made. Irrespective of the reason for the apparently normal speed of simple reaction, the choice reaction deficit occurs whether or not linguistic stimuli are involved, and regardless of whether the stimuli are visual or auditory.

Now consider motor skill. There are severe initial deficits in bead threading, pegboard manipulation and normal balance, but the last two do at least improve with age. By contrast, the deficit in blindfold balance persists into the D16 group, with performance worse than that of the C8 group. In phonological skill it is clear that the deficit in segmentation remains into adolescence.

Of course, the reading deficit or spelling deficit is normally taken as the index of dyslexia. For our groups we found the spelling deficit to be the more severe. This is in line with Thomson (1984), who reported typical achievement ratios of only 0.27 for spelling, compared with 0.40 for reading, i.e. improvements of 3 months and 5 months respectively in any 12-month period (see also Frith, 1985; Thomson, 1988, 1991). It is therefore worth considering, for each group, which deficits are more severe than the spelling age deficit. It is reasonable to assume that these exceptionally severe deficits may reflect the fundamental problem more clearly than does the spelling deficit. For the D8 group these tests are: speech rate, visual search and balance. For the D12 group, the only such test is blindfold balance. For the D16 group the tests are: rhyming, bead threading and blindfold balance.

Discussion

Our initial motivation was to explore the pattern of performance across the skill spectrum in the belief that it might be premature to opt for one or another hypothesis in the absence of this information. It seems clear from the results that our caution in advocating the collection of wide-ranging data before committing oneself to one or other theory was just-ified. It is not possible to account for the range of deficits shown in terms merely of one of phonological deficit, visual deficit, speed deficit etc. The true cause or causes must surely lie deeper within the cognitive system.

Before returning to the primary objective of theoretical understand-ing, it is worth considering the important secondary issue of diagnosis. If a suitable explanatory framework could be found that was less reliant for diagnosis on the skill of reading, it might be possible to identify diagnostic procedures less susceptible to environmental factors and may be applicable at an earlier age than the current reading-based approach. Only one of the cognitive tests shown in Figure 4.1 involves reading accuracy, and *a priori* there is no reason to consider reading accuracy any more valuable a diagnostic criterion than any other of the tests of skill used here. It seems very likely that some suitable combina-tion of tests may be employed for diagnosis, using discriminant func-tion analysis to provide a series of scores: one for dyslexia, one for specific language delay, another for general learning disability and so on. This hope rests on research as yet unfinished, with perhaps the greatest need being to identify the qualitative performance of 'slow-learning' children on the battery of tests developed above. Our prelimi-nary studies suggest that slow-learning children show equal or greater problems in phonological skill, memory and processing speed, whereas their blindfold balance is better than that of the dyslexic children. Turn-ing now to predictive screening, again we see reason for optimism, with perhaps scope for a multi-purpose battery of tests, providing a vector 'at risk' score for several childhood disorders. Many of the tests may be used, in suitably simplified form, with 5-year-old children. Indeed we have nearly completed a 3-year screening study, having tested children at age 5 and 6 on many of the tests noted above, and we are now wait-ing to see which of our sample of children will prove dyslexic by the normal criteria, thereby allowing a retrospective analysis to be carried out (Fawcett, Pickering and Nicolson, 1992).

It is also important to stress that, although we have found deficits in a range of primitive skills, this should not be taken to indicate any lack of mental ability. Far from it. We believe that the cognitive system (including intelligence and learning) is functioning at normal or above normal levels, as witnessed by the high achievements of many dyslexic people (West, 1991). Dyslexic people are fortunate in having the ability to 'consciously compensate' for these underlying difficulties in primitive skill, to the extent that these difficulties are apparently overcome in normal life.

It remains to consider the theoretical interpretation of the results. First let us consider our initial question 'They can't all be right, can they?'. In one sense they all are. There are indeed phonological deficits, visual deficits, motor skill deficits and speed deficits. Furthermore, the overall performance is well described as showing an automatisation deficit. But in this case, being right is not enough. Each of these theoretical positions, even the automatisation deficit, is merely a description of one facet of the underlying problem(s). It does not explain the cause.

Our results therefore raise as many questions as they resolve. All we can do at this time is speculate, and sketch out possible ways forward. In deference to Tim Miles, we offer a series of 'buzzes' – speculative but interesting ideas which could prove fruitful research avenues. We can consider the cause at three levels of description, each 'deeper' in the brain. At the directly observable, performance level, dyslexic children may be well characterised by our suggestion that they show a lack of automatisation of skill. Indeed, this suggestion provides a remarkably parsimonious account of the data, accounting for difficulties in phonological skill, visual skill, motor skill, information-processing speed and, of course, reading. Furthermore, in many circumstances dyslexic children and adults are able to compensate for this underlying lack of fluency by concentrating harder or using strategies (our 'conscious compensation' hypothesis), thereby resulting in the characteristic signs of rapid tiring and distractibility. However, an automatisation deficit is itself merely a description. It does not explain, *inter alia*, the pattern of deficits – why simple reactions appear to be of normal speed, whereas choice reactions start slow but then improve at a normal rate; why motor skills and phonological skills are poor, but balance skills appear to be worst and least amenable to improvement. Most important, it does not explain why difficulties are most marked immediately, but then tend to diminish with practice. An explanation must appeal to deeper levels within the brain.

First, consider Galaburda's neuroanatomical discoveries (Galaburda, Rosen and Sherman, 1989) of both abnormal connectivity in the cortex (and the magnocellular pathways to the cortex) and microscopic abnormalities ('brain warts') in cortical assemblies. What effects would one expect such abnormalities to cause? Arguably the most important development within the past decade in terms of modelling neural behaviour was the development of the 'parallel distributed processing' framework in which techniques were developed for modelling the development of skill using the analogy of a network of neurons (a 'neural network') which functioned as a distributed form of memory and which learned by modifying the strengths of the connections between the elements of the network (a landmark in this area was the publication of two volumes by Rumelhart and McClelland and their group in 1986 – Rumelhart and McClelland, 1986). One of the most convincing features of this 'connectionist' approach is that processing by real brains must be somewhat similar. After all, we do know that there are networks of neurons and that learning in them does take the form of modification of connections between them – see Eccles (1991) for a fascinating and accessible exposition. Very impressive results have been obtained using connectionist modelling techniques, to the extent that demonstrations have been made in all the areas of skill discussed in this chapter. One of the recent developments in connectionist modelling techniques (McClelland, 1992) is the acceptance that for modelling reaction-time parameters it is necessary to introduce the concept of 'intrinsic noise' (background activity that is essentially unrelated to any of the events taking place, analogous to 'snow' on old-fashioned television sets or hiss and crackle on audio recordings). Returning to dyslexia and the human brain, it seems inevitable that deviations from the normal neural organisation, as identified by Galaburda and his colleagues, will lead to an increase in this background 'noise'. In a qualitative analysis reported in Nicolson and Fawcett (1994b) we argued that such noise (in the absence of any other cognitive difficulties) should lead to the need for greater input of attentional resources to obtain normal performance (in much the same way as one has to concentrate very much harder when driving in foggy conditions). This would lead to exactly the pattern of results obtained here, with marked initial difficulties, essentially normal speed of learning, and final performance that was more error-prone and required further effort than normal. We are currently investigating direct tests and models of this hypothesis.

Assuming for the moment that our 'noisy neural networks' hypothesis has some merit, it must be pointed out that it is still too general, in that it does not explain which skills should be more affected and which less. It is here that we turn to a third level of theoretical description, the brain itself. Two striking features of our results were the apparent difficulties in automatisation and the severe problems in motor skill, especially balance. These types of deficit point strongly to the cerebellum, an ancient brain structure known to be responsible for balance and for motor skill in humans and lower animals. Furthermore, Ito (e.g. Ito, 1984) has argued strongly that the human cerebellum is responsible for motor skill automatisation. The cerebellum is also known to be centrally involved in eye movement control, an area also known to be problematic in dyslexic children (Stein, 1989). However, the cerebellum has until now been discounted in the dyslexia literature owing to its supposed lack of involvement in linguistic and cognitive skill. The human cerebellum is in fact very much more developed than that of other primates (with a development ratio second only to that of the cortex – Dow and Moruzzi, 1958), and researchers have wondered quite why this was, given that our motor skills are not that much better than the other primates (except for manual dexterity). Recent research has revealed that, in addition to the established role of the cerebellum in motor skill and automatisation, the neocerebellum is significantly involved in timing (Ivry and Keele, 1989) and in cognitive performance, including language – for recent tomographic and magnetic resonance studies see Decety et al. (1990) and Akshoomoff et al. (1992). Indeed, Leiner, Leiner and Dow (1989, 1991) argue that the loop between the cortex and the cerebellum, the cerebro-cerebellar loop, enables the cerebellum to moderate the learning of cognitive and language skills. This discovery makes mild cerebellar dysfunction a prime candidate for the underlying cause of dyslexia. In preliminary research into the possible role of the cerebellum in dyslexia, we investigated relative performance of our six groups on temporal estimation (known to be a sensitive index of cerebellar dysfunction) and loudness estimation (an apparently very similar task known not to be affected by cerebellar dysfunction). The dyslexic children showed the predicted dissociation, with a significant deficit on temporal estimation (even when compared with reading age controls) but no deficit on loudness estimation. The dissociation between time and loudness estimation provides strong support for a cerebellar deficit hypothesis, but further research is needed to explore this hypothesis, in view of the existing findings of neuroanatomical irregularities in the cortex (Galaburda, Rosen and Sherman, 1989), and the magnocellular pathway (Livingstone et al., 1991).

In conclusion, then, it seems that the single-mechanism explanations of dyslexia, which rely on a deficit in phonological, visual, motor or temporal processing skill, are overly restrictive. There are deficits in *all* these facets of skill, and therefore the true cause of dyslexia must lie deeper in the brain. Rather than an awkward embarrassment, we believe that this finding not only makes sense of what were previously rather disparate findings, but also points the way to an exciting research programme which explores the link between the brain and the mind. Our current framework involves an automatisation deficit at the performance level, noisy neural networks at the subsymbolic level, and a deficit somewhere within the cerebro-cerebellar loop at the brain level. No doubt further research will prove us wrong, but we feel that we are at least asking important questions, and that the answers to our questions will point towards the real answer.

Chapter 5
The cognitive psychology of developmental dyslexia

Introduction

This chapter reviews some of the work undertaken at University College of North Wales concerning the cognitive psychological description of developmental dyslexia. Tim Miles started this programme of research and 17 years later he continues to inspire hundreds of other students, psychologists, teachers, parents and children who all share a concern with developmental dyslexia. His researches address not only theoretical aspects of the disorder but also clinical and applied issues concerning remediation and education, and his training in linguistic philosophy ensures that no one associated with him can rest in a false security of woolly language and fuzzy definitions (Miles, 1957, 1961). Comparison of hundreds of individual cases has allowed him to see the syndrome pattern in the apparent labyrinth of diverse presenting symptoms (Miles, 1978, 1983). The Dyslexia Unit at University College of North Wales was set up to research and develop effective remedial teaching programmes, to train teachers, and to ensure a local provision for the assessment and education of dyslexic children (Miles, 1970; Miles and Miles, 1975, 1990). Tim has urged us that people, science, scholarship, and, particularly, dyslexia really do matter.

Tim first wrote on developmental dyslexia in a 1961 article 'Two cases of developmental aphasia' which reported detailed clinical case studies of two children, Brenda and Michael. In this chapter I will briefly illustrate the major issues and approaches introduced in that article and then review how these have progressed over the subsequent three decades.

The four major issues concern the following:

1. Developmental dyslexia as a syndrome – a specific deficit in reading

I express grateful thanks to my co-workers, Alan Baddeley, Gordon Brown, Suzanne Cataldo, Barbara Large, Tim and Elaine Miles.

and spelling which occurs despite high intelligence and which is commonly associated with other difficulties in symbolic processing.
2. The similarities between developmental dyslexia and acquired disorders of language.
3. The understanding that can be gleaned from analyses of the spelling mistakes of dyslexic individuals.
4. The possibilities of successful remediation given the proper choice of method.

The importance of these themes is indexed by the large amounts of work that have addressed them since that date. I argue here that:

- the most general information processing deficit in developmental dyslexia lies in phonological processing; developmental dyslexic subjects resemble acquired surface dyslexic subjects but are even more similar to younger children of equivalent reading ability;
- an understanding of the development of reading can only come from longitudinal investigations of development itself;
- such studies demonstrate typical sequences of interactive growth of related skills;
- a key stage in the development of reading is the acquisition of an alphabetic strategy and we can trace the evolution of this skill from implicit phonological awareness through explicit phonological awareness to spelling and hence to reading itself.

A cognitive psychological description of specific dyslexia

Miles (1961) showed that his two case histories demonstrate specific dyslexia, i.e. a failure to read and spell *despite high intelligence* 'as opposed to an ordinary manifestation of dullness or stupidity' (p. 63). Furthermore, their literacy problems were not the only symptoms:

> to say that a child suffers from dyslexia is not, as some have supposed, simply a high-faluting way of saying that he is weak at reading; it is to link such weakness with comparable weakness in brain-damaged adults, and to recognise the existence of a specific syndrome.
>
> (p. 49)

Thus the children had other difficulties concerning, for example, letter reversals and, particularly, short-term memory (Michael's poor reverse digit span and difficulty in repeating polysyllabic words). It was emphasised that these associated difficulties were predominantly concerned with symbolic rather than concrete processing:

> I am not of course suggesting that there is any failure of integration when *things* lie side by side, but only when *symbols* lie side by side.
>
> (p. 68)

How have these claims fared over subsequent investigations?

By the late 1970s it *appeared* that there were a wide variety of other difficulties associated with dyslexia. The then-current knowledge of dyslexia, reflected in reviews of hundreds of individual studies (e.g. Critchley, 1970; Vernon, 1971; Gibson and Levin, 1975) suggested a host of problems. Critchley's (1970) index is illustrative with its coverage of dyslexic subjects' perceptual problems, weak cerebral dominance, a constellation of minor neurological signs and clinical manifestations and maternal and socioeconomic correlates. Admittedly these were presented alongside an emphasis on language problems and the similarities with aphasia, but nevertheless it was still easy to reach the jaundiced conclusion that those with developmental dyslexia differed from normal readers in just about every assessed respect if investigators looked hard enough (Ellis and Large, 1987). These reviews arose predominantly from studies using *ex post facto* bivalent designs with little or no attempt to look for differential abilities. The investigations had been performed by different investigators, with children of different cultures, education, age and socioeconomic background, and they had involved radically different numbers of subjects. They had taken place over the previous 50 years when educational practices had been changing. It was quite possible therefore that these reviews constituted a nomothetic generality which, from a heterogeneous population, reflected none of the individuals studied.

By the end of the 1970s there began to appear more analytical and theoretically focused meta-analyses. Vellutino (1979) marshalled a strong case that just about all of the published experiments demonstrating the difficulty of those with developmental dyslexia used measures which involved some element of *verbal* processing; Ellis and Miles (1981) and Miles and Ellis (1981) analysed experimental, psychometric and clinical correlates of developmental dyslexia and argued that they all reflected problems with processing words as symbols (thus returning to the original etymological characterisation of dys*lexia* as a 'lexical encoding deficiency'); and Frith (1981) editing the 1981 special issue of *Psychological Research* on dyslexia concluded that dyslexic subjects' major problems with verbal processing arose because of a core deficit in phonological processing.

This will be illustrated with details of cross-sectional studies, studies from University College of North Wales and an in-depth longitudinal investigation.

Cross-sectional studies

When two letters of the same case are presented simultaneously and the child has to report whether they are the same (OO) or different (OB), dyslexic and control children do not differ either in the speed or in the accuracy with which they can perform this task. Nor are the dyslexic children or poor readers slower than age-matched controls when the letters, though different, are visually confusable (OQ, RP, EF, CG) (Ellis, 1981a,b). It appears unlikely, therefore, that dyslexic children have difficulty in dealing with the visual characteristics of letters as such. In contrast, when two letters of different case have to be adjudged the same (Gg) or different (Gw, Gd) on the basis of name characteristics, the dyslexic children are reliably slower and more error-prone than age-matched controls. It thus seems that dyslexic children have no extra difficulty in dealing with the visual aspects of letters as such, but that they show an impairment when the task demands the access and analysis of phonological features. This dissociation is similarly demonstrated in the study of Done and Miles (1978), who presented dyslexic subjects and age-matched controls with arrays of digits and afterwards made the correct digits available and asked the children to place them in the original order. At this task, where the stimuli were nameable, the dyslexic children scored considerably lower than the controls, but when non-verbal nonsense shapes were used as stimuli in place of digits the differences were minimal. Finally, when both groups had been given Paired Associate Learning, where names were learned for the nonsense shapes, the performance of the controls again became significantly superior.

This deficit in phonological access is confirmed in the wide range of demonstrations of dyslexic children being slow in naming letters, objects, colours, digits, pictures, non-words and words (Ellis and Miles, 1981) and their difficulties in verbal short-term memory, which are often taken as symptomatic of the syndrome.

These findings underpin the now modal view of developmental dyslexia as a deficiency in phonological processing: developmental dyslexic children are specifically impaired on tasks requiring perception, access or analysis of phonological material and they evidence no dramatic disability to function with concrete or visual material (Spring and Capps, 1974; Vellutino, 1979; Ellis and Miles, 1981; Frith, 1981; Miles and Ellis, 1981).

A longitudinal study

If we want to understand *developmental* dyslexia then we must do so directly. Only when the same persons are tested repeatedly over time does it become possible to identify developmental changes and processes of organisation within the individual. Cross-sectional studies which compare different groups of people at different stages of acquisition must always come a poor second when small but reliable changes with age are to be detected, where teaching methods and teachers change with time and where we do not wish to make the false assumption that the abilities of a younger cross-section were necessarily present in the older cross-section at a previous time. They also fail us with regard to the determination of causality: a cross-sectional study may show an association between two phenomena, but only a longitudinal investigation can determine which came first.

At Bangor we embarked on a study of the first three years of reading development in the same children using a longitudinal differential design (Ellis and Large, 1987, 1988). The longitudinal nature of the study allowed a meaningful analysis of the changing nature of individual children's reading skill and the determination of which skills promote reading development and which benefit from it. The differential design allowed not only the determination of which skills are associated with reading, but also their relative importance.

A cohort of 40 children was assessed for their abilities on 44 variables; besides the full Wechsler Intelligence Scale for Children (WISC; Wechster, 1976) there were a variety of measures of reading, spelling, vocabulary, short-term memory, visual skills, auditory–visual integration ability, auditory/language abilities, language knowledge, and rote knowledge and ordering ability. The children were assessed on these measures each year, from 5 to 8 years old. In the first of our reports (Ellis and Large, 1987) we extracted three groups at age 8 on the basis of reading and IQ scores. Group A showed a specific reading disability (high IQ, low reading), group B were good readers of similarly high IQ, group C showed a more generalised reading deficit in that they were at the same level as group A in reading but their IQ scores were low. The data were then searched retrospectively to describe the development of these patterns of ability from the very beginnings of reading acquisition.

The children with specific reading retardation differed from their better-reading peers in terms of the relatively few variables that concerned phonological segmentation, short-term memory and naming. The children with generalised reading disability differed from their better-reading peers in almost every respect, but the strong discriminators concerned phonological processing. The children with specific reading disability differed from those with generalised reading disability in terms of intelligence and abilities that involve visual processing. These patterns of ability were broadly replicated at each age from 5 to 7 years old.

From the wide and varied test battery there were few tests which discriminated between the children with specific reading disability and their age- and IQ-matched controls, and they all concerned phonological processing, short-term memory or some aspects of accessing the articulatory equivalents of visual material. The most important discriminators were the rhyming tasks that require implicit use of phoneme segmentation and which had previously been demonstrated to be reliable discriminators between dyslexic and adequate readers in group studies

(Snowling, Stackhouse and Rack, 1985), and to be reliable predictors of later reading difficulty (Bradley and Bryant, 1983). The next strongest discriminator was auditory digit span, a most common finding in the developmental dyslexia literature (see Vellutino, 1979; Ellis and Miles, 1981; Jorm, 1983; Ellis, 1990, for reviews). Next came other tests of short-term memory for verbal material (auditory sentence span, auditory word span) and of phonological processing (sound blending, phoneme segmentation). We additionally found that the rate at which children can access the articulatory equivalents for colours discriminated between the groups, and we confirmed the typical WISC profile of dyslexic children where they had problems with the Digit Span, Comprehension, Information and Coding subtests (Spache, 1976). The only discriminator which was not of a phonological type was visual serial ordering which squeezed in at the bottom of the list, a suitable placement because of the dispute over whether visual encoding problems fall out of group studies as being associated with dyslexia: some affirm this to be the case (Benton, 1962; Ingram, 1971), some deny (Yule and Rutter, 1976; Ellis, 1981a,b), some find it to be dependent on spatial frequency with the deficiency only in the transient subsystem (Lovegrove, Martin and Slaghuis, 1986), and some reinterpret the 'visual' tasks to involve implicit verbalisation strategies (Vellutino, 1979), but most would agree that such problems are negligible when compared with short-term memory and phonological processing deficiencies.

None of the other tests, the larger part of the battery, significantly discriminated between these groups – the children with specific reading problems did not seem to show reliable patterns of problems of visual processing (on tests of visual closure, picture completion, letter search, coding, block design, object assembly or picture arrangement), nor syntactic skills, nor rote knowledge and ordering.

Tim's earlier claims in this regard have thus stood the test of time: the developmental dyslexic children were really quite different from both their normal reading-ability peers and those with general reading retardation – see also Ellis (1994), and the commentary by Stanovich (1994). Furthermore, there is a characteristic pattern of associated difficulties all concerning phonological processing, suggesting that a core problem in this area may underlie the various presenting symptoms of developmental dyslexia (Frith, 1990).

Relationships between developmental and acquired disorders of language

Miles (1961) also saw that the language problems of developmental dyslexia might be enlightened by comparison with other acquired disorders:

our understanding of these [developmental dyslexic] disabilities in children can be helped by an examination of the whole group of aphasic disabilities in adults.

(p. 49)

The term 'dyslexia' is applied both to the difficulty a child may experience in learning to read and to reading problems resulting from brain damage in previously normal adults. Research on acquired dyslexia has recently undergone an intensive period of theoretical development and has led to a number of agreed categories of dyslexia, each having a characteristic pattern of reading errors, a different pattern of sensitivity to the characteristics of the material read and a concomitant description in terms of deficit in information-processing routes in models based on the analysis of normal adult reading (Coltheart, Patterson and Marshall, 1980; Patterson, 1981; Patterson, Marshall and Coltheart, 1985). For example, deep dyslexics have more difficulty reading orthographically regular non-words than real words, function words than content words and low-imageability words than highly imageable words, but they are largely unaffected by word length or orthographic regularity. Surface dyslexic subjects show the converse in that they are largely unaffected by lexicality, parts of speech or imageability, but are affected by word length and spelling regularity. Most current models of reading suggest that an isolated word may be read aloud by either of two routes. Those words that are in the reader's sight vocabulary may directly access both the word's phonological representation and its meaning. These will be read rapidly and accurately. In the case of words that are less familiar, reading is assumed to proceed via the application of either grapheme-to-phoneme translation rules or analogies between groups of letters in the word being read and similar groups of letters in known words. Deep dyslexic patients are assumed to have the former direct route relatively less impaired than the grapheme-to-phoneme or analogy-based route. Those with surface dyslexia, on the other hand, are assumed to be capable of using the grapheme-to-phoneme route, but to be impaired in the operation of the whole word route; hence, the use of their relatively automatic sight vocabulary is impaired but the ability to sound out words and non-words is relatively intact. When we compared developmental and acquired dyslexic subjects (Baddeley et al., 1982; Baddeley, Logie and Ellis, 1988), we found that people with developmental dyslexia were more akin to those with surface dyslexia, with both groups being susceptible to the effects of spelling regularity, somewhat susceptible to word-length effects, and insensitive to the content–function word distinction. On the other hand, our subjects with developmental dyslexia were clearly highly susceptible to the lexicality effect, being much better at reading words than non-words, an effect which is not said to be prominent in the pattern of reading disability exhibited by people with surface dyslexia. The pattern of results for those with developmental dyslexia was very similar to that of normal, younger children of an equivalent reading age.

People with developmental dyslexia and young children resemble people with surface dyslexia in having a poorly developed sight vocabulary, and thus having to rely more extensively on the indirect rule-based route. They differ from them in that adults with acquired dyslexia have previously had a fully developed reading system and their grapheme–phoneme route is well developed, extensive and automatised. The system of people with developmental dyslexia has simply not yet developed and their phonological deficits slow and restrict their reading through this rule-based route; hence their exceptional difficulties with novel words.

The role of spelling in reading development

It is interesting that Miles (1961) identified that dyslexic children's spelling errors might hold a clue to the nature of their problems:

> [Brenda's] spelling, despite its oddity, is nonetheless not unintelligent spelling, . . . her spelling is an attempt to put onto paper the written symbols for tongue and lip positions and movements, not the written symbols for words as such.

He explained spelling errors like 'kach' for *catch*, 'disdons' for *distance* by pointing out that 'there are no tactile–kinaesthetic cues for distinguishing a soft *c* from an *s* nor a hard *c* from a *k*, and, more generally, that many of the spellings are "phonetically intelligible"' (p. 57).

The importance of this observation has been reinforced by subsequent studies which have shown that analysis of children's spelling throws light both on the normal development of alphabetic strategies of reading and on the difficulties that developmental dyslexic children have at this stage of literacy development.

The idea that children's misspellings reflect a developing sense of phonetic properties of words was pioneered by Read (1971, 1975, 1986) who found evidence that young inventive spellers used a system of grouping sounds together according to shared phonetic features. Thus they might represent a particular vowel sound in their spelling by substituting a letter whose *name* shared a salient phonetic feature with the sound. Read's exhaustive studies of invented spellings attuned further research to the analysis of misspellings in an attempt to uncover a developmental sequence for spelling that reflects a heightening awareness of the internal sound structure of words, and this has led subsequent researchers to categorise developmental strategies in spelling. Henderson and Beers (1980) analysed samples of children's creative writing and assigned each error to a category according to the completeness of phonetic information mapped by the misspelling. They charted movement from pre-phonetic to phonetic stages of spelling. As a result of their work and that of Gentry (1982), it is now generally agreed that children move through distinct stages of spelling, namely precommunicative, semi-phonetic, phonetic, transitional and correct spelling. It is the first three of these developmental stages that are relevant to the question of how phonological awareness plays a role in children's early spelling. Pre-communicative spellings are characterised by the strategy of randomly selecting letter strings to represent words. Although at this stage children can produce letters in writing, their spellings reflect a complete lack of letter–sound or letter–name knowledge. Semiphonetic spellings contain a partial mapping of phonetic content. Phonetic spellings contain a complete description of the sequence of sounds in pronunciations.

Theoretical analyses which assign spelling a major role in the development of phonological as well as reading skills include Elkonin (1973), Chomsky (1977), Lewkowicz (1980) and Ehri and Wilce (1987). Frith (1985) suggested a theoretical framework within which spelling and reading interact to advance the learner towards increased proficiency in each ability. In her model, spelling plays a fundamental role in the movement from a visual, or logographic, reading strategy to an alphabetic approach: alphabetic spelling is the pacemaker for the use of an alphabetic strategy in reading. Early spelling practice involves dividing spoken words into phonemes and representing these phonemes with letters. In this way experience in spelling words affords the opportunity for making comparisons between the phonetic information in individual letters and sounds as they are embedded in the spoken word. Through repeated practice in spelling, the child may come to appreciate the subtle relationship between a symbol in the written word and its corresponding sound in the context of the spoken word. The discovery of this relationship is the key to alphabetic insight. The crux of the problem is 'knowing how to combine the letters into units appropriate for speech' (Liberman and Shankweiler, 1979, p. 141). Early efforts in spelling may provide the opportunity to experiment in a very concrete way with the properties of this abstract concept. As children struggle to decompose words into individual phonemic units, they commonly experiment with various articulatory rehearsals of word parts and they search for distinguishable articulatory units that correspond to letter–sound units. This process of their separating sounds in a word through consciously monitoring their own articulations may serve a dual purpose: it may both help the development of phonological awareness and enhance knowledge of the alphabetic principle.

Cataldo and Ellis (1988, 1989; Ellis and Cataldo, 1990) adopted a longitudinal design to measure directly these early sequences of interactive development in reading, spelling and phonological awareness skills. We elucidated the early causal relations among these three variables by following the development of each skill in a group of children as they moved from preliteracy through the beginning stages of learning to read and spell. In this study the early interactive development of reading, spelling and phonological awareness was charted in a group of 28 children during their first three years in school. During this time the children were tested at four intervals in reading and spelling real and nonsense words, phoneme segmentation and auditory categorisation. A test of phoneme segmentation was given as a measure of explicit phonemic awareness and a test of auditory categorisation was taken as a measure of implicit phonological awareness. The majority of the sample had only begun to attend school when the initial assessments were taken at the beginning of the school year in which their mean age was 4;6 years. The children were re-tested at the end of their first school year, at the beginning of the second year and finally at the beginning of the third school year. Exploratory (LISREL – Joreskog and Sorbom, 1984) causal path analyses were used to investigate the contribution of each ability to the subsequent growth of skill in word recognition, spelling and phonological awareness. The patterns of interaction among these three abilities provided a preliminary framework for mapping the early stages in the acquisition of literacy.

By broadening the phonological awareness–reading paradigm to include spelling, we were able to see a clear picture of the early interaction among these abilities. There were three measured phrases of development. Phase 1 spanned the children's first year in school. Phase 2 charted the development from spring of the first school year to autumn of the second year. Phase 3 looked at development from the beginning of the second year in school to the beginning of the third year. The phase 1 pathweights from spelling to reading real words and nonsense words identified spelling as an important contributor to the early formation of reading. This pattern of influence was repeated much more strongly in phase 2 with high pathweights from spelling to reading real words and nonsense words. The pronounced influence of spelling on reading contrasted with a negligible contribution of reading to spelling in both phases 1 and 2. Implicit phonological awareness initially predicted early attempts to read as well as to spell but lost its influence on both reading and spelling in the following two phases. In contrast to the diminishing predictive power of implicit phonological awareness, explicit phonological awareness consistently predicted spelling in all three phases, this influence increasing with phase. Explicit phonological awareness only emerged as a strong predictor of reading in phase 3.

This early interactive sequence describes the pattern of growth from pre-alphabetic to alphabetic stage reading (Frith, 1985). Although implicit knowledge of the sound properties of words helps children forge initial connections between the printed word and its pronunciation, spelling acts as a mediator for the use of explicit phonological awareness until the child begins alphabetic stage reading by directly applying explicit phonological awareness to reading. Our data suggested that, as children practise spelling, so they develop proficiency in the use of the alphabetic principle and apply this knowledge to the task of reading. In the beginning, as spelling begins to take form, the beginner relies on a phonological strategy based on a perception of the overall sound content of words. In turn, these early endeavours in spelling contribute to an awareness of the general sound properties of words. In the next stage, children begin to demonstrate proficiency in spelling with increasingly complete phonemic descriptions and a more analytical approach to pronunciations. This progression from holistic to analytical phonological strategy is analogous to the movement from semiphonetic to phonetic spelling proposed by Gentry (1982). Recognising that children's misspellings provide valuable insight into the formation of spelling ability, we also explored the relationships among different groupings of misspellings and different levels of phonological awareness.

We classified misspellings in five categories that reflect increasing insight into the phonetic structure of the word. It was a hierarchical classification of spelling errors based on work by Henderson (1980), Gentry (1982) and Morris (1983). The most rudimentary spelling skill, first letter strategy, preserves only the information for the initial letter. Closer approximations have both boundary sounds intact. The highest level of informed error are partial-sequential and sequential errors where only the middle phoneme is in doubt: the representation of consonant sounds is 'safer' than vowel sounds in that consonant sounds are more reliably 'matched' to letters on a one-to-one basis than are vowel sounds.

Our analyses showed that when young children in this age band made a spelling error which bore any phonetic resemblance to the target, it was more often the case that only information for the initial consonant was preserved. The next most typical responses were those where both boundary sounds were correct (either with or without an incorrect intervening vowel). By the time the children were at the beginning of year 3, the total numbers of errors had declined. Errors which fell into this hierarchical classification system became predominant (54% at the beginning of years two and three versus 23% at the beginning of year 1) – the children did indeed move from being precommunicative to semi-phonetic spellers. And this progression was also found within the semi-phonetic stage: the lowest phonemic content errors (first letter intact) declined with age and higher-order errors (sequential and partial-sequential), which preserved more of the phonetic content, came to the fore.

In conclusion, it is clear that Tim was right to identify spelling as an important clue to the nature of reading and reading disability. It is an important clue for researchers of these phenomena, but even more, it is important to the very children who are learning to be literate. Although implicit phonological awareness is the precursor of early developments in spelling, reading and explicit phonological awareness, it is the growth of *explicit* phonological awareness that allows the acquisition of alphabetic spelling. Awareness of rhyme and alliteration is not sufficient for accurate spelling; rather the child has to be able explicitly to segment the sounds of a spoken word, to strip it apart sound by sound and then look for the graphemes that represent these sounds. In turn, spelling makes this ability relevant to the child for the first time, both phonological awareness and spelling grow through practice and the alphabetic insight is gained. This insight is then available to allow its application in reading and the child shifts from a logographic to an alphabetic strategy of reading – see also Frith (1985) and Ehri and Wilce 1987).

Dyslexic children's problems with phonological analysis and awareness makes this passage very difficult for them, as Frith (1985, p324) says: 'Classic developmental dyslexia is the failure of alphabetic skills'. Hence children with developmental dyslexia need special remedial teaching which concentrates on phonological awareness. Although he did not use these terms, Tim's interventions concentrated on exactly these processes, as we will see in the next section.

Remedial teaching

Tim's description of the teaching programmes for Brenda and Michael reads as follows:

> The main problem was that of vowels. To start off, Brenda was required to make five columns in an exercise book; the first was headed by the word 'bag', the next by the word 'beg', and the third, fourth, and fifth by the words 'big', 'bog', and 'bug'. Each column had a 'noise', which was its vowel sound with the consonants removed... Brenda was required to make the 'noises' for each column in turn, concentrating on the tongue movements and the vibration of the vocal bands as she did so. The 'noise' could easily be associated with a particular letter, and thus any word with the same 'noise' as, say, 'bag' would necessarily have to have the same letter, viz. *a*, as its vowel. 'Cat', 'ham', etc. would go in the 'bag' column; 'cot', 'dog', etc. would go in the 'bog' column, and so on. The consonants were left in the main to look after themselves, since apart from *f* and *v*, etc., the phonetic distinction between them is not difficult.
>
> The next stage was to introduce a new set of 'noises'. The 'noises' chosen were the long *a*, the long *i*, and the long *o* and the three columns were headed by the words 'tame', 'time', and 'tome'. Brenda was required to pay attention to the contrast between the *ae* 'noise' (short *a*) and the *ei* 'noise' (long *a*), and was told that when the long vowel occurred an *e* was necessary at the end. Thus 'mate' carries a final *e*, 'mat' does not... In general the purpose was to give her

rules to follow whenever this was possible, rather than present her with the formidable task of remembering every word of the language by heart.

(Miles, 1961, pp. 56–57)

Such remedial teaching continued over about a year with her form mistress reporting 'steady (although not spectacular) progress in spelling' (Miles, 1961, p. 58).

This approach is clearly heavily influenced by 'phonic' methods (Flesch, 1955; Daniels and Diack, 1956; Downing, 1973). Did Tim back the right horse when he chose such an intervention? This question relates to *The Great Debate* (Chall, 1967) concerning the 'best' ways of teaching reading, at the core of which vie methods based on 'whole language', 'look-and-say', 'phonics', spelling and meaning. Over the decades each has ascended and waned in almost predictably recurrent cycles. It is a huge question and the debate still rages. However, since 1961 there have been a number of findings which suggest that, again, Tim was correct.

There is now an accumulation of evidence from evaluative studies of differing teaching methods that phonic and spelling-pattern training is particularly effective. Chall's (1967) exhaustive meta-analysis of the studies performed between 1910 and 1965 concludes that:

1. A code (phonics) emphasis tends to produce better overall reading achievement by the beginning of the fourth grade than a meaning emphasis, with greater accuracy in word recognition and oral reading from the very beginning, and better vocabulary and comprehension scores by mid-second grade. With a code emphasis the child seems initially to read more slowly because of the greater emphasis on accuracy; however, by the third or fourth grade when he is more fluent his rate is equal to, or may ultimately exceed, that produced by a meaning emphasis.
2. Systematic-phonics programmes that rely on direct teaching of letter–sound relationships are as successful as, or perhaps more successful than, programmes that rely on 'discovery' – the so-called linguistic approaches that do not teach letter–sound correspondences directly.

For the particular case of children with specific reading disabilities we find, similarly, in Bradley and Bryant's (1983) training study that when children who were backwards in reading at 4 and 5 years old were trained on sound categorisation (very similar in method to that of Miles (1961) described above) they showed markedly greater improvements in reading over the next two years than those who were given semantic categorisation training. However, those children who were given sound categorisation and, with the help of plastic letters, were additionally taught how each common sound was represented by a letter of the alphabet, showed even greater improvement. Furthermore, less than 10 hours of such training spaced over two years led to these superiorities in reading being sustained through until the children were 13 years old (Bradley, 1989). We can conclude from these results that phonic training is particularly effective for individuals who are retarded in reading, and, furthermore, training in sound categorisation is even more effective when it is linked to spelling and involves an explicit connection with the alphabet.

A perennial question in clinical and educational psychology concerns whether training for individuals with a particular information-processing deficit should attempt to remedy that deficit directly or whether it should play to individuals' strengths, helping them to circumvent their weaknesses by capitalising on other skills. It is becoming clear that, at least for those with developmental dyslexia, their problems with reading stem from underlying phonological problems and these are best countered by reading tuition which helps them to acquire phonological awareness and analysis skills.

Conclusions

This brief review has confirmed the phonological deficits in developmental dyslexia. It has shown how reading changes in nature as it is learned and that an important early stage in its development is the adoption of an alphabetic reading strategy. It has traced the precursors of the phonological knowledge that forms the foundations of grapheme–phoneme reading back through spelling, through explicit phonological awareness and in turn to its source in implicit phonological awareness. It has confirmed that the reading and spelling development of developmental dyslexic children is limited by their prior failures to acquire this knowledge. Furthermore, it has demonstrated Tim Miles's keenness of insight in identifying these over 30 years ago as important areas of research.

Chapter 6
Elementary symbol processing in less skilled readers in a componential analysis framework

CHE KAN LEONG

Introduction

In his cumulative research and clinical programmes on developmental dyslexia over many years, Tim Miles has investigated a number of significant issues. These 'dyslexia matters' studied by Miles and his Bangor team include, among others:

- estimating the prevalence of dyslexia and testing the hypothesis of 'normal' and 'anomalous' variations of dyslexia from a large survey (Miles and Haslum, 1986; Miles, 1991);
- diagnosing, specifying 'patterns of difficulties', remediating and helping dyslexics (Miles, 1970, 1982, 1983; Miles and Miles, 1990);
- verifying experimentally and delineating verbal processing deficits in dyslexics (Ellis and Miles, 1981; Miles and Ellis, 1981; Miles, 1986).

These important theoretical and practical issues continue to be investigated by a number of researchers with varying findings. Take, for example, the question of developmental dyslexia as a bimodal or continuous distribution of reading abilities studied by Miles (1991; Miles and Haslum, 1986). Dobbins in his more recent study of 600 9- to 11-year-old children found some qualified support for severe underachieving readers as a 'naturally occurring' group different from those merely backward in reading (Dobbins and Tafa, 1991). In some contrast to Dobbin and Tafa are the findings of the large-scale Connecticut Longitudinal Study of 414 children entering kindergarten in 1983 and followed by birth cohort (Shaywitz et al., 1992). Using the aptitude achievement approach, with discrepancy defined as the difference between observed achievement predicted by regression on intelligence, Shaywitz et al. demonstrate a univariate normal distribution pattern for the discrepancy scores. The Connecticut results show dyslexia as occurring at the tail end of a normal distribution of reading ability with some fluctuation of long-term outcomes in diagnosis. These recent studies are but samples of the varied nature of dyslexia studied with different approaches and methods.

If there are disagreements, there is also general consensus on some issues. One important consensus finding is dyslexic people's persistent deficit in all aspects of automatic word identification (Perfetti, 1985). This verbal deficiency is traceable to some elementary lexical encoding deficiency across input and output modalities (Ellis and Miles, 1981) and is verifiable clinically (Miles and Ellis, 1981; Miles, 1986).

In this chapter, I offer further evidence of information processing of elementary symbol identification as a source of individual differences in reading performance. The experimental task is a variation of the sentence verification paradigm (Clark and Chase, 1972; Carpenter and Just, 1975) and one used by Miles (1986, Experiment 3). The target subjects of less skilled readers comprised the lowest 25–30% in scaled aggregates of vocabulary and reading comprehension standardised tests for each of grades 4, 5 and 6 in a two-phase, two-cohort study of component processes of reading in about 300 children (Leong, 1988, 1992a). These target less skilled or below-average readers, as compared with average and above-average readers of similar chronological ages, including what Miles (1991) terms underachievers with stronger and weaker evidence of dyslexia and 'normal' achievers with stronger and weaker evidence of dyslexia. The results will need to be interpreted within this broader grouping. As the experimental task of sentence–letter verification is part of the measurable tasks used in the componential analysis, I will first outline this broader aspect.

Componential analysis of reading

Component processes

It is hypothesised that reading deficits characterising less skilled readers can be better understood and remediated by conceptualising 'macro' reading processes as more 'micro' components and sub-components acting and interacting, one on the other (Frederiksen, 1982; Carr and Levy, 1990). These mutually facilitating processes are emphasised: word analysis; discourse analysis above the word level; and integrative analysis. In particular:

1. Skilled reading performance derives from integrated, automatic processing of various knowledge-based subskills.
2. The integration of the subskills operates in an orderly cascade system, enabling outputs from a particular level (e.g. word processing) feeding into adjacent levels (e.g. sentence processing) and also distant levels.
3. The efficiency or automaticity of the processing is particularly important.

4. Mechanisms for the interaction of the components may differ for 'expert' or fluent readers and for 'inexpert' or less skilled ones. While poor readers are generally inefficient in processing component reading tasks, there are individual differences and the locus of inefficiency varies from component to component and from subskill to subskill.

Postulates

Based on the above logic, it was hypothesised in the two-phase, two-cohort study that for readers in grades 4–6, reading proficiency results from a complex operation of at least these components which also interact with one another:

● orthographic and phonological component,
● morphological component,
● sentential comprehension component.

These components were conceptualised as latent or unobserved domains subserved by some manifest or measurable variables tested via the microcomputer with response latency measures as indices of automaticity or processing efficiency (Leong and Lock, 1989).

These unobserved, parsimonious, latent variables, subserved by measurable laboratory reading or reading-related tasks, were tested for their goodness of fit with the latent reading competence, subserved by measurable standardised vocabulary and reading comprehension tests, in liner structural relation (LISREL) modelling. Details of the logic, *a priori* theory and the modelling of reading processes in 10- to 12-year-old readers (298 in the phase 1 cohort and 252 in the phase 2 cohort) of varying reading proficiency are provided elsewhere (Leong, 1988, 1992a).

In addition to the linear structural relation modelling, the developmental study also yielded fine-grained information on the readers' differential processing of the interrelated components and subcomponents such as derivational morphology (Leong, 1989a,b). The micro and macro analyses further provided the basis for remediation to enhance word knowledge and reading comprehension in those children most deficient in both reading and spelling (equivalents of the underachievers with stronger and weaker evidence of dyslexia and normal achievers with strong evidence of dyslexia in Miles (1991) (Leong, Simmons and Izatt-Gambell, 1990). I outline below the nature of the components and their measurable tasks as used in the phase 1 study (Leong, 1988). The measurable tasks used in phase 2 (Leong, 1992a) were basically the same as those for phase 1 with refinements after item analysis using the Rasch model (1960/1980).

Modelling orthographic and phonological knowledge

The orthographic and phonological domain was subserved by the orthographic subskill, phonological subskill and rhyme-matching subskill tasks. The orthographic subskill task required individual children to distinguish accurately and rapidly words from homophonous letter strings matched for length and pronunciation (e.g. *RAIN*, RANE; CLOUN, *CLOWN*). The assumption is that a correct lexical decision has to be based on knowledge of the orthographic code of the letter strings. The phonological subskill task required subjects to designate accurately and rapidly the pseudohomophonic letter strings that sound like real words in item pairs matched for length and orthographic similarity (e.g. BLOG, *BLOE*; *KAKE*, DAKE).

The rhyme-matching task tests the hypothesis that the cognitive and linguistic demand, and by inference the latency for decision, of rhyme matching is markedly increased where there is a conflict between orthographic and phonological cues. This notion was tested with matched non-rhyming word pairs which contain identical rime but different onsets (e.g. PAID–SAID; GOLF–WOLF). This rhyme-matching condition with conflicting orthographic and phonological cues was compared with other word-pair conditions which rhyme (e.g. BLUE–FLEW), and word pairs which both rhyme and are orthographically similar (e.g. PAIR–FAIR). Statistical analyses of the response latencies show clearly the different rhyme-matching conditions vary significantly according to the cognitive and linguistic demands of the conditions and for readers of varying reading abilities in different grades (Leong, 1991a).

Modelling morphological knowledge

The morphological domain relates to declarative knowledge of the structural composition of words with particular emphasis on derivational morphology and morphemic parsing (Leong, 1989a,b). The complementary derived form morphology and base form morphology subskills examined individual subjects' automatic morphological knowledge of the derived forms and base forms of words embedded in sentence frames in relation to reading proficiency. Latency results of the automatic processing in vocalising the appropriate derived or base words from the target base or derived forms, embedded in short sentence frames, show clearly the increased cognitive and linguistic demand from the no change (e.g. WARM#TH; ENJOY#MENT) through the orthographic change (e.g. SUN – SUNNY), phonological change (e.g. DRAMA – DRAMATIC) to the orthographic and phonological change (e.g. EXPLAIN – EXPLANATION) processing conditions (Leong, 1989a,b).

The morphological decomposition subskill relates Taft's (1987) Basic Orthographic Syllabic Structure (BOSS) principle and its corollaries to reading proficiency in the two-phase, two-cohort study (Leong, 1988, 1992a). This task is based on the logic that the parsing mechanism conserves the underlying morphological relationship among semantically related words. For example, ACTOR or LANTERN should be recognised visually more efficiently as the morphologically BOSS-headed ACT-OR or LANT-ERN rather than as the articulation-defined AC-TOR or LAN-TERN. There is also a processing 'cost' associated with the parsing of pseudo-affixed words containing affix-like segments (e.g. enOUGH, CLIMate) as compared with truly affixed words (e.g. LEADer, NATIONal). The results of studies using similarly constituted words and pseudo words with different reading subgroups and different grades suggest that the efficiency in lexical decision via the Taft BOSS-headed morphemic division of words is a source of individual differences in reading proficiency (Leong, 1989a, Study 1; Leong and Parkinson, 1992).

Modelling verbal comprehension

The sentential comprehension domain was subserved by several sub-skills. The sentence lexical decision task is predicated on the rationale that the grammatical structure of incomplete sentences affects lexical latencies. Modal verb contexts, followed by main verb targets, and preposition contexts, followed by plural noun targets, should lead to faster response latencies than do the opposite pairings. This principle of grammaticality and parsing procedures should differentiate response latencies and provide another indicator of reading performance. In this task the subject was asked to press a YES/NO key to denote if the target word would make the anomalous sentence 'better' (but still anomalous) or 'not so good'. Sample couplet sentences were: 'If the ball falls, it will LAUGH.' (YES); 'If the ball falls, it will CROPS.' (NO).

The sentence pattern task is essentially a sentence decision task assessing functional grammar such as subcategorisation, particle movement, selection restriction, and transformations including negation, question formation and passivisation. Examples of parallel sentences were: 'The runner turned off the road.' (YES); 'The runner turned the road off.' (NO). Efficient access to knowledge of functional grammar is another source of individual differences in reading proficiency.

The paragraph comprehension task aimed at assessing the child's ability to detect quickly and accurately the one incongruous or inconsistent sentence embedded in running texts of six sentences each. An example was a passage with the schema of a boy going into a barber shop, waiting and finally getting a hair cut, but the title of 'Visit to a Doctor' was incongruous. It was hypothesised that the ability to detect inconsistency in connected discourse would affect reading performance.

Sentence–picture/sentence–letter verification task

The sentence verification task was predicated on the psycholinguistic processing models of sentence–picture verification of Clark and Chase

(1972) and Carpenter and Just (1975), and their precursor 'The processing of positive and negative information' by Wason (1959). There were two parts to the present task with 16 sentence–picture verification pairs to part 1 and 16 sentence–letter verification pairs to part 2 (this part being similar to the experiment 3 task in Miles (1986)). The emphasis was on the cognitive and linguistic processing needed in a deceptively elementary sentence verification task and the different effects on readers of varying reading proficiency.

In essence, typical sentence–picture pairs are constructed by taking four binary dimensions (STAR, PLUS), (IS, IS NOT), (ABOVE, BELOW), and (*, +; +, *) for part 1 and the binary concepts of the graphemes <b>, <d> or phonemes /b/, /d/ (bness, dness), (IS, IS NOT), (LEFT, RIGHT), and the 'pictures' or symbols of b and d in part 2 in all possible combinations. These permutations yield 16 sentence–picture pairs and 16 sentence–letter pairs with four truth conditions: true affirmative (TA), false affirmative (FA), true negative (TN) and false negative (FN). The sentence–picture (or sentence–letter) combination is displayed simultaneously on the microcomputer screen such that individual subjects might see the sentence 'Star is above plus' and a picture of a star above a plus (TA condition) or 'The b is to the left of the d' with a 'picture' of d to the left of b (FA condition) (see Table 6.1 for details). The subjects are then asked to verify accurately and quickly if the sentence is a true or a false description of the picture (or sentence–letter) combination with a key press, which terminates the timer to provide precision verification timing in milliseconds. This standard procedure was followed in the present study with the part 2 task.

This type of verification task taps the cognitive process involved in holding a series of reading units in memory until their meaning is accessed, and this process is used irrespective of the linguistic or the pictorial strategy employed. The response latency thus reflects the combined time taken to encode and comprehend the sentence–picture or sentence–letter pair and also to verify the match or mismatch of the TA, FA, TN or FN truth conditions. Despite some technical differences between the Clark and Chase (1972) and the Carpenter and Just (1975) psycholinguistic models, there is general agreement that verification latencies show increasing linearity according to the degrees of match or mismatch or the number of constituent comparisons. Furthermore, the robust linearity results account for a very large proportion of the variation in latencies across truth conditions. True negative (TN) sentence–picture pairs should take the longest processing time because of the mismatch between the embedded strings of the sentence and the picture encoded in propositional forms and the embedding strings. The next longest latencies are the FNs, then the FAs, and the TAs are processed the fastest. In other words, the cognitive and linguistic demands of the truth conditions as reflected in response times can be hypothesised as: TA < FA < FN < TN. The information-processing mechanism of the sentence–picture or sentence–letter verification task is shown in Table 6.1.

It should be noted that the TN condition is the most complicated in terms of the mental operations needed for verification. It is likely that in the verification process subjects mentally delete the negative, then verify the truth or falsehood of the statement, and then change the answer to accommodate the deletion of the negative. It is TN, not FN, which is a double negative in that TN denies a falsehood. Hence it is reasonable to expect TN to take the longest processing time.

Within the above logic, the linearity of processing as a function of the number of constituent comparisons was borne out with the phase 1 grades 4, 5 and 6 children ($n = 298$) trichotomised into below-average (BA), average (AV) and above-average (AA) readers on the aggregate of standardised word reading and reading comprehension tests. Space limitation precludes detailed discussion and the results for the part 2 sentence–letter verification can be summarised as follows. The means and standard deviations of the verification times (TRUE/FALSE) of the correct answers, after editing for outliers for the three grades by reading, and for the four verification conditions, are shown in Table 6.2. These results are displayed graphically in Figure 6.1.

Without going into details and without loss of generality, the analyses of variance of the verification time measures indicate highly significant

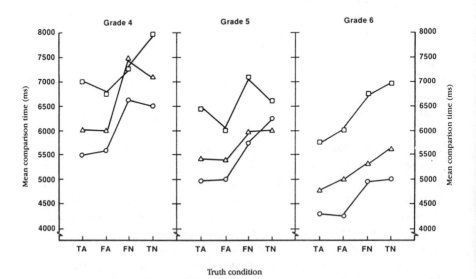

Figure 6.1 Sentence–letter verification time (ms) for grades 4, 5 and 6 children (n =298) by reading level (below-average (BA) – $\square$, average (AV) – $\triangle$, above-average (AA) – $\bigcirc$), and by truth condition (true affirmative (TA), false affirmative (FA), false negative (FN), true negative (TN))

Table 6.1 Sentence verification task, part 2

	Truth condition		Sentence representation	Letter representation	Number of constituent comparisons
The *b* is to the left of the *d* / The *d* is to the right of the *b*	True affirmative (TA)	*b d*	[AFF(*b*, LEFT)]	(*b*, LEFT)	K
The *b* is to the left of the *d* / The *d* is to the right of the *b*	False affirmative (FA)	*d b*	[AFF(*b*, LEFT)]	(*d*, LEFT)	$K+1$
The *b* is not to the left of the *d* / The *d* is not to the right of the *b*	True negative (TN)	*d b*	{NEG[AFF(*b*, LEFT)]}	(*d*, LEFT)	$K+5$
The *b* is not to the right of the *d* / The *d* is not to the left of the *b*	False negative (FN)	*d b*	{NEG[AFF(*b*, LEFT)]}	(*d*, LEFT)	$K+4$

Table 6.2 Means and standard deviations (in parentheses) of sentence–letter verification times (ms) by condition and reading level for grades 4, 5 and 6 children ($n = 298$)

	Grade 4 readers Below average (BA)			Grade 5 readers Average (AV)			Grade 6 readers Above average (AA)		
Truth conditions	BA	AV	AA	BA	AV	AA	BA	AV	AA
True affirmative (TA)	7053 (2706)	6074 (2006)	5548 (1934)	6449 (2561)	5406 (1577)	4909 (1660)	5766 (2277)	4772 (1547)	4347 (1502)
False affirmative (FA)	6742 (2655)	6017 (2377)	5658 (2138)	6021 (2664)	5335 (1657)	5030 (1256)	6077 (2490)	5024 (1835)	4292 (2026)
True negative (TN)	7910 (3095)	7184 (3003)	6495 (2437)	6623 (3039)	6086 (1538)	6259 (3006)	6897 (2674)	5614 (2060)	4992 (1919)
False negative (FN)	7364 (3169)	7456 (2868)	6603 (2486)	7190 (3494)	5900 (2285)	5775 (2070)	6737 (2966)	5362 (1642)	4892 (1540)
Sample size	35	34	34	27	30	31	36	34	37

performance differences at the 0.001 level among the three grades ($F[2, 288] = 10.57$) and varying reading levels ($F[2, 288] = 9.52$). In particular, the three (grade) by three (reading level) by four (truth condition) ANOVA results with the last factor repeated show significant differences in response latencies among the four verification conditions ($F[3, 867] = 30.20$). Essentially the same results are obtained in adjusting for the very slight different general ability scores for the different subgroups. All the differences vary linearly accordingly to the level or complexity of match or mismatch in the mental operations, especially for the grade 6 readers. These results are in accord with the earlier robust findings with adults (Clark and Chase, 1972; Carpenter and Just, 1975), and further support the analyses of the part 1 sentence–picture verification task with the same 298 children (Leong, 1991b).

Of the four verification conditions, the TA condition involves no mismatch between the sentence and picture representation and should be processed the fastest. The base number of constituent comparison denoted by K is incremented by one mental operation in the FA condition where there is a mismatch between the sentence and picture propositions. Similarly, for the FN condition the number of constituent comparisons is $K + 4$; and for the true denial of a falsehood or TN condition the number of constituent comparisons is $K + 5$. The ANOVA results summarised in Figure 6.1 show that the response latencies among the four verification conditions generally vary linearly according to the levels of match or mismatch in the mental operations. The verification of truth conditions as a form of verbal comprehension is not so much a function of affirmation or negation *per se*, but of the number of constituent comparisons between the mental representations.

Discussion and implications

Verbal efficiency

One of the purposes of the longitudinal two-cohort study as outlined here and discussed in detail elsewhere (Leong, 1988, 1992a) was the modelling of reading processes with a number of laboratory reading or reading-related tasks sampling interrelated reading subskills under rather stringent experimental conditions. The administration of all the experimental tasks via the microcomputer with response–time measures as the dependent variables aims at capturing the on-line, real-time nature of reading. In analogy with other complex skills (Downing and Leong, 1982, Chapters 2 and 3), reading involves the concurrent computation of different kinds of cognitive and linguistic information in a relatively short time. The immediacy nature of reading is best repre-sented in the latency measures derived from the various lexical and sentence decision tasks and the vocalisation tasks. The computerised tasks also encourage automaticity (due care being taken to guard against speed–accuracy trade-offs) at 'lower' levels of processing so that resources can be devoted to 'higher' levels of processing. The underlying notion is the promotion of verbal efficiency (Perfetti, 1985).

The present results indicate that less skilled readers are much less efficient or less 'automatic' in encoding and verifying the truth condition of the deceptively simple sentence–letter verification task and the parallel sentence–picture verification (Leong, 1991b). It should be pointed out that left–right directionality did not pose a problem for the children as determined during the practice sessions. The reaction-time measures discriminating grades and reading levels (Figure 6.1) suggest that an elementary information-processing task such as sentence–picture or sentence–letter verification might be one of the sources of individual differences in reading performance. Whether this inefficiency or lack of automaticity would extend beyond the verbal domain to more general skills for dyslexic subjects, as argued forcefully by Nicolson and Fawcett (1990), needs further investigation.

Interrelated components of reading

Details of the interrelatedness of the three latent components of reading (orthographic and phonological, morphological, and sentential comprehension) and their 'causal' effects on grades 4, 5, and 6 readers' reading performance, subserved by standardised word reading and reading comprehension tests, have been reported elsewhere (Leong, 1988, 1992a). Briefly, linear structural relation (LISREL) modelling (Jöreskog and Sörbom, 1984) with competing models shows that the three-component modelling, with nine to ten independent variables, seems to provide a good fit for phase 1, grade 4 and a reasonable fit for grade 5, but was less unambiguous for grade 6 (Leong, 1988). This 'loose' fitting suggests that the model and its variant forms need to be formulated more rigorously, and 'clean' manifest tests should enhance the contribution of the interrelated domains to school reading performance. It should be pointed out that for the second cohort of 252 children in phase 2 of the longitudinal study, the manifest or indicator tests were in fact 'purified' on the basis of item analysis using the Rasch model (Leong, 1992a). Furthermore, results from the multi-sample linear structural relation modelling using LISREL indicate reasonable stability over time and across cohorts in terms of the goodness of fit of the model and its variants with the data.

Results of the analyses of variance of the experimental tasks (Leong, 1989a,b, 1991a,b; Leong and Parkinson, 1992) and the LISREL analyses should add to the argument for the multi-level and multi-component model of reading proposed by Carr and Levy (1990) and Frederiksen

(1982). Conscious awareness of knowledge of phonology, as represented by the orthographic and phonological component in the developmental study, has been shown to be important in early reading (Leong, 1987, 1991a), and phonological processing of lexical access is not diminished with age or with familiar words (Van Orden, 1987). At the same time, knowledge of the compositional and relational nature of lexical items as reflected in the morphological component is also important. This is shown by the finding in multiple regression analyses that the derived morphology task accounted for 32%, 34% and 44% of the variance of the criterion of reading performance for grades 4, 5 and 6 readers respectively (Leong, 1988). Then verbal comprehension as subserved by the sentence decision, sentence pattern, paragraph comprehension and sentence verification tasks is equally important, because reading revolves around the learning of concepts from texts, in addition to acquiring and developing word knowledge.

As shown by the classic studies of Wason (1959), Clark and Chase (1972) and Carpenter and Just (1975), and as can be inferred from the heuristic values of my results with children summarised here (Tables 6.1 and 6.2, and Figure 6.1), the basic mental processes involved in sentence–letter verification are part of a larger system of mental operations used in verbal comprehension. In comprehending linguistic materials, readers (and for that matter listeners) need to encode the lexical and syntactic information, access the concepts and simultaneously compute the interpretations on the basis of previous knowledge. The efficiency with which readers encode and verify elementary information, as suggested here, may be a source of their reading proficiency.

Training of components of reading

The delineation of functionally defined information processing domains and their interactions, as suggested by Frederiksen (1982) and Perfetti (1985), among others, emphasises the linking of the components and the possibility of training individual subskills. The cognitive framework and actual training procedures are well stated by Frederiksen and his colleagues (Frederiksen, Warren and Rosebery, 1985a,b; Frederiksen and Warren, 1987). The underlying notion is that '. . . tasks high in a skill hierarchy (e.g. the inference task) depend on the effective, integrated operation of a number of skills that are functionally linked, either through shared data structures or shared processing resources, to the skills explicitly acquired to perform such tasks . . .' (Frederiksen, Warren and Rosebery, 1985b, p. 334).

Frederiksen and his colleagues have developed microcomputer training environments focusing on individual components of reading and have carried out training studies to evaluate transfer effects to other functionally linked components. These 'enabling' processes in word analysis and parallel, frame-based analysis of text demonstrate the feasibility of componential approach to instruction and remediation.

Our intervention efforts during the phase 2 follow-up of the second cohort of children were much more modest. Two twin-training studies, extending over five weeks and involving poor readers akin to Miles's (1991) underachievers with stronger and weaker evidence of dyslexia, together with their controls, were carried out (Leong, Simmons and Izatt-Gambell, 1990). The emphasis was on verbal efficiency and its interaction with the underlying mental representation systems (Beck and Carpenter, 1986). Study 1 stressed the development of word knowledge component in poor readers through multiple exposures and multiple sources of information (McKeown and Curtis, 1987; Miller and Gildea, 1987). Study 2 aimed at elaboration training in the prose comprehension component (Palincsar and Brown, 1984; Wong, 1985). Analyses of the quantitative and qualitative data show some measure of success in the modest five-week training programme in promoting word knowledge and efficient self-questioning among these poor readers. Both study 1 and study 2 also suggest that direct, explicit teaching with discussion of learning strategies and feedback could go some way in helping not only less skilled, but also skilled, readers. Extending the Frederiksen concept and his microcomputer training environments, colleagues in Colorado, Guelph and Umeå, and I have also been using the sophisticated text-to-speech computer system (DECtalk) to enhance word knowledge and reading comprehension in children (Leong, 1992b).

In summary, this succinct report with data on the inefficient lexical system of less skilled readers, as shown by their less efficient processing of the elementary sentence verification task, within a cognitive componential framework of reading processes is in accord with some of the findings of Miles and his colleagues (Ellis and Miles, 1981; Miles and Ellis, 1981; Miles, 1983, 1986, 1991). The Bangor team has also pointed to further directions for added exploration.

Part III
The Identification
of Dyslexia

Chapter 7
Diagnosing dyslexia in the classroom: a three-stage model

PETER GARDNER

Introduction

This article outlines a three-stage model to help teachers diagnose dyslexia. It aims to be relevant to the needs of teachers, already busy not only with their teaching role, but with the increased responsibilities and curricular changes brought about by the 1988 Education Reform Act. It aims to be simple to follow and practical in application whilst not cutting too many theoretical corners.

There is ample research evidence that the earlier a child's difficulties are diagnosed and appropriate treatment given, the better is the prognosis for remediation. Most researchers agree on the inappropriateness of diagnosing dyslexia in children less than seven or eight years old. However, it is still sensible to assess a child's areas of strength and weakness at an early stage, so that an appropriate remedial programme can be provided.

Assessment can be of many types; two are considered here. First, there is the informal type of assessment, which occurs routinely as part of a teacher's in-class skills, where the teacher observes aspects of the child's functioning in reading, spelling, handwriting and mathematics, particularly with regard to the errors that the child makes. Second, there is the psychometric approach which is quantitative and normative and which assesses the child both in relationship to other children and in comparison to other aspects of his or her own performance. Stage 1 of this model corresponds to the informal type of assessment and stages 2 and 3 are progressively specific approaches using a psychometric model.

A definition of specific learning difficulties/dyslexia

Many such definitions exist. Some are controversial; few are specific or 'conceptually-leakproof' (Pumfrey and Reason, 1991). One current definition of specific learning difficulties is:

organising or learning deficiencies which restrict the student's competencies in information processing, in motor skills and working memory, so causing limitations in some or all of the skills of speech, reading, spelling, writing, essay writing, numeracy and behaviour

(Dyslexia Institute, 1989)

Incidence of dyslexia in schools

Estimates of the incidence of dyslexia vary considerably, with 'a wide range of apparently conflicting percentages: some are as low as 0.05% and some as high as 30%' (Miles, 1991), but the British Dyslexia Association suggests a figure of 4% of the population being severely dyslexic, indicating that, as a rough rule of thumb, there will be one severely dyslexic child in every classroom.

The three-stage model of diagnosing dyslexia

Stage 1. Teacher observation of the child's areas of difficulty

A number of checklists of symptoms associated with specific learning difficulties or dyslexia exist (Spreen, 1968; Miles, 1970, 1983; Word Blind Centre, 1970; Bannatyne, 1971). Such lists often highlight the presence in the dyslexic child of:

1. An apparent discrepancy between the child's apparent intellectual capacities and his or her attainments in basic literacy and numeracy skills.
2. Reversal of letters such as *b, d, p, g, q*, inversion of letters *u* and *n*, *m* and *w*, and confusion of numbers 3 and 5, 6 and 9, possibly reflecting poor visuospatial ability.
3. Poor auditory sequencing and poor short-term auditory memory in the pupil who finds difficulty in reciting common sequences, e.g. days of the week, months of the year.
4. Poor visual sequencing and poor short-term visual memory.
5. An incomplete knowledge of laterality, e.g. left and right knowledge, of himself and of others, with perhaps associated directionality problems which may be associated with telling the time or tying shoelaces.
6. Crossed lateral dominance, where the dominant eye is on the opposite side of the body to the dominant hand, though there is research evidence to counter this hypothesis (Clark, 1970; Rutter, Tizard and Whitmore, 1970; Moseley, 1988).
7. Poor visual tracking, i.e. the tendency to scan from right to left,

rather than (necessary in Western cultures) from left to right with, at times, the lack of a fixed reference eye.

8. Verbal retrieval difficulties, where the pupil appears slow or unable to access words from his or her wordstore, sometimes meaning that he or she cannot put names to familiar objects.

9. Poor concentration, an inability to settle to the task in hand and restless distractability.

10. Poor organisational skills, meaning that the child may arrive at lessons with insufficient or the wrong equipment, may have difficulty in acknowledging time limits and appear to become scruffily dressed rather quickly.

11. *Secondary* emotional or behavioural difficulties, which may take the form of increased aggression or temper tantrums, withdrawal or isolation, feelings of depression, hopelessness and inferiority etc. It is clearly important to distinguish behavioural difficulties which appear to arise as a result of the child experiencing difficulties in learning, particularly when confronted at school by the need to acquire literacy and numeracy skills, from similar behaviour, which may arise from other causative factors such as parental divorce or the birth of a new sibling, for instance, and from pre-existing primary behavioural difficulties, i.e. those which were present before the onset of the need for formal learning in basic educational attainments.

Whatever identifying characteristics of dyslexia observation or research appear to suggest, great care should be exercised in defining such characteristics as causative of failure to achieve satisfactory attainments. Young and Tyre (1983) argue that, for instance, *b–d* confusion, often considered to be a 'classic' dyslexic sign, may itself be the result of reading inexperience rather than the cause of reading failure; likewise, Bryant and Bradley (1985) quote evidence suggesting that the hypothesis that a poor memory for words often leads to poor reading ability is not proven; rather, it seems, it may be the other way round, i.e. 'reading probably determines memory'.

Developmental indicators of possible dyslexic difficulties

It is sensible for the teacher to liaise with the child's parents:

- to gather from parents information about the child's development which is an aid to the diagnosis of dyslexia;
- in order to involve them in discussions about their child's difficulties and possible future treatment plans.

Developmental indicators

1. Since dyslexia, when defined 'narrowly', is seen as language difficulties, it is unsurprising that many dyslexic pupils (60%) show a history

of late talking (Hornsby, 1984) or unusual 'scrambled' pronunciation of words.

2. Some history of the delayed passing of motor milestones may be present, including both gross coordination, i.e. walking, where 20% of dyslexic students were late walkers (Hornsby, 1984) – the average age for the onset of walking unaided in the general population of children is 13–14 months (Gesell et al., 1940) – and fine motor coordination, sometimes associated with a child's poor-quality, jerky handwriting with inadequate pencil control and poorly formed letters.

3. There is evidence that dyslexic difficulties may be genetically transmitted (Miles and Miles, 1990; DeFries, 1991). This goes beyond the widely accepted finding that a child with literacy difficulties is likely to have parents who show similar difficulties, which finding only supports a familial, rather than a genetic, association.

4. Evidence exists from post-mortem studies that the brain structure of dyslexic differs from that of non-dyslexic subjects, indicating that there is likely to be a neurological basis to dyslexia (Galaburda et al., 1985), which can result in unusual brain rhythms in dyslexic children (Duffy et al., 1988). In the case of children with brain injury occurring at or after birth, where similar developmental and educational symptoms can occur, the resulting syndrome is deemed to be 'acquired dyslexia', of which several subtypes are held to exist (Marshall, 1984).

Factors which do not define dyslexia

There are a number of factors which are often found commonly associated with educational retardation in basic literacy and numeracy skills, but which are not considered to be defining characteristics of dyslexia:

• very low intellectual ability
• peripheral sensory deficits in visual and auditory modalities
• a serious lack of, or inadequate, education
• serious health problems
• obvious brain damage
• emotional or behavioural difficulties which preceded the formal learning process
• cultural deprivation.

However, it is quite possible for a dyslexic child to show a number of such characteristics, i.e. cultural deprivation or inadequate education, though these themselves are not defining characteristics of dyslexia.

Stage 2. Assessment of the child's levels of attainments and intellectual abilities

The aim of the stage 2 assessment is to get accurate baseline information on the child's abilities in reading, spelling, handwriting and mathematical skills, together with an assessment of intellectual capacities. The concept of 'intellectual abilities' is, I believe, preferable to 'intelligence', because the latter term tends to imply a single and unitary ability, whereas in reality a person can be intelligent in a whole variety of more or less unrelated ways (Gardner, 1983). Thus, though the IQ figures are useful in themselves, it is often – and particularly in the case of children or adults with learning difficulties – more instructive to consider a person's specific strengths and weaknesses in abilities, and several tests actually can do this.

Tests of intellectual ability are overwhelmingly successful in their practical application. Very large numbers of carefully planned research studies support the conclusion that tests of intellectual ability, properly constructed, administered and interpreted, are good predictors of success or otherwise of the child at school or the person in further or higher education, though they do not, of themselves, take account of other factors important in determining success, such as motivation and perseverance (McCall, Appelbaum and Hogarty, 1973), type of school (Rutter et al., 1975) and parental support (Hanson, 1975).

For instance, with regard to type of school the child attends, although the average IQ is 100, there can be much variation from school to school, depending on the type of socioeconomic background of the area, quality of teaching etc. Thus, in an area where the comprehensive system is a true comprehensive system, 100 will be the average IQ; in some schools, the average is approximately 110, whereas in some independent schools and in a few grammar schools, the average may be 125 or even 130.

Good tests of intellectual ability have been found in research studies to be superior to the subjective judgements of adults, which sometimes are influenced by a person's performance in just one or two areas or abilities, language factors, attributes of personality – and even physical presentation, clothes, accent etc. (see, for example, Berscheid and Walster, 1972).

Criticisms of IQ tests are numerous and have often centred on their lack of prediction (Hudson, 1971), their limiting effect on our understanding of intellectual processes (Sigel, 1963), their cultural bias (McGuire and Hirsch, 1977) and their 'labelling' effect (Kagan, 1971). Anxiety can depress performance, though not usually to a significant degree, and the examiner is on the lookout for such signs and makes appropriate allowances in reporting the results. IQ figures do vary from occasion to occasion, though not, in usual circumstances, to a marked degree. They become increasingly valid as the child gets older and, after about eight years of age, they have considerable predictive power (Butcher, 1968). This is not to decry their use before that age; revealing a child's areas of relative strength and weakness at an early age often suggests areas where further help is valuable. Clearly, IQs should not be 'labels' on people. They provide very useful information on an important aspect which differentiates one person from another.

Intelligence measurement

An IQ (Intelligence Quotient) is a type of standardised score, based on an average (arithmetic mean) score of 100. Statistical analysis demonstrates that the relationship between IQ and the percentage of any sample of people obtaining a certain IQ is as shown in Table 7.1. The percentages are reasonably, rather than exactly, correct and can be translated into the concept of percentile, which is a very useful way of understanding an IQ figure. A *percentile* means a person's position on a scale from 0 to 100 compared to a randomly selected group of his age. Thus, if a person falls at the 90th percentile, he is more able than 89% and less able than 10% of people of his own age. Age-equivalent scores, i.e. in years and months, are also useful.

Tips to guide the assessment process

1. It is usally sensible to support any subjective qualitative observations of a child's strengths and weaknesses with quantitative, norm-referenced data, in order to ensure that the most accurate information possible is obtained. Tests are, thus, necessary.
2. It is usually preferable to use published tests rather than to construct in-house tests. Though their content may not entirely match the pupils' curriculum, their advantages of standardisation, validity, reliability etc. outweigh the disadvantages in many instances.

Table 7.1 Categories of intelligence (as approved by the British Psychological Society)

IQ level	Categories of intelligence	Percentage of people obtaining an IQ within these limits
<55	Severe learning difficulties	1
55–69	Moderate learning difficulties	2
70–84	Below average	13
85–94	Low average	34
95–104	Average	34
105–114	High average	13
115–129	Above average	2
130+	Superior	1

3. There are schools which screen a new intake of children *en bloc* in a number of basic attainments. They often use NFER or other group tests of verbal and non-verbal intellectual ability and reading skills. When group tests are used, it should be accepted that their results may be somewhat less accurate than those provided by individual tests, partly arising out of the characteristics of the tests themselves and partly because each child's level of motivation and on-task behaviour cannot so easily be controlled as in a one-to-one, face-to-face setting. It is sensible to screen the whole class initially, probably in late September or early October, i.e. when the children have had time to settle down with their teacher.

4. It should be accepted that no test adequately and completely meets every need; further, it is very rare indeed to come across a test which is universally acclaimed. Texts by Vincent et al. (1983), Levy and Goldstein (1984), Pumfrey (1985) and Ridgway (1987) provide detailed critiques of a wide range of tests of educational attainment.

Tests which fulfil the following criteria are preferred, bearing in mind that no single test is likely to fulfil all the following stated criteria:

   (a) are appropriate for the age range being considered;
   (b) contain detailed publication data;
   (c) have an adequate standardisation, which states the sampling method (preferably random), the sampling design, an adequate size of standardisation sample together with an evaluation of the sample representativeness, and the date of standardisation – it is surprising to note how, even for some well known and popular tests, no standardisation information is given;
   (d) fulfil the stated purpose of the author;
   (e) give adequate detail of item preparation and analysis, the relationship between items and appropriate pupil curricula, and trialling;
   (f) are relatively straightforward to administer, with clear and unambiguous instructions;
   (g) are valid:
      (i) in terms of content and theoretical base (content and construct validity), they measure what they are supposed to measure,
      (ii) relate to other similar measures now or in the future (concurrent and predictive validity), and that such validity coefficients (on a range 0–1.0) are clearly stated with estimates of confidence limits, i.e. to what extent can we be certain that the obtained scores in fact do represent the pupil's true score;
   (h) are reliable, in being reasonably replicable between testers or over a period of time;

(i)   are easily scored;

(j)   give some cues as to interpreting test results;

(k) are short and do not take up too much valuable teaching time.

Specific tests of educational attainments and intellectual abilities

Assessment of educational attainments

As noted above, one of the defining features of a pupil with a pattern of specific learning difficulties is that his or her attainments are not at the level one would expect, bearing in mind the pupil's age and level of intellectual abilities. This helps distinguish such children from children who are globally retarded.

In order to assess current levels of attainment accurately, it is traditional practice to assess reading, spelling and mathematical skills using appropriate attainment tests.

Tests of reading ability

It is useful to assess a number of different aspects of reading, including word recognition, sentence reading, reading comprehension and reading speed.

1. *Word recognition tests*. With regard to word recognition tests, many psychologists use the word reading test from the British Ability Scales (Elliott, Murray and Pearson, 1979, 1983) which has five forms and yields reading ages from 5;0 years to 14;5 years, together with percentiles and T-scores; the latter scores are based on an arithmetic mean of 50. However, this is a test limited to use only by psychologists (referred to as a 'closed' test) and, in its absence, teachers may use a test such as the Burt Word Reading Test (1974 Revision – Scottish Council for Research in Education, 1976), which yields reading ages from 6;4 years to 12;0 years, the Schonell Graded Word Reading Test (1971 Revision) giving reading ages of 6;0 years to 12;6 years (Schonell and Schonell, 1942–1955), or the Carver Word Recognition Test (Carver, 1970), an individual or group word recognition test up to a reading age of approximately 8;6 years. This last test not only provides a level of attainment, but, in the opinion of the author, is an excellent diagnostic test. The Burt and Schonell tests take approximately 5–8 minutes to administer, whereas the Carver Test may take a little longer, approximately 15 minutes.

2. *Sentence reading tests*. Single-word recognition can be considered to be an important skill, inasmuch as a number of single-word signs do exist in society at large; further, multiple-choice examination questions often penalise children with poor word recognition skills. However, they have been criticised (Vincent et al.,1983; Pumfrey,

1985) inasmuch as they only assess a very limited aspect of the total reading process and ignore a child's reading in the total linguistic context. For this reason, it is good practice to give also a prose reading test. If time is limited, the Salford Sentence Reading Test (Bookbinder, 1976), with three parallel forms, is a sentence reading test which gives reading ages from 6;0 years to 10;6 years. This, like word reading tests, has the advantages of being short and simple to administer; indeed, many pupils complete this test in approximately 3–5 minutes. To cope with pupils with higher reading ages, the Edinburgh Reading Tests (Moray House, 1981), stage 3, age range 10;0–12;6 years, and stage 4, age range 12;0–16;0 years, may be used, though they take a considerably longer time to complete. Alternatively, the Wide-span Reading Test (Brimer and Gross, 1972), taking approximately 30 minutes, being a test of silent reading comprehension, covers an age range of 7;0–15;0 years. The Edinburgh and the Wide-span Tests are group tests and could be used for screening purposes.

However, many psychologists, and indeed teachers, prefer the detailed individual analysis of a child's reading accuracy, reading comprehension and reading speed, given by the Neale (1989) Analysis of Reading Ability – Revised British Edition, which asks a child to read passages of graded difficulty and answer appropriate questions, while the child's reading is timed. Typically, an administration of the Neale Analysis of Reading Ability to a single child, together with its scoring, takes between 15 and 25 minutes.

A closed test which has recently appeared on the market is the Wechsler Objective Reading Dimensions (WORD – Rust, Golombok and Trickey, 1993), assessing children from 6;0 years to 16;0 years in basic reading, which includes word recognition and sentence reading, reading comprehension and spelling.

Spelling tests

The range of spelling tests available is considerably more limited than that of reading tests. Many teachers will be well acquainted with the Schonell Graded Spelling Tests A and B (Schonell and Schonell 1942–1955), whose two parallel forms provide spelling ages of between 5 and 15 years. However, the 1955 standardisation is now virtually 40 years out of date. For this reason, the Vernon Graded Word Spelling Test is often preferred, with its more recent date of publication (Vernon, 1977), providing spelling ages of between 5;7 years and 15;10 years. The Spar (Spelling and Reading) Tests (Young, 1976) with the value of ten parallel spelling tests, with spelling ages ranging from 7 years to 15;11 years, but taking approximately 30 minutes, provide a possible alternative.

Although it is valuable to assess children's spelling on a normative test, it is also highly desirable to make an assessment of their spelling in unaided free writing, because free writing, in making the additional demands on a child of sentence construction, punctuation and grammar, often leads to a deterioration in spelling ability. It is thus desirable to measure a child's spelling error rate in free writing and to express it as a percentage, i.e. the child who misspells, in a 5-minute period of free writing, 10 words out of 50 which he writes, is said to have a 20% spelling error rate.

Assessment of handwriting

Asking the child to complete a piece of free writing in a five or ten minute timed period can yield important information in this crucial skill; it may be that handwriting has been considered to be an underrated skill. Certainly, a child's handwriting is one of the most visible signs of his achievement and, as so much work is presented by the child in written form, the child's handwriting is often one of the most visible aspects of his abilities, noticed by both pupils and teachers (Cotterell, 1970).

Initially, observations may be made as to whether the child has any difficulty in thinking of what to write. It is then sensible to observe whether the child adopts the usual and correct position for approaching the handwriting task (Alston and Taylor, 1987; Jarman, 1988). It is then important to observe whether the child anchors the paper with the non-writing hand. Further, does the child hold the pencil in the usual tripod grip, or in an unusual grip, or is the grip particularly low or high on the pencil? It is important to consider letter formation skills, in order to assess whether a child starts and finishes letters correctly, reverses or inverts letters and closes letters when necessary.

With regard to style and presentation, observations can be made as to whether the child uses print, a cursive script or a mixture of the two. Are letters of a correct relative size to each other? Is the spacing between letters and words regular and appropriate? Is the writing of an appropriate size for the child's age and does it discriminate in size between capital and lower case letters? Does he or she keep to the lines?

An assessment should be made as to the child's speed of handwriting. For instance, a GCSE candidate who writes at only ten words a minute is likely to be severely disadvantaged in public examinations, unless he or she receives a concession of extra time.

Lastly, an overall rating should be made as to the presentation of written work, bearing in mind crossings out and alterations. This is inevitably subjective, but can be rated on a one to ten scale, bearing in mind age and ability. Further assessments of punctuation, grammar, sentence structure, sentence length and content can also be made.

Tests of mathematical skills

A child may show a specific learning difficulty with mathematics, either in mental arithmetic or in written computation skills or in both. Mental arithmetic in particular places a heavy burden upon a child's short-term auditory memory coupled with sequencing skills, drawing upon recall of mathematical tables. A mental arithmetic sub-test is contained on the Wechsler Intelligence Scale.

Perhaps of more importance, particularly in the days of calculator usage, are written mathematical skills. In order to assess basic computational skills, using the four rules and involving fractions and decimals, is the basic number skills test of the British Ability Scales (Elliott, Murray and Pearson, 1979, 1983). Again, this is a closed test. An alternative to this can be found in the 30-minute Graded Arithmetic–Mathematics Test (Vernon, 1979) which has both junior and senior versions, providing a range of mathematical ability ages from 5;0 years to 17;1 years, and samples a wide range of arithmetic and mathematical skills, including basic computation, time, money, distance etc., graph-work, equations and trigonometry. It has the advantage of being a group test.

An alternative to this is the France (1979) Profile of Mathematical Skills, which again has junior and senior versions, is a group test, provides separate mathematical ages for addition, subtraction, multiplication, division, operations, measurement and money and extensions, has the considerable benefit of providing mathematical ages, standardised scores and percentiles, but has the disadvantage of being very detailed and untimed. Many schools assess one component in a single lesson. Nevertheless, it provides excellent diagnostic information and a profile of mathematical scores for each child.

Assessment of intellectual capacities

Despite some initial differences in conceptualising intellectual processes between, on the one hand, the so-called British school of thought, represented by Spearman (1927), which considered that whilst each task carried a specific factor loading, every task also shared a factor loading of g (general factor), and, on the other, the American school of thought, represented by Guilford (1967) and his followers, which proposed a multi-factorial model of intelligence, whose essence is the presence of many separate individual factors, there grew up a general agreement of a model which allowed both a general factor, specific individual factors and some group factors. Burt (1917) found evidence, through examining children in school subjects, of verbal, numerical and practical group factors; Vernon (1960) generally supported this model. The most widely used test of intellectual ability in the Western World, i.e. the Wechsler Intelligence Scale for Children, is now in the WISC-III UK edition. This gives evidence of a Verbal Comprehension factor and a

Perceptual Organisation factor being the two major factors of ability measured by the scale, and those broadly correspond to verbal and practical (non-verbal) abilities respectively. Most teachers, therefore, will wish to assess both a child's level of verbal intellectual ability and a child's non-verbal intellectual ability.

The measurement of verbal intellectual ability on an individual basis by teachers can be carried out by using either the English Picture Vocabulary Tests (Brimer and Dunn, 1970) or the British Picture Vocabulary Test (Dunn, et al., 1982). Both tests have an ability age range up to 18 years and are quick to administer, require no necessary verbal response from the child and are simple to score. They yield standardised scores (equivalent to IQs), percentiles and, by extrapolation, receptive vocabulary ages.

An alternative test is one which not only taps a child's receptive vocabulary (understanding of words), but also assesses a child's expressive language (his ability to understand and express language). Vocabulary tests have long been known to be an excellent predictor of verbal intellectual ability. The ones which are most widely available and subject to a considerable amount of research are the Vocabulary Scales (Mill Hill and Crichton) of Raven (1958, 1981–1988). Here the child is asked to define individually a series of words. The test takes approximately 10 minutes. One of the drawbacks of this test is that it appears to give scores only in terms of percentiles at the 5th, 10th, 25th, 50th, 75th, 90th and 95th percentile points or in terms of grades on a five-point scale from verbally superior to verbally impaired.

Perhaps the most widely used tests of non-verbal intellectual ability available to teachers are the Coloured Progressive Matrices and Standard Matrices of Raven (1958, 1981–1988). These tests require a child to study a pattern, part of which is missing. The child has to perceive relationships and then select a piece of a pattern from a number of such pieces in order to complete the diagram. The test thus uses a logical method of reasoning with non-verbal materials. Again, it has the disadvantage of giving scores in terms of a limited number of percentile points and in terms of grades. However, it has the advantage of being well standardised.

Of course, it is perfectly possible for teachers to select verbal and non-verbal reasoning tests from the NFER catalogue and to administer them individually, instead of as group tests.

Interpretation of results

Many teachers compare a child's attainments in the basic skills to his or her chronological age. Thus, a child who is 9;0 years old will, if he or she achieves a reading age of 8;0 years, appear to be 1;0 year retarded in reading. However, this line of reasoning discounts the importance of a child's intellectual potential in determining achievement, and just as no educator would expect, for instance, a child of 9;0 years with profound and multiple handicaps to achieve at a 9-year-old level (for such a child, an overall developmental level may be less than 1;0 year), it is just as appropriate to expect a more intellectually able pupil of 9;0 years to have basic literacy and numeracy levels which are at a level above his or her own chronological age. Thus, a child whose overall IQ is 110 might be expected to achieve at or near to a 9;11 years level, one with an overall IQ of 120 at 10;10 years, and one whose overall IQ is 130 at 11;8 years. Table 7.2, provides details of differential retardations based upon the difference between a child's expected attainment level and the actual attainment level, based on age and level of intellectual maturity. Note that it is very often the bright and able child, i.e. child number 5 or 6 in Table 7.2 who, being only a year retarded behind his or her own chronological age, may not be picked up as showing a considerable true retardation, i.e. behind his or her own level of mental maturity.

Clearly, this model has drawbacks, but it does serve to support generally held assumptions relating achievement, at least in part, to intellectual ability. Educational law supports this understanding: the 1944 Education Act specifies that children should be educated according to 'age, ability and aptitude', thus determining the right of the child to have his or her ability levels taken into account in determining the appropriate education (and, by inference, his or her level of educational retardation).

This model of attempting to specify a pupil's expected reading/ spelling/mathematical score has been criticised (Gaddes, 1976), and other approaches have been suggested. Ravenette (1961), Rutter, Tizard and Whitmore (1970) and Dobbins (1986, 1988) have preferred a 'regression approach' using regression equations, which are designed to 'predict the most likely measurement in one variable from the

Table 7.2 Differential retardations based on the differences between a child's expected and actual attainment levels

Child number	Child's age (years)	Intellectual level (IQ)	Expected attainment level (predicted from IQ) (years)	Actual attainment level (years)	Retardation (years)
1	9;0	100	9;0	9;0	nil
2	9;0	90	8;1	8;1	nil
3	9;0	100	9;0	8;0	1;0
4	9;0	110	9;11	8;0	1;11
5	9;0	120	10;10	8;0	2;10
6	9;0	130	11;8	8;0	3;8

known measurement in another' (Guilford, 1981). Such an approach is not, however, despite its statistical rigour, in widespread use.

Having completed stage 2 of the assessment, the teacher will now be in a position to do the following:

1. Ascertain those children who show some global intellectual retardation.
2. Ascertain those children who, despite a good level of intellectual abilities, appear to show specific learning difficulties in one or more of the basic educational attainments.
3. Ascertain which children show features of specific learning difficulties, observations gleaned from the teacher's informal assessment of stage 1.

Stage 3. Tests of important subskills underlying literacy and numeracy development

At the end of stage 2, the teacher is unlikely to have detailed knowledge of the important subskills which underlie achievements in the basic educational skills. It is the function of stage 3 to diagnose such difficulties.

In the hands of an experienced teacher, many 'level of attainment' tests can yield useful diagnostic information. Nevertheless, specific diagnostic tests of certain important subskills exist and are likely to deepen the teacher's understanding of the child's problems. Table 7.3 shows a selection from a wide range of tests useful for this purpose; they have the additional benefit of being readily available.

At the end of stage 3, the teacher will have a detailed profile of the child's developmental history, an indication of current levels of difficulty in basic literacy and numeracy skills, and evidence of abilities in verbal and non-verbal intellectual abilities, together with diagnostic information concerning important subskills. It is at this stage that a diagnosis of specific learning difficulties/dyslexia can be made, with a level of certainty that reflects the emergent pattern and the teacher's own professional experience and expertise in recognising such difficulties. If the teacher is in any doubt, a consultation with an educational psychologist is strongly advised.

Consultation with an educational psychologist

Children may be assessed by an educational psychologist for a variety of reasons, and these include assessment for Statementing purposes, assessment for the provision of a remedial programme, assessment for educational placement, assessment and treatment for emotional and behavioural difficulties or for vocational and career guidance purposes. If the pupil's difficulties appear relatively severe, it may be necessary to instigate a multiprofessional assessment to ascertain whether or not the

Table 7.3 Tests of subskills

Name of subskill	Tests used by Teachers
Short-term memory – auditory	Aston Index *Auditory Sequential Memory Macmillan† Diagnostic Reading Pack
Short-term memory – visual	Aston Index *Visual Sequencing Memory (Pictorial) Aston Index *Visual Sequential Memory (Symbolic) Macmillan† Diagnostic Reading Pack
Discrimination – auditory	Aston Index *Sound Discrimination Macmillan† Diagnostic Reading Pack
Discrimination – visual	Aston Index *Visual Discrimination
Sound-blending	Aston Index *Sound-blending Macmillan† Diagnostic Reading Pack
Auditory organisation	Bradley (1980) Test of Auditory Organisation
Visual perceptual and visual motor skills	Frostig (1964) Developmental Test of Visual Perception
Grapheme-to-phoneme correspondence	Many, including Neale (1989) Analysis of Reading Ability Supplementary Diagnostic Test 1: Names and Sounds of the Alphabet Macmillan† Diagnostic Reading Pack
Phoneme-to-grapheme knowledge	Ask the child to write the letter of the alphabet from each sound given individually in an oral manner. Sounds should be randomised, not in ABC order
Knowledge of key words	Many, including Macmillan† Diagnostic Reading Pack, Thirty Two Key Words, Sixty Eight Key Words
Knowledge of laterality	Harris (1974) Tests of Lateral Dominance Aston Index*
Checklist of dyslexic symptoms	Bangor Dyslexia Test (Miles, 1982)

*Aston Index (Thomson and Newton, 1982).
† Macmillan Diagnostic Reading Pack (Ames, 1980).

child has special educational needs as defined under Sections 1(1) and (2) of the Education Act 1981, with a resultant Statement of Special Educational Needs under Section 7 of the same act. Education authorities must, as a minimum, seek educational, medical and psychological advice, and the psychological advice will, in most cases, be provided by an LEA educational psychologist.

However, only 30% of educational psychologists find 'dyslexia' to be a helpful term and approximately 9% find the less 'emotive' term of 'specific learning difficulties' not helpful (Pumfrey and Reason, 1991). Such figures may well change as research confirming a neurological aetiology to dyslexic difficulties, but there are schools and individual teachers who, with an educational psychologist unsympathetic to such problems, may either ask for a second opinion or advise parents to seek the opinion of a psychologist outside the state system who finds the descriptive diagnostic terms acceptable and helpful.

It is not the purpose of this chapter to detail the approach or tests used by psychologists; they lie outside its scope. However, it is appropriate for the psychological report to do the following:

1. Use a sufficient variety of psychological and educational tests, which detail the child's strengths and weaknesses in a range of skills and subskills.
2. Describe the child's difficulties in simple terms, where jargon is either avoided or explained.
3. State how each area of weakness affects his or her current functioning within his or her class and school setting.
4. State how each area of weakness affects the child's self-esteem, social relationships and functioning within the home environment.
5. Detail clearly what remedial measures need to be taken, in terms of curricular details, details of any extra remedial help and remedial equipment, details of the amount of time to be spent on remedial work and whether this is on an individual withdrawal basis, a small group basis or an in-class support basis or a combination of more than one of these types of involvement.
6. State clearly what the process is for monitoring the child's future progress.

In conclusion, this three-stage model is presented as an aid to help teachers diagnose more accurately children with specific learning difficulties in their care. It is offered in the belief that accurate diagnosis is an effective use of time by specifically targeted remedial strategies rather that adopting a scatter-gun approach. It is offered in the hope that children's learning difficulties are not overlooked, that such problems are not thus compounded and that each dyslexic child is helped to achieve to his or her potential.

Chapter 8
Towards a rationale for diagnosis

T.R.MILES

A significant feature of the present dyslexia scene is the absence of agreed criteria for diagnosis. There are many practitioners – parents, teachers and those who carry out professional assessments – who have wide experience of dyslexia and who have no difficulty in picking out standard cases. Such people, however, are not always of the same mind as researchers; the latter have sometimes tended to 'do their own thing' without checking whether the criteria which they formulate are acceptable to the practitioners. In the 'rationale for diagnosis' which follows I shall attempt to formulate principles which hopefully will be acceptable to practitioners and researchers alike.

A common procedure among researchers has been to equate 'dyslexia' with 'reading disability' and then to make use of 'exclusionary' and 'discrepancy' criteria. Excluded are those whose poor reading is due to lack of intelligence or lack of opportunity, along with those who have significant sensory defects or severe problems of personal adjustment. The 'dyslexics' are those among the remainder whose reading, despite adequate opportunity, is less than would have been expected in view of their intelligence level. Researchers who (with minor variations) have followed this line include Vellutino (1979), Treiman and Hirsch-Pasek (1985), Shaywitz et al. (1990), and many of the contributors to Pennington (1991b).

It is somewhat puzzling that some of the more recent published papers refer to their subjects not as 'dyslexic' but as 'reading disabled' or 'RD'. It is not clear whether this expression is intended to imply less by way of theoretical commitment than 'dyslexia' or whether the two terms are intended to be synonymous. In the case of Shaywitz and her colleagues the references to dyslexia in their literature review strongly suggest that they are equating the two, and this is certainly how their research has been interpreted*. Pennington (1991b, p.3) speaks of 'dyslexia *or* reading disability (RD)' (my italics), which again suggests

---

*A letter sent to various American newspapers on behalf of the Orton Dyslexia Society contains the following plea: 'We hope that the study will receive more than the cursory, sometimes unclear and misleading interpretations it has received in some of the media.'

that he is not making any distinction. In contrast, however, Yule et al., (1974), though using similar selection criteria, chose to speak of 'specific reading retardation' precisely so as to avoid any theoretical commitments which could be associated with the word 'dyslexia'. There have therefore been differences in terminology as well as differences of substance.

Now if we reflect on what are the requirements for a good definition of dyslexia it would seem that two conditions in particular need to be satisfied. The first is that the outcome must be a classification which has firm foundations in research. The second is that the criteria specified must lead to the picking out of those whom practitioners know to be dyslexic – people, that is to say, who are dyslexic in the commonly accepted sense of the word. I shall argue that if dyslexia is equated with 'reading disability' and diagnosis is made on the basis of exclusionary and discrepancy criteria, then neither of these conditions is satisfied.

To take the second point first (because it can be disposed of more briefly), the equation of 'dyslexia' with 'reading disability' would never be accepted by practitioners. For them the emphasis on poor reading diverts attention from the many other needs which, at least in the case of older people with dyslexia, are far more important – the ability to spell, to calculate, to keep appointments, to organise study skills and to retain self-respect. Even more relevant is the fact that by the age of about ten or eleven many intelligent dyslexic children will have learned to read reasonably adequately, and it follows that researchers who diagnose in terms of poor reading will miss many individuals ('false negatives') who by other criteria are clearly dyslexic. Anyone with experience of dyslexic university students knows well that reading is among the least of their problems. The position has been admirably stated by Rosenberger (1990, p. 103) who writes:

> It is entirely possible for a dyslectic youngster, by virtue of proper tutorial assistance, to read at grade level; and selection criteria that require an achievement deficit of one or two grade equivalents, even those that take IQ into account, will miss this important subgroup.

There is also the risk of including a significant number of 'false positives' – those who are poor readers without being dyslexic. It is plain that what we call 'reading' involves a variety of complex skills, and there is no reason why someone should not be a poor or retarded reader when other manifestations of dyslexia are not present. Evidence has been put forward (Miles and Haslum, 1986; Miles, Wheeler and Haslum, 1993) which suggests that the distinction between dyslexic and non-dyslexic underachievers is a valid one.

With regard to the first requirement, it is essential that those who formulate diagnostic criteria should take into account the relevant advances which have been made in research in the last ten years.

Among the most striking of these have been the anatomical investigations of Dr Albert Galaburda and his colleagues (Galaburda et al., 1987, 1989; Sherman et al., 1989; Galaburda, 1993). The part of the brain selected for special study was an area of the temporal lobe known as the planum temporale. When post-mortem examinations were carried out on the brains of eight individuals known to have been dyslexic in their lifetime it was found not only that there were many disturbances of cell layers but that in all eight cases the two plana were symmetrical and approximately equal in size. In contrast it had earlier been found that in about 75% of unselected brains there is asymmetry, with the left planum usually being the larger. A probable interpretation is that the symmetry in those with dyslexia gives rise to an unusual balance of skills. This would make sense of the fact that those skills usually associated with the right cerebral hemisphere – a talent for thinking visuospatially and for thinking holistically – are often well developed in dyslexic people, whereas those usually associated with the left hemisphere – in particular the ability to organise language in a sequential way, which is a skill needed in reading and spelling – are relatively weak. Such an interpretation would certainly make sense to the practitioners. Although the matter has not so far been adequately documented, it is widely agreed that some of those with dyslexia have distinctive talents in such fields as art, engineering and modelling, as well as in areas where high creativity is at a premium, such as mathematics, imaginative literature and business management. For further discussion of the distinctive skills of those with dyslexia see Geschwind (1982) and West (1991).

It is even possible in the light of recent research to offer a tentative theory of causation. It is now known that within the visual system of primates there are two separate divisions, which have been named the magnocellular subdivision and the parvocellular subdivision. The former has been found to carry fast low-contrast information, the latter slow high-contrast information. A particularly exciting finding was that, when Dr Albert Galaburda carried out post-mortem examinations of five of the dyslexic brains which he had earlier studied, he found that there were no abnormalities in the parvocellular layers but considerable disorganisation in the magnocellular layers (Livingstone et al., 1991). The authors consider the possibility that other systems besides the visual have a fast and a slow subdivision; and if this were true of the auditory system it would make sense of the so-called 'phonological' difficulties – inability to deal with fast-changing speech sounds – which are widely believed to be a central feature of dyslexia (Tallal, 1980; Catts, 1989; Rack, 1994). In an attempt to summarise the situation I have written as follows:

> The most likely causal chain . . . seems to me to be this: for genetic or other reasons certain individuals have a weakness in the magnocellular pathways of the visual and auditory systems, with the result that it is difficult for them

adequately to synthesise sequences of sounds – including speech sounds – if they are presented at too fast a rate. This in its turn leads to a weakness at the 'phonological' level: dyslexics have more difficulty than non-dyslexics in associating things and events in the environment with their spoken equivalents. The consequence is the whole range of weaknesses which have been described in this book

(Miles, 1993, pp. 236–237)

It may be in the future that anatomical criteria will take the place of behavioural ones. In the meantime, however, it is clear that if diagnosis is to have a firm scientific basis a key concept on the behavioural side must be that of an imbalance of skills. The dyslexic person has many strengths but will often be relatively weak at any task which has a significant phonological component – at tasks, that is, where the appropriate speech sound has to be produced at speed. The job of the diagnostician is to check for such an imbalance.

Now if this account of the matter is correct, then for researchers to rely primarily on reading scores is insufficient. As I have argued elsewhere (Miles, 1994), the term 'reading' does not provide an adequate taxonomy (classificatory principle). A strong taxonomy is one that investigators can *do* things with. Thus in the field of medicine, for example, 'tuberculosis' and 'phenylketonuria' provide strong taxonomies in contrast with the very much weaker taxonomies of 'fever' and 'nervous breakdown'. In the case of weak taxonomies there is, indeed, a general indication of what to look for and what to expect, but there is no agreed causal theory – the phenomena in question are untidy and constitute a 'mixed bag'. The reason why 'tuberculosis' and 'phenylketonuria' are different is that in both cases the appropriate experts know the causes and the correct treatment. My argument in the above paper was that 'poor reading' is in this respect like 'fever' or 'nervous breakdown': its manifestations are a 'mixed bag' and do not form the basis for any classification of permanent scientific value. In contrast 'dyslexia', though as yet without the assured foundations of tuberculosis or phenylketonuria, provides a classification which has already led to significant progress and is likely to continue to do so.

There is also something very unsatisfactory about 'definition by exclusion'. It is difficult to think of any other diagnostic category either in medicine or education where membership is determined not by what signs are present but by what signs are *absent*. To be mischievous for a moment, there is a child's riddle which asks, 'Why is an elephant like a teapot?', to which the answer is, 'Because neither can climb trees'. It is plain that 'inability to climb trees' is unlikely to be of much use as a taxonomy; and to say that people with dyslexia are alike because they do not have certain characteristics seems scarcely less absurd.

If the above arguments are correct it follows that the commonly used diagnostic procedures – involving tests of reading and of intelligence and the use of discrepancy and exclusionary criteria – are not so much wrong as in need of modification. In the appropriate context reading tests may indeed pick out some cases of dyslexia because an important component of reading is that of relating the written or printed letters to the correct speech sound. In particular, if the investigation takes place in a socially prosperous area or at a fee-paying school, the number of children who are poor readers as a result of lack of opportunity is likely to be very small compared with the number who are poor readers because they are dyslexic; the risk of false positives is therefore significantly reduced. Another necessary condition is that the children should be relatively young, aged not more than, say, ten or eleven. This is because, although phonological weakness regularly shows itself in *lateness* in learning to read, many older people with dyslexia, as was noted above, will have learned to read fairly adequately; and with increasing age there will therefore be an increasing number of false negatives.

Individual assessors can of course take such factors into account, and, whether a child is dyslexic or not, for practical purposes his performance at a reading test on a given occasion is of course likely to be very informative. In population studies by researchers, however, no such safeguards exist.

A further relevant point is that there are different kinds of reading test – those which involve single-word reading, those which also involve comprehension, those which involve nonsense words, and so on. More research is needed in this area, but it seems likely that those with dyslexia will be more disadvantaged at single-word reading and less so if the central requirement is that of reading comprehension. Practitioners know well that dyslexic subjects are often very skilful at guessing from the context.

It is also likely to be informative if the subject's reading performance is timed. This makes sense in view of the magnocellular weakness in those with dyslexia (see above), because one of the functions of the magnocellular system is to deal with information which changes rapidly: people with dyslexia, one might say, are at a disadvantage if the stimuli fall too thick and fast.

Although for practical purposes a knowledge of the subject's reading level is essential, there are many advantages from a research point of view in placing more reliance on the results of a spelling test. There is the same problem over false positives as there is in the case of reading tests, but the risk of false negatives is much reduced. Practitioners know that even when dyslexic people have learned to read adequately they almost always continue to have a spelling problem; and, indeed, if a person can spell adequately it is arguable that his dyslexia can at most be only mild. There is also an advantage on the practical side if spelling tests are used in preference to reading tests: they can be given to many individuals at once, whereas most reading tests have to be administered in a one–one situation. There is thus a considerable saving of time.

It remains to discuss the problems which arise if reading or spelling scores are contrasted with IQ. As Stanovich (1991) has pointed out, the concept of IQ as a measure of 'intellectual potential' has largely been abandoned, yet it appears to be central to the notion of 'discrepancy' because this requires the identification of those whose reading or spelling performance is discrepant with their 'potential'. It appears to follow, therefore, that discrepancy definitions of dyslexia rest on an insecure foundation. Stanovich himself suggests that a more relevant discrepancy measure would be that between reading ability and listening comprehension. The great advantage of this proposal is that it preserves the concept of imbalance while deftly avoiding the difficulties connected with the concept of IQ.

The case, however, for wholesale exclusion of intelligence test items does not seem to me to be made out. One of the criteria which practitioners use in picking out those with dyslexia is the fact that they are often *intelligent*; and there are many items in traditional intelligence tests which demonstrate this. The main requirement is to avoid measures which are inappropriate.

Thus in the case of the Wechsler Intelligence Scale for Children (Wechsler, 1976) there are good reasons for regarding it as inappropriate to look for discrepancies between 'Verbal IQ' (VIQ) and 'Performance IQ' (PIQ). To use this measure is to ignore the existence of the 'ACID profile' – a pattern of scores found in the case of many dyslexic subjects comprising relatively low scores on the Arithmetic, Coding, Information and Digit span sub-tests. This phenomenon is well documented (Richards, 1985), and makes sense theoretically (Miles and Ellis, 1981). A similar pattern of weaknesses on the part of dyslexic children has also been found by Thomson (1982) on the sub-tests of the British Ability Scales (Elliott, Murray and Pearson, 1979, 1983). It has been argued by Miles (1993, pp. 8ff.) that traditional intelligence tests in fact involve a variety of component skills and that sometimes the scores of those with dyslexia are pulled down because they lack skills that are irrelevant to the purpose in hand. For example, in the Terman–Merrill test (Terman and Merrill, 1960) there is a complicated item involving cans of water; and it is possible for someone with dyslexia to carry out all the appropriate reasoning yet fail to recognise the solution because he does not know that $9 + 4 = 13$. An IQ figure which has been obtained from strict adherence to the instructions in the test manual may therefore provide only an impure measure of the intelligence of a dyslexic person – often sufficient in practice to show that he has 'special educational needs' (Warnock, 1978) but lower than it would have been if these irrelevant factors had been ignored.

What is needed, therefore, is an uncontaminated measure of intelligence. If such a measure can be obtained one can then check on how far there is an imbalance between it and the person's score on a spelling test. For convenience I shall speak in what follows of a measure of 'reasoning ability'. 'Reasoning ability' can be treated as approximately equivalent to 'intelligence' but need not be tied to the concept of 'IQ' in the traditional sense; in particular one need not think of it as a kind of fixed possession which does not change over time and which sets limits to what the person is considered able to achieve.

My suggestion is that the appropriate kinds of reasoning power are those which were identified by Spearman, over half a century ago, as involving 'the eduction of correlates' and 'the eduction of relations' (Spearman, 1927). In the one case the subject is given a term and a relationship and is asked to supply the correlate term; in the other the subject is given two terms and has to determine the relationship between them. Many test items of Spearman's day in fact involved a combination of the two. Thus 'Here is to There as Now is to . . . ' (Spearman, 1927, p. 179) involves first educing the relationship between 'here' and 'there' and then, given 'now' and the educed term, educing the correlate. This is not unlike the situation in the 'similarities' items which are found in many intelligence tests (Terman and Merrill, 1960; Wechsler, 1976; Elliott, Murray and Pearson, 1979, 1983); and similar skills are also needed when the subject has to choose the appropriate figure in a matrices test (for example Raven, 1958; Elliott, Murray and Pearson, 1979, 1983). Spearman also refers (p. 177) to the situation where 'some relation already observed between any two spatial ideas is applied to a third, whereby is generated a fourth idea, the correlate'. The example which follows (p. 178) involves a complicated combination of rods and pivots, and part of the skill required is that of 'imagining changes of position'. The requirements are not unlike those which play a part in the Block Design and Object Assembly items in the Wechsler Intelligence Scale for Children (Wechsler, 1976). In all such items the phonological components are small: the subject needs to understand the instructions and the meaning of words such as 'now', 'alike' etc. but he is not required to 'retrieve' such words at speed.

In brief, what is needed in diagnosis is to check for a discrepancy between reasoning skills such as those discussed by Spearman and phonological skills.

My final proposal is that neither reading nor spelling performance should be regarded as the only criteria for determining if a phonological weakness is present. There is also a need for what my colleagues and I have elsewhere called 'supplementary' items (Miles, Wheeler and Haslum, 1993). When the Bangor Dyslexia Test (Miles, 1982) was first devised it lacked any firm theoretical basis: the items in it were chosen simply because they appeared to work. However, it can now be seen that many of them tap phonological weakness (Miles, 1993, Chapter 25), and I and my colleagues have recently argued that they are less susceptible than tests of reading and spelling to what may be called 'learning overlay' (Miles, Wheeler and Haslum, 1993). Considerable time and effort is spent in teaching children to read and spell; and any child's performance on reading and spelling tests will necessarily be influenced by the amount of teaching which he has received. In contrast, schools do not hold classes for teaching children how to remember digits or the months of the year, and even though the difference between 'left' and 'right' may well have been taught to them at some stage, whether in the home or at school, those with a phonological weakness have regularly been found to show 'telltale signs' such as hesitations, pauses or requests for the question to be repeated (Miles, 1993, Chapter 10); this is taken into account in the scoring.

There are various ways in which the items in the Bangor Dyslexia Test could be modified or supplemented. There would be many advantages in a computerised – or semi-computerised – version, in which, for example, the time taken to respond to the left/right and other items was systematically recorded.* What is particularly needed, in view of the research of Livingstone et al. (1991), is one or more tests which tap speed of processing. A possible idea would be to compare the performance of dyslexic subjects on a cancellation task involving every fifth letter with their performance on a cancellation task involving every fifteenth letter. As the latter requires an extra amount of counting one might expect that the difference between the two scores would be greater in the case of those with dyslexia than in the case of controls. A recent pilot study† suggests that this may well be the case. Recall of visual material in timed conditions is also likely to be informative (Miles and Wheeler, 1977; Ellis and Miles, 1977).

It has not been the purpose of this chapter to stipulate in detail what tests should be used. Still less has it been my intention to specify test items in such a definitive way as not to allow for any modification. What I have attempted to do is to provide a rationale on which any future diagnostic criteria for dyslexia can be based. The central requirement is that of discovering whether or not there is an imbalance between reasoning skills on the one hand and phonological skills on the other. Suitably chosen items from traditional intelligence tests will provide a measure of the former; a spelling test, items in the Bangor Dyslexia Test and tests involving speed of information processing will provide a measure of the latter. What constitutes 'imbalance' can then be operationalised with no difficulty.

---

*The first steps in the provision of such a test have already been taken by my colleagues Dr Rod Nicolson and Dr Angela Fawcett, and I should like to express my gratitude to them both for this and for much else.
†I am grateful to Steven Morgan for developing this idea which he successfully tried out on 17 dyslexic subjects and 17 matched controls of various ages.

Chapter 9
Quantifying exceptionality: issues in the psychological assessment of dyslexia

MARTIN TURNER

Introduction

The case for a psychometric approach to specific learning difficulties (dyslexia) may be too obvious to be readily perceived. It is that skilled cognitive performances can and should be measured.

Interest in psychometric methods has waxed and waned over the years and the pendulum of fashion has swung far in a contrary direction. There is, in differential psychology, a concentration upon the world as it is, which dismays those whose primary concern is with the world as it ought to be. And in this as in every age, subjectivism, 'qualitative methods' and denial of the applicability of science to human behaviour do not lack for supporters. Yet:

> The only course open to the social sciences is to forget all about the verbal fireworks and to tackle the practical problems of our time with the help of the theoretical methods which are fundamentally the same in all sciences. I mean the methods of trial and error, of inventing hypotheses which can be practically tested, and of submitting them to practical tests.
>
> (Popper, 1945)

The advantages of quantitative methods in clinical work are, as I hope to show, very considerable. I hope also to address the rationale for identifying dyslexia as a cognitive deficit, the role of emotional factors, strengths and weaknesses of the major child assessment batteries and their revisions, a methodology for ipsative assessment and discrepancy definition, the level of interpretation, the question of norms in relation to sex and, finally, ways forward for diagnostic investigation of the individual's language and reading processing system.

Dyslexia: a cognitive deficit

After decades of controversy and confusion, progress in the base sciences (cognitive psychology and neurobiology in particular) has gone a considerable way towards resolving many, if not all, of the key questions about specific learning difficulties, their origins, nature and treatment. Cultural inertia may persist which prevents professionals from acclimatising themselves to the relevant disciplines: it remains the case that one can study psychology to doctoral level, in the UK and in North America, without ever taking a course in biology. And psychoanalysis casts a long shadow, especially in the applied field. But there are now the materials for an agreement that dyslexia is best understood and located at the cognitive level.

A recent clear statement of this view is to be found in Frith (1992). Here it is argued that behind the manifest learning difficulty there lies a multiplicity of little-understood biological, including genetic and neurochemical, factors, whereas in the foreground there is an equal profusion of behavioural phenomena. But, it is argued, the locus of the learning difficulty lies at the cognitive level where, as with autism, an analysis becomes meaningful.

One implication is that an individual clinical examination for an hour or so in a quiet setting may be more effective than hours – or weeks – of classroom observation, where the behaviour to be observed may be nothing out of the ordinary or at best inconsequential for an analysis of the learning difficulty. The rationale for a situational assessment has been developed for social behaviour and problems of maladjustment in particular and is typically unproductive in the case of a cognitive learning difficulty.

The individual and the curriculum

Though the cognitive level would seem to be the appropriate one at which to analyse the failure of some system or subsystem of cognition, it would be naive to look at within-child factors only. Nevertheless this is commonly done. In a recent study, Alessi asked 50 school psychologists to comment on the 5000 referrals they accepted within a year. In no single case was the curriculum identified as the problem; in every case the child himself, together with home environment factors, received the main attribution of cause of failure (Alessi, 1988).

This may be diplomatic, but may there not be equal truth in a contrary view, namely, that, as Engelmann asserts, 'The central cause of all failure in school is the teaching. When the teaching fails, the [children] fail' (Engelmann, 1992, p. 79). In which case, what is the relevance of all the differential data gathered in individual assessments, if '. . . learning styles and individual differences have a relatively minor effect on [child] performance' (Engelmann, 1992, p. 86)? Clinical diagnosis is an end in itself, surely, but research needs to establish far more carefully than has often been done what the rationale is for directing remedial attention to cognitive subsystems whose deficiency is revealed in assessment.

Only exceptionally, then, is the learner's cognitive individuality the key to his or her learning, and in any case it must be taken in conjunction with both the curriculum and the teaching methodology (Engelmann and Carnine, 1982).

Emotional development and the direction of causality

So what is the role of the much sought-after social and emotional factors in learning disability? No one doubts that a happy child learns: an unhappy child learns only about unhappiness. Yet, though literacy has always been felt to be important in the personal development of the individual, this importance may if anything have been underestimated. Chapman, Lambourne and Silva (1990) report a longitudinal study in New Zealand in which reading attainment at seven proved to be the most important single building-block of later academic self-concept and attitude towards school and school work. This was so even in relation to the well-known negative effect of maternal depression on the development of language in children pre-school.

The prime concern, therefore, should be to consider the extent to which learning failure causes emotional and behavioural disturbances. Although 'working memory capacity is regarded as the locus of the effects of anxiety on cognitive task performance' (Pumfrey and Reason, 1991, p. 6), impaired working memory is normally demonstrated by the dyslexic subject in an unstressed and relatively anxiety-free state.

Assessment frames of reference

By convention, normative assessment, that is, assessment which ranks an individual's performance in relation to performances of others of the same age, is contrasted with criterion-referenced assessment, which establishes an individual's level of performance in relation to an objective curriculum sequence. However, there is in the measurement literature a third kind of assessment, the ipsative. This is often found in tests and schedules of personality assessment, especially of the self-report kind (e.g. the Edwards Personal Preference Schedule – Edwards, 1953). Here an individual's profile of strengths and weaknesses is made apparent by contrasts and congruences within his or her individual pattern of responses.

Normative psychometric tests are the best established in the marketplace: tests of intelligence, reading, number and various other special aspects of performance (e.g. psychomotor response in trainee pilots) are in frequent use. Such tests are usually thought of as summative, as giving a report on an established level of skill following a period of instruction. Criterion-referenced tests remain largely hypothetical but may be developed for domains already well structured in terms of progression, such as self-help skills (Dockrell and McShane, 1993). They are conceived as curriculum-referenced assessments and are thus intended as formative tests, yielding indications as to what needs to be taught next in a given curriculum sequence. In ipsative assessment, the development of an individual in different cognitive domains is compared with that expected from a child of the same age.

However, no single mode of assessment exists independently of the other two (Figure 9.1). The convention is to define the three concepts of assessment in distinction to each other (e.g. Anastasi, 1988, p. 581). Nevertheless it may be seen that each makes a tacit or explicit acknowledgement of the other two. Normative assessment, though mainly silent on the details of the curriculum being followed and assessed, in fact reflects progress in this curriculum. This is most obvious in tests of attainment, especially number ('We haven't done division yet'). In cognitive development, instead of curricular there is a developmental sequence, though this cannot be prescriptive. Criterion-referenced assessment, which claims to ignore age norms, in fact makes assumptions about which tracts of curriculum are relevant to children of a given age. Ipsative assessment, though it compares performances on one dimension with another, does so with the individual as a frame of reference: without reference to age norms, no such comparison can be made. Here too profiling is dependent on knowing what levels of skill

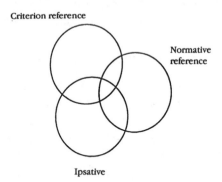

Figure 9.1 The overlap between the three concepts of assessment

are appropriate for each age or stage.

Thus all forms of assessment entail each other in ways which are sometimes tacit, sometimes explicit. Where normative or summative testing is appropriate, this information will have relevance also to the curriculum followed and to an individual's pattern of strengths and weaknesses. A teacher may choose among a number of curriculum-referenced inventories or schedules which have a formative purpose. These will serve to record pupils' progress, but such assessment assumes the progress to be expected from children at this age and may hold normative implications. Where a child performs poorly in either of these two modes of assessment, diagnostic or ipsative assessment is called for. This entails the use of standard techniques and implies both judgements about normal levels of performance to be expected of the individual in relation to others and choice as to appropriate curricular targets.

Use of the discrepancy definition

Conventionally the diagnosis of dyslexia is an ipsative assessment based on a discrepancy between ability and attainments, together with clinical observations and judgements. Without clinical evaluation of diagnostic measures, such a discrepancy identifies only 'underachievement'.

This is not the only possible approach: alternative methodologies are regularly proposed. Three may be mentioned. Stanovich (1991) wishes to do away with intellectual assessment altogether, in favour of a measure of listening comprehension. This proposal has yet to gain wide acceptance but can be evaluated by the kind of analysis presented in Carroll (1993, pp. 178–181). Seymour (1987) suggests a laboratory-style evaluation of response times to word and non-word stimuli. Elena Boder in her Boder Test provides a methodology for identifying sub-types of dyslexia using reading and spelling measures only (Boder, 1973). (A posthumous identification of Lee Harvey Oswald's dyslexia has been made by 'experts' from samples of free writing only.) But all such single-strand methodologies run the risk of idiosyncrasy and the comprehensive analysis of individual cognitive profiles remains popular. However, both components of this methodology – the discrepancy and the clinical judgement – need to be looked at carefully.

Objective performance data and subjective ('personal' – Polanyi, 1951) clinical interpretation may be seen as complementary. Objective data are derived from test performances and rely heavily upon the technical efficiency of the tests used. Psychometric tests function as a 'platform' upon which stand the clinician's skills of interpretation and judgement, as represented schematically in Figure 9.2. The former may be improved as newer, more highly developed tests become available; the latter increase with clinical experience and are improved by the discipline of relating the individual's profile to known research findings.

New testing resources

In the UK the Wechsler Intelligence Scale for Children – Revised (WISC-R) (Wechsler, 1976), and the British Ability Scales (BAS) (Elliott, Murray and Pearson, 1979, 1983), remain the best established individual child cognitive assessment batteries. Each has its strengths and weaknesses and these are summarised in Table 9.1. The Wechsler tests sacrifice psychometric efficiency for valuable continuity with the past. Both exist in

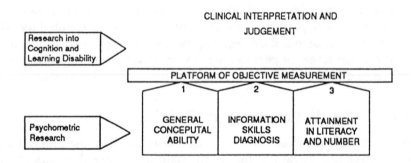

Figure 9.2 Schematic representation of psychometric tests as a platform for the clinician's skills

important revisions (see below). The BAS remains a versatile battery for the primary-aged child: it includes useful perceptual and motor tests for the 3–8 year age group and enables observed/expected frequencies to be calculated up to the age of 13;11 years. (Visual/verbal IQ differences may

Table 9.1 Stengths and weaknesses of the Wechsler Intelligence Scale for Children – Revised (Wechsler, 1976) and the British Ability Scales (Elliott, Murray and Pearson, 1979, 1983)

Weschler Intelligence Scale for Children – Revised	
Strengths	Weaknesses
Research tradition	Block Design only 'pure' measure of spatial ability
Continuity	
	Arbitrariness of Object Assembly and Comprehension
Wechsler 'family' of tests	
'ACID' diagnostic profile	Factor structure does not separate IQ from information skills.
WISC – *the* intelligence test worldwide	

British Ability Scales	
Strengths	Weaknesses
Tailored resting	Short Form IQ dyslexia-sensitive
Arbitrary nature of composition is clear	Discrepancies anchored to Short Form IQ
Achievement tests integral	Block Design ceiling effect
Expectancy tables relevant to specific learning difficulties	Standard IQ procedure sacrifices flexibility
Good range of spatial and perceptual tests	
Tests are more theory-compatible (good sub-test specificity)	

be precisely quantified up to 14;5 years.) An automated scoring system (for IBM and Apple machines) makes such calculations very much easier.

The year 1992 was one notable for developments in the field of psychometric tests. The US development and extension of the British Ability Scales was produced – the Differential Ability Scales (DAS – Elliott, 1990a); and the third generation of Wechsler tests, the WISC-IIIUK (Wechsler, 1992), with the benefit of a UK validation sample, made its appearance. Both these systems are published by The Psychological Corporation and enable the psychologist to say precisely, from within the standardisation sample, what is the observed frequency or infrequency of any particular pattern. The DAS includes tests of word recognition, spelling and number, and allows one to say how infrequent is any observed pattern of underachievement. WISC-IIIUK has been co-normed with the Wechsler Objective Reading Dimension (WORD – Rust, Golombok and Trickey, 1993), and permits unexpected failure in word recognition, spelling and (most usefully) reading comprehension to be quantified in the same way.

Where these newer test materials are not available, a discrepancy definition may be derived direct from the normal distribution: $(O - E)$/s.d. gives the difference between observed and expected values in points of z-score and the frequency of the result may be looked up in a table or expressed using a modern calculator. Though this rudimentary method fails to take into account regression to the mean, which may be important at the extremes, Elliott (1990a) reports that in most cases the outcome is very little different from that obtained using the statistical apparatus of a sophisticated test battery.

From measurement to skilled inference

The higher the 'platform' of technical instrumentation, the greater is the advantage with which the clinician starts when making inferences from observations. This is particularly so when the assessing psychologist, using a discrepancy definition of specific learning difficulties (dyslexia), is able to report observations about an individual which show, in an objective way, that a given pattern of low attainment in basic skills is both statistically significant and of a given level of demonstrable infrequency among others of his or her contemporaries.

The validity of clinical judgement often seems to receive defence in the psychological literature, as if the realm of intuition were threatened. But the limitations of psychometric test results may be seen quite simply, when an individual obtains an unexceptional score after demonstrating enormous effort to obtain it! Further, an average score may be made up of some harder items correct, together with easier items wrong. (On Rasch-scaled tests the probability of obtaining such a paradoxical result, too, can be quantified.)

A methodology for diagnosis

Thus the tide of technical improvements in testing raises the clinician's baseline. The strategy that is pursued may be described in terms of three phases (the three 'pillars' in Figure 9.2). The first phase of investigation may be thought of as the measurement of a selection of general (i.e. non-dyslexic) abilities wider than that encountered in the ordinary classroom.

IQ itself (a composite or average score showing statistical stability) is essentially a measurement artefact. It may conceal wide anomalies in development and thus mislead in an individual case. But more fundamentally it reports a value which is not there until the measurement is made. A window is of a given height before a tape-measure is applied to it, but an individual's IQ is a by-product of the measurement process itself, depending crucially, for instance, upon the particular measurement procedure adopted; alternative 'IQs', comprised of different selections of sub-tests, for example, lack validity through being non-standard. Hence the legalistic anxieties associated with correct procedure.

In both the DAS and WISC-IIIUK there is, at last, a separation of diagnostic from intelligence-measuring tests. Thus in WISC-IIIUK the well-established factor structure associated with learning disability (Freedom from distractibility, Speed of processing) may be reported separately for any individual, though this revision brings the test up to date only with research published by the end of the 1970s (Kaufman, 1979). The wide margin of clinical verbal decision-making is reduced. On the DAS the diagnostic tests – Recall of Digits, Speed of Information Processing, Recall of Objects Immediate and Delayed – are evaluated separately from, and in relation to, General Conceptual Ability.

Whatever the findings of tests, the pattern or profile of any individual needs to be related to the very considerable body of research literature on dyslexia and cognition. It is useful to think of this second phase of investigation as that of information skills. Of principal importance, perhaps, are measures of working memory. Tests of phonological memory are a valuable supplement to conventional psychometric testing. Research implicates speed of information processing, too, as a common area of weakness in the learning-disabled child. Also, 'dyslexics typically have poor motor skills' (Bishop, 1990, p. 129). The motor component of Coding (WISC) or Speed of Information Processing (BAS/DAS) may be a problem, rather than the manipulation of symbols in memory; this is a decision for the clinician. For an evaluation of visual sequential memory (and much else), the Harrison–Winter Computerized Visual Assessment System provides precisely timed measures of Visual Attentional Span, conceived as visual memory capacity that is grounded in developmental norms (Harrison, 1988).

Good clinical work, in summary, rests upon a platform of objective, precise and quantitative data and requires that the psychologist relate an individual to known clusters, types or sub-types of dyslexia (or other conditions) where possible, through an evaluation of cognitive processes. Test results in themselves, however, may provide no more than a framework for clinical detection work. In this, a good working knowledge of recent neuropsychology is perhaps the most useful guide, so that, for instance, disorders in phonological processing may be distinguished from executive function or spatial cognition disorders (Pennington, 1991a); a similar approach to psychosocial development is also fruitful (Rourke and Fuerst, 1991).

The third, final, phase of investigation is that of scholastic attainments. These are usually the presenting problems (poor reading, spelling, writing, arithmetic) and it is the aim of the first two phases to provide a context in which parents and teachers may understand the uneven development of these key skills. For the non-psychologist, assessment materials currently available are numerous, though there are significant gaps (Turner, 1993). Generally speaking, current research is favourable (e.g. Frederiksen, 1982; Beech, 1989) to a componential theory of skills, including the skills of literacy, and this supports both the assessment methodology outlined above and the specialist remediation or training of subskills which may follow a positive diagnosis.

This assessment methodology represents the most complete attempt at present to identify the kinds of learning disabilities which, in the USA, now account for 47% of all children with Individual Educational Programs (Elliott, 1990b, p. 22) and which remain the most common source of educational misery. Such a framework, even if increasingly accepted, should not be a straitjacket but a structure for development. Let us turn, next, to some central issues which are showing strong signs of evolution within the field of dyslexia assessment.

Levels of interpretation

Increasingly the attention of cognitive scientists is turning to specific processes, whether thought of as modularised or not. This raises the possibility that the notorious pragmatism of psychometric science may at last be harnessed to some well-defined theoretical purpose, as Wittrock and Baker (1991) among others would propose. One such line of development is towards greater sub-test specificity and sub-test homogeneity (Elliott, 1990a). This offers process-specific analysis at what is, in effect, the lowest level of interpretation.

We have seen that the highest, summary level of interpretation, that of the single-value IQ, is a construction from measurements rather than a measurement *per se* and may in any case incorporate bias against

dyslexic subjects. (This is especially the case with the Short Form IQ in
the British Ability Scales, essentially a verbal ability measure, which
comprises, among four scales, two that are dyslexia-sensitive.) There
remains the largely unexploited intermediate level of Verbal and Performance Scales (WISC; scale here means composite) or, in the Differential
Ability Scales, Clusters. In the Differential Ability Scales, in place of the
conventional two (verbal, non-verbal), there are three intermediate
composites or Clusters: Verbal, Non-verbal and Spatial. The difficulty
dyslexic children often have with non-verbal sequential reasoning, even
when their spatial ability is good, may now be highlighted in a useful
way, i.e. a way which resolves to a greater degree than verbal/perfor-
mance discrepancies the difficulties which may be experienced with
convergent, analytical processes.

Profile visualisations may be seen for two individual cases, MW and
TS, who were tested about three years apart, first on the WISC-R, then
on the DAS, in Figures 9.3–9.6.

The distinction between non-verbal reasoning (sequential, 'succes-
sive' processes with a strong submerged element of verbal rehearsal
and mediation) and spatial ability (holistic, 'simultaneous' processes
with a much reduced verbal element) appears to make sense of their
learning difficulties. Dyslexic subjects tend to be poor at convergent,
level 1 (Jensen, 1970) or information skill activities. In these analyses,

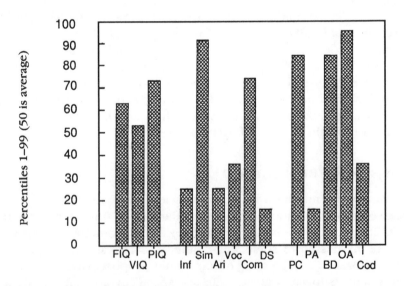

Figure 9.3 WISC-R profile for MW (F) aged 13;9 years. Abbreviations: FIQ, Full-
scale IQ, VIQ, Verbal IQ, PIQ, Performance IQ (the three composites); Inf, Information, Sim, Similarities, Ari, Arithmetic, Voc, Vocabulary, Com, Comprehension, DS,
Digit Span (the six verbal sub-tests); PC, Picture Completion, PA, Picture Arrangement, BD, Block Design, OA, Object Assembly, Cod, Coding (the five non-verbal or
performance sub-tests)

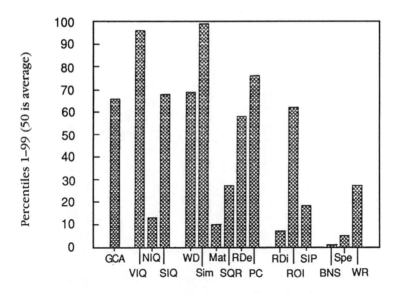

Figure 9.4 DAS profile for MW (F) aged 16;7 years. Abbreviations: GCA; General Conceptual Ability (the IQ composite); VIQ, Verbal IQ or Cluster, NIQ, Non-verbal IQ or Cluster, SIQ, Spatial IQ or Cluster (three composites based on the three following pairs of tests); WD, Word definitions, Sim, Similarities (the verbal pair); Mat, Matrices, SQR, Sequential Quantitative Reasoning (the non-verbal pair); RDe, recall of Designs, PC, Pattern Construction (the spatial pair); RDi, Recall of Digits; ROI, Recall of Objects – Immediate; SIP, Speed of Information Processing (the three diagnostic tests; ROD, Recall of Objects – Delayed [see Figures 9.7 and 9.8] is based on a further administration of the Recall of Objects test after 15–20 min); BNS, Basic Number Skills, Spe, Spelling, WR, Word Reading (the three attainment tests)

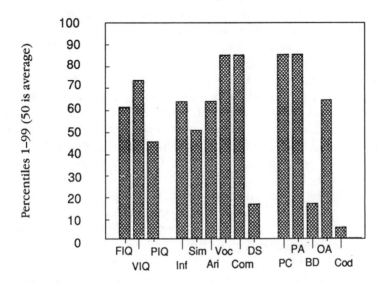

Figure 9.5 WISC-R profile for TS (M) aged 8;0 years. Abbreviations as for Figure 9.3

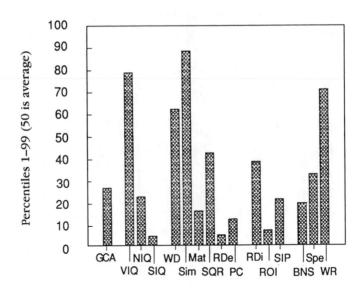

Figure 9.6 DAS profile for TS (M) aged 10;8 years. Abbreviations as for Figure 9.4

verbal as well as spatial ability strengths are resolved through separation from memory-intensive phonological and sequencing tasks. In addition light is shed on two tests which sometimes seem to behave in an unexplained diagnostic fashion: Picture Arrangement (WISC) and Matrices (BAS/DAS).

At 13;9 years, MW's scores appear to fall into two separate groups: high and low. The latter includes all four dyslexia-sensitive tests (ACID: Arithmetic, Coding, Information, Digit Span) and tends to a positive identification. But Picture Arrangement is also inexplicably depressed, more so than Coding (Figure 9.3). Three years later, with the Differential Ability Scales, the picture is resolved. MW's underlying strength in language ability is now obvious (Word Definitions, Similarities, Verbal IQ); her Spatial Cluster, although lower, is not a significant area of difficulty; but, acutely, it is the non-verbal reasoning processes involved in Matrices and Sequential and Quantitative Reasoning that are highlighted as her prime area of difficulty. This is confirmed by improved levels of reading but a dire level of written number skills (Figure 9.4).

At age eight TS showed only an incomplete picture of dyslexia: two ACID sub-test scores. But his Performance IQ is depressed by an extremely low Block Design score. However, in isolation this score does not invite interpretation (Figure 9.5). Two and a half years later, much more distinctive internal contrast is visible in his profile. But the conjunction of good scores in vocabulary, verbal reasoning, verbal memory and reading may have hindered the provision of specialist teaching appropriate to his kind of learning difficulty, because this profile is unlike that of most dyslexic children. Yet he now clearly shows acute difficulties with spatial ability that could not be easily detected using the WISC: Recall of Designs and Pattern Construction both defeat him. But the verbal rehearsal and control elements in the Non-verbal Reasoning Cluster (Matrices, Sequential and Quantitative Reasoning) suffice to raise this group of abilities, which is otherwise also low. Number, spelling and reading attainment conform to this pattern (Figure 9.6).

Percentile values for the y-axis, chosen for their utility in conveying information to the lay parent or teacher, nevertheless exaggerate inter-test differences.

The value of ipsative assessment may be seen in Figures 9.7 and 9.8. In Figure 9.7, DAS composite scores, core, diagnostic and attainment scales, together with two WISC-R diagnostic sub-tests (Digit Span and Coding), are shown in standard form as T-scores for a dyslexic boy of nearly 12 of average ability. In Figure 9.8, for contrast, the same results for core and diagnostic sub-tests only are converted into z-scores and then arranged about the subject's own mean. Based on the premise of sub-test specificity, that cognitive strengths and weaknesses illustrate the essential anomalies in learning development, without reference to composite or attainment scores, Figure 9.8 shows clearly the phenomena to be interpreted. Here again one may note the difficulty with non-verbal reasoning relative to spatial ability (only 5% of the standardisation sample show this degree of discrepancy), the poor consolidation of items into intermediate memory (Recall of Objects – Delayed) and the difficulty with verbal sequences shown up by the two WISC-R sub-tests.

It may perhaps be thought that 'Ability and achievement tests are more efficient than inventories, self-ratings and projective tests in assessing personality structure when properly analysed and interpreted' (Jastak, 1992, p. 28). If so, and given the importance of attitudes and affects in educational progress, a Jastak Cluster Analysis permits interpretation of attainment on the Wide Range Achievement Test (Revised) (Jastak and Wilkinson, 1984) and the Wechsler tests separately for the sexes and in terms of motivational as well as group factors (Jastak and Jastak, 1979). So at this intermediate or group-factor level, further technical and professional development may be anticipated.

Normative differentiation of the sexes

For 15 years evidence has been accumulating on sex differences in cognitive style and cognitive development (Ansara et al., 1981; Moir and Jessel, 1989; Halpern, 1992). The Jastak Cluster Analysis is one of the few instruments which take into account developmental and occasionally

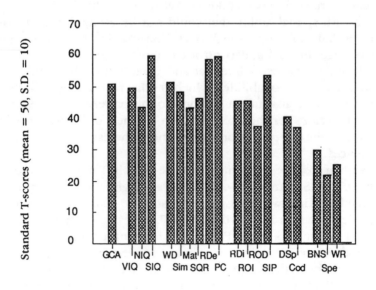

Figure 9.7 Profile of DAS and two WISC-R sub-tests for TT (M) aged 11;10 years. Abbreviations as for Figures 9.3 and 9.4, with ROD = Recall of Objects – Delayed

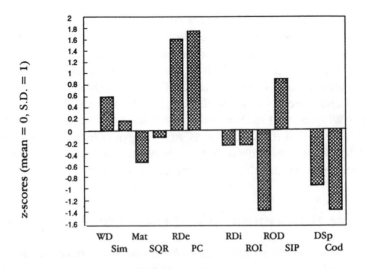

Figure 9.8 Strengths and weaknesses (ipsative) for TT (M) aged 11;10 years. Abbreviations as in Figures 9.3 and 9.4

life-long cognitive differences between the sexes. This is important at the margin (the dyslexic individual) because the diagnostic procedures are often those (Coding, Digit Span, Speed of Processing) at which girls show an advantage and must therefore perform exceptionally to attract a label. Females are of course under-represented among dyslexic subjects. Another rare example among published tests, the Edinburgh Reading Test (Moray House, 1981), at stage 1 (7;0–9;0 years) offers separate norms for early reading attainment for the sexes, a feature which could help to attenuate the under-detection in girls of specific learning difficulties. Differing levels of maturity and cognitive 'preference' between the sexes should therefore be taken into account in future development of, especially, diagnostic tests.

Inclusive definitions

Frith (1985, p. 306) observed that the controversy about the existence of dyslexia was 'still faintly burning'. One version of the sceptical view which remains respectable is that literacy failure occupies one tail of a specific distribution of such skills (Perfetti, 1985; Shaywitz et al., 1992). Less creditable, perhaps, is the tendency to ascribe undue importance to issues of definition. 'The chief danger to our philosophy,' as Frank Ramsey wrote in *The Foundations of Mathematics*, 'apart from laziness and woolliness, is *scholasticism* . . . which is treating what is vague as if it were precise' (Ramsey, 1931, p. 269).

I hope it will be apparent that the quantitative, process-oriented approach outlined above is tolerant of differing schools of thought in fast-moving research. Indeed a two-word summary of this methodology would be that it quantifies exceptionality. Two further advantages deserve mention.

There is no reason to suppose that only individuals of average or above intelligence should have specific learning difficulties (dyslexia). *A priori* grounds are lacking; epidemiological grounds suggest otherwise. So it is important to note that the regression approach is fair with regard to pupils of all levels of ability. A school pupil with an WISC-IIIUK IQ of 70 and a basic reading standard score of 62 would be found in only 2% of the population, according to the WORD norms.

Second, the terminology of specific learning difficulties strongly implies that general and specific learning difficulties are mutually exclusive. Indeed this is an accepted feature of the exclusionary diagnostic procedure. However, once again there are no grounds for supposing that individuals with global learning difficulties are exempt from specific disturbances in working memory and phonological processing, though these may be harder to demonstrate in the presence of extensive language impairments. An approach which quantifies exceptionality, however, is able occasionally to describe general and specific learning difficulties in the same individual.

Conclusion: the reading sequence

Much of the above has assumed, justifiably I hope, that learning difficulties originate in impairments in the cognitive system or subsystems ('architecture'); these subtend the manifestations of failure in reading and spelling which are usually described in curricular terms.

However, reading skills are much less easily so described than are number skills, which as mentioned earlier depend more obviously on current instruction. Explanations of reading and spelling acquisition are put forward that operate on different levels. For instance, stage models of children's progress are confirmed or otherwise by fine-grained studies of reading strategies and their interaction with teaching; the predictiveness of phonology and vision factors in the learning process are gradually being explained by careful methodological consideration; information-processing and computational models provide perhaps the most coherent theoretical base; and research into heredity and brain anatomy has converged on the structures which mediate working memory and phonological processing. Rack, Hulme and Snowling (1993) offer a useful provisional synthesis of these four levels of theory, showing that there is now considerable agreement among them.

A final prospect, therefore, is that reading will yield a curriculum sequence to compare with that for early number skills. This would permit an assessment procedure closer to true curriculum-referencing, but without the arbitrariness of many current inventories. Researchers use lists of words, regular and irregular, with and without homophones, to detect skills in non-word reading, morphemic knowledge, rime analogies and many other features of word recognition ('the limiting skills in reading development': Rack, Hulme and Snowling, p. 100). We know that in principle children can learn to read and spell English words in many ways, though not all ways are optimal. Given the high heritability of phonological processing, as well as its prominence in reading failure, it is to be hoped that a 'natural' progression may emerge from studies of how children learn best, other things being equal. At present skilled teachers perform just such diagnostic assessments but often through 'feel' justified by experience. An empirically based procedure would not only serve as a test for placing a pupil in a teaching sequence, but also offer a coherent developmental path for the learner for whom norms have become an irrelevance.

Part IV
Education Management of the Dyslexic Child

Chapter 10
How children with dyslexia respond to specialised teaching: some practical and theoretical issues

MICHAEL THOMSON

Introduction

Among the many contributions Professor Miles has made to the teaching of dyslexic children, was a publication in 1970 called *On Helping the Dyslexic Child*. This was one of the few books available at the time that described the teaching procedures and educational management for dyslexic children. It led in due course to various publications with Elaine Miles (e.g. Miles and Miles, 1975). There have, of course, been other approaches to teaching which have since been published including the Alpha to Omega (Hornsby and Shear, 1976), Aston Portfolio (Aubrey et al., 1982), Hickey (1977; Augur and Briggs, 1993) method and many others. Professor Miles has not been slow in discussing ways in which teaching could be evaluated, and pointing to the importance of how dyslexic children can be helped, as well as looking into the aetiology and diagnosis of dyslexia. It seems eminently appropriate, therefore, that one of the papers in this series looks at the way in which teaching dyslexic children can be evaluated. This paper is the latest in a series of papers that I have written examining this issue (Thomson, 1988, 1990a,b, 1991). The aim of this chapter is not to describe teaching procedures in any great detail, but to look at ways in which we can, both as educators and researchers, examine ways in which dyslexic children respond to various teaching approaches. The chapter will begin by looking at attainment monitoring and examining ways in which we can evaluate children's progress. I will then look at some specific teaching techniques and the evaluation of those. Finally, I will try to relate the findings to one or two theoretical issues in dyslexia.

Developmental considerations

It is very important for teachers and researchers to bear in mind the developmental aspects of dyslexia. It is a truism that, when describing developmental dyslexia (as opposed to acquired dyslexia, often the result of brain dysfunctions of various kinds), one should take into account the way in which children develop. Yet this is often not done, and there are a number of factors which we need to take into account.

Researchers in the past, myself included, have often described auditory and visual dyslexic children. These purport to be individuals who either have a sub-test pattern on, say, the Wechsler Intelligence Scales for Children (Wechsler, 1976) or the British Ability Scales (Elliott, Murray and Pearson, 1979, 1983) suggesting more of an auditory or visual deficit. Alternatively, these descriptions were applied to children with reading and spelling errors reported as being auditory, visual or mixed types. (A review of this research can be found in Thomson (1990).) One of the things that I have noticed since being at East Court is that children who are purportedly 'auditory' dyslexics often become 'visual' dyslexics after having been at the school for two or three years. This is apparent on the basis of their reading and spelling errors, e.g. a 'bizarre' or phonetically inaccurate error like 'kss' for 'snake' might become 'snak'. The reading and spelling performance, rather than being a function of some underlying cognitive difference, seems to be a reflection of the teaching procedures which have been received. For example, training in analysing syllables, in rhyming, in sound coding will inevitably improve the application of these auditory skills as they relate to written language learning.

Another important aspect of the developmental perspective is the expectation of change over time. Again, this may sound obvious but it is a point often overlooked. A dyslexic child who is 9 years old often has quite serious attentional, organisational and short-term memory problems as well as reading, writing and spelling difficulties. This can be different from a 13–14 year old with dyslexia whose problems in these areas are considerably less marked and do not affect everyday life in the same sort of way. Children respond to teaching procedures in very different ways; sometimes children respond steadily over a period of time, but in most cases there are sudden spurts and plateaux.

The issue of control groups is also an important one. Where control groups have been used in the studies outlined below, they often use matched reading-age controls as well as matched age controls. The argument here goes that children who are matched on chronological age with dyslexic children, but have greater reading and spelling skills, do not present a proper comparison. This is because the process of learning to read from (say) 7 years reading age to (say) 10 years reading age may developed, as a *result* of the learning process, skills such as short-term memory or phonological coding, which are the particular variables in question. In examining dyslexia as a developmental disorder, it is often helpful to look at stages in spelling. Frith (1985), for example, proposes a number of stages in reading and spelling. These are outlined in Table 10.1. Of course, these stages do not follow on neatly one after the other, and children do vary. Even those children who are at the so-called logographic stage will have some sound representation skills. For example, children may attempt to spell 'cheese' as 'tzjes' which is an approximation to the sound patterns which they say in spoken language. Later on they may spell 'jumt' for 'jumped', 'buks' for 'books' and so on, which are clearly phonological alphabetic skills.

There does not appear to be much evidence that knowledge about what things *look* like in reading gives rise to spelling later on. There may well be a dissociation between reading and spelling strategies, where children can spell words that they cannot read (this is rare, of course). However, there is evidence that in the early stage of learning the phonological or explicit knowledge of sound/symbol associations required for spelling may give rise to generalising these skills in reading. Thus, the reading of unfamiliar *regular* words is possible. The reading of these words may then result in stored memory of spelling patterns. These orthographic patterns can then improve spelling skills. Goswami (1993) argues that the use of orthographic analogies, for example, a clue word 'beak' helping the spelling of 'peak' and 'weak', is important in the development of phonological knowledge. This applies particularly when the analogous sound shares a spelling pattern, e.g. head/bread as against head/said.

Before moving on to some studies on teaching it may be helpful to

Table 10.1 Frith's three phases

Stage	
1. Logographic	Associate speech signs with symbols read as logograms. Shape recognition, visual memory in environment. Particular words/spoken/written. Reading logographically helps to spell logographically
2. Alphabetic	Chunking letter sounds and morpheme identification. Grapheme–phoneme translation route, sound-to-letter correspondence; requires phoneme awareness, decoding of novel words. Using phonological–letter sound approach in spelling creates alphabetic approach in reading
	In spelling this involves: 1. Correct sound analysis (within word) 2. Phoneme–grapheme translation 3. Conventionally correct graphemes selected
3. Orthographic	Automatic recognition of graphemic clusters: -tion etc. Access to lexical representations set up relating to letter-by-letter sequences. Use of lexical analogies. Uses orthographic code first in reading, then transfers/develops spelling.

present these in the context of a model of developmental disorders. This was originally described by Frith (1992) as a general model of developmental disorders with specific reference to autism. I have represented it here (Figure 10.1) as applied to dyslexia, as it does give quite a nice framework for examining dyslexic difficulties. It may be seen from the above, therefore, that research into neurological components of dyslexia can easily be accommodated by other biological causes and brain differences. Current research suggests that the cognitive deficit is in the phonological mechanism/short-term memory/sound–symbol area. As far as the core problems are concerned, i.e. naming, short-term memory for words and letters and phonemic segmentation, these are the key features upon which teaching needs to focus. Most of the teaching procedures in fact do this by their overlearning and multisensory approaches. What is different is that some-

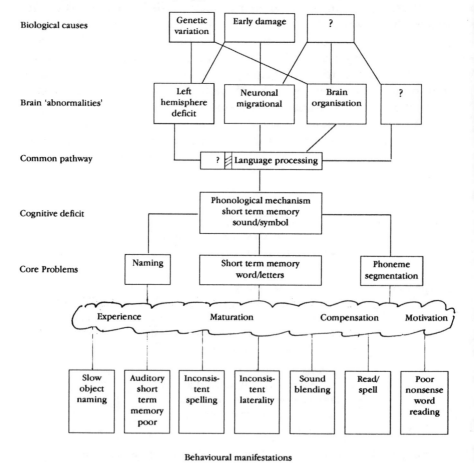

Figure 10.1 Model of developmental disorders applied to dyslexia (adapted from Frith, 1992)

times the rationale for these teaching techniques is based on early ideas of weakness in auditory–visual integration as a cause of dyslexia. Recent research has not found much evidence for these as prime causes, but nevertheless the teaching techniques still work. The notion that developmental experiences affect these core problems is an important one and may be as a result of experience, maturation, learning strategies or teaching. The behavioural manifestations observed are those that the teacher would observe. The wide variety of these manifestations may well account for the notion argued by some researchers that dyslexia is not a common disorder but a disparate group of children with various reading difficulties. The model described above is able to accommodate different strategies resulting from a common cause.

Attainment monitoring

At the time of writing, there is a good deal of debate concerning the testing of children following the introduction of the National Curriculum. It seems appropriate that the debate should focus on *how* children are assessed, but it seems to me that the question of whether they should be assessed is clear cut. The answer should be 'yes'. At a basic level, how can we be sure that what we do in our teaching actually benefits the children? How can we be accountable for our teaching? These are fundamental questions which are answered by some form of test. As far as reading is concerned, Pumfrey (1990) proposes (among others) the following as important uses of reading tests:

- accountability (public information);
- maintaining and improving reading standards at local, regional and national levels;
- comparing reading skills between pupils;
- measuring the progress of individuals and groups to find starting points for instructions;
- to evaluate teaching approaches;
- identifying pupils' strengths and weaknesses (diagnosis);
- to increase the teacher's understanding of the processes involved in reading;
- to help early identification (screening and prevention);
- research.

There may obviously be problems in any particular test that is chosen – for example, whether one should examine individual word reading, comprehension, speed of reading, use of inference in text, accuracy in reading and so on. It also begs the question of how one should examine spelling, handwriting, fluency in expression of ideas in written form and a plethora of other skills which are weak in dyslexic children and one is trying to remediate.

Typically in the field of specific learning difficulty (dyslexia), children are given individual tests of word reading. These may be the Schonell Graded Word Reading Test (Schonell and Schonell, 1942–1955), the British Ability Scales (Elliott, Murray and Pearson, 1979, 1983), the Wide Range Reading Tests (Jastak and Wilkinson, 1984) or others. They are also commonly given the Neale (1989) Analysis of Reading Ability, looking at Accuracy, Comprehension and Fluency. They are also typically given a graded word spelling test such as the Vernon (1960). By presenting some data gleaned from children taught at East Court over the last ten years, it is possible to illustrate the way in which one can monitor attainments and look at some of the issues involved.

The data presented in Table 10.2 are taken from 173 children who have attended and since left East Court School up to 1993. East Court is a specialist school for dyslexic pupils. All the children receive small-group teaching for their dyslexia. This involves a structured and multi-sensory approach following the basic principles of teaching dyslexic children that have been outlined elsewhere in this book and are described in detail in Thomson and Watkins (1991). The children are assessed on their written language attainments twice a year during their time at the school. In addition to the mean scores shown below, an achievement ratio based on the number of months improvement over 12 twelve-month period is also given. Discussion of this and other aspects of the data is given below.

There are a number of discussion points which emerge from the above. The first is examining the data on their own. It does seem that dyslexic children exposed to a very structured teaching programme do make good improvements. This has been shown elsewhere (Hornsby and Miles, 1980; Thomson, 1988, 1990). It should be noted that the higher score on the British Ability Scales Word Reading Test (BASR) is not simply due to higher abilities in individual word reading. The BASR

Table 10.2 East Court attainment monitoring up to 1993 (n = 173): written language attainments of children at East Court School

	Mean scores*	
	In	Out
Reading		
BAS Word Reading	8.3	12.8
Neale Analysis		
Accuracy	8.5	11.5
Rate	8.4	10.0
Comprehension	9.1	12.2
Spelling		
Vernon Graded Word	7.7	11.3

*Mean chronological age on entering school (in) is 10.3 and leaving school (out) is 13.0.

has a ceiling of 14.6, whereas the Neale Analysis (Accuracy) has a ceiling of 13 years. Inevitably, children who are reading at the ceiling level on the Neale will not bring up the Mean Score as much as children performing at the ceiling level on the BASR.

It is also helpful to compare the results with children who are not given help. Data available from the University of Aston Clinic (Thomson, 1991) show that dyslexic children not given help will tend to make only five months of improvement in reading in a year and three months of improvement in spelling in a year. This improvement is shown in Figure 10.2 (see below). These children lag further and further behind. We also notice from the children at East Court that development is in fits and starts – sometimes there is a plateau, sometimes a sudden increase in development and this reflects different degrees of achievement. An alternative way of looking at this attainment improvement is by examining them in relation to the 'normal growth' of development. This can be done in reading, for example, by looking at centile growth charts. This approach has been developed by Cook and Cook (1988) and the above data on reading and spelling are shown in Figure 10.2.

It may be seen from the above that the children's development is well below their expected centile on entering the school, and comes up to the norm on leaving the school. The data from dyslexic children not given help are also shown and the contrast is marked. These growth curves are a useful way of evaluating attainments, as are comparisons with ability scores which can be used with the British Ability Scales.

Specific techniques of teaching

It is generally agreed that dyslexic children should be given teaching that is multisensory, structured and cumulative. It is also generally agreed that there should be plenty of scope for undertaking the same work again and again, i.e. so-called 'over-learning', and most teachers of dyslexic children use a specific written language programme. Different teachers have different techniques which they like using, but in most cases there is some kind of analysis of phonics and a multisensory approach (that is, integrating sound with symbol with the written form). It is not the purpose here to describe in detail the particular techniques – these can be found in Thomson and Watkins (1991). However, it is quite useful to examine the results of a number of studies which we have undertaken at East Court which examine different teaching techniques. A number of studies have been undertaken. These involved comparing 'look and say' or visual approaches to spelling with more phonetic approaches; the use of syllable analysis in spelling and the use of 'simultaneous oral spelling' (where children were required to say words, spell them out letter by letter, write them down saying each letter as it was written and then read them). In many of the studies

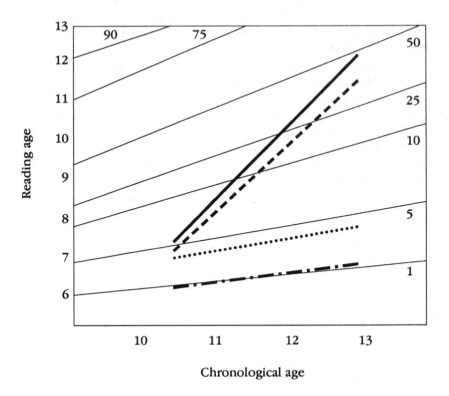

Figure 10.2 Reading and spelling of dyslexic children given help at East Court and dyslexic children not receiving help – showing percentile growth. Numbers on fainter lines represent percentile points. ━━━ , BAS reading at East Court, ━ ━ ━ , Vernon spelling at East Court, ••••••, reading without help, ━ • ━ , spelling without help

the children were asked to read regular and irregular words. The reason for this is that children required to read regular words may use an alphabetic strategy, i.e. they use sound/symbol correspondence rules to work out what the words are saying, and/or a direct route to read. The latter implies that they will go directly from the visual input into meaning. Irregular words, on the other hand, can *only* be read by the direct route. As grapheme/ phoneme correspondence rules cannot be applied – these would give wrong words – they must learn to read the words directly from visual input to meaning. Most models of the reading process assume that going from printed word to spoken response involves these two routes. In addition to grapheme/phoneme translation, the so-called alphabetic route involves phoneme segmentation and use of the speech system as well as blending, or putting together the sounds to make the words, then assembling the sounds at the phonological stage prior to saying the word. The direct route implies some kind of visual input system with a link to the semantic or meaning system and then straight through to the output or assemblage of sounds prior to the spoken response. In relation to the stages that are outlined earlier in the chapter, Frith (1985) predicates that dyslexic children have particular difficulty in the alphabetic stage of phases.

Table 10.3 summarises the results of various evaluation studies. Further details and full data are given in Thomson (1988, 1990, 1991).

Table 10.3 Evaluation of specific teaching technigues and skills: summary of studies

Teaching technique	Measures	Results
Visual versus phonic spelling	Reading and spelling regular and irregular words	Dyslexic children better at regular word reading when younger. In spelling, equally poor at both, regular spelling improving more rapidly
Syllable analysis	Spelling one-, two- and three-syllable words before and after syllable analysis training	Significantly better improvement following teaching syllables (syllable types) against copying the whole word out
Simultaneous oral spelling (SOS)	Spelling regular and irregular words before and after SOS	Significantly better spelling for dyslexic children (multisensory) using SOS against visual inspection; both methods equally effective for non-dyslexic controls
Feuerstein Enrichment Programme*	Cognitive (visualisation of cubes; block design; similarities). Attainments and focus of attention	No improvement on measures given comparing dyslexic children receiving programme against those not.
Phonological skills†	Reading regular/irregular words of different frequency. Homophonic confusion	Dyslexic children have more homophonic confusions than non-dyslexic controls

* Preliminary data based on a study undertaken by Cate Farrall (Farrall, 1993).
† Preliminary data based on a study undertaken by Cate Farrall (Farrall, Thomson and Watkins,1994).

General discussion

We need to place the above results in the context of changing attainments and changing strategies. It is often the case that children receiving specific help do change the way they approach their work and the comments made in the beginning concerning developmental perspectives need to be noted. Given these, however, one can draw a number of conclusions.

First, general teaching regimes can overcome an apparent cognitive weakness. If one examines the model of developmental disorders described earlier, one sees that a cognitive deficit in the phonological mechanism or short-term memory sound/symbol association was posited. Earlier descriptions of dyslexia as a condition were often resisted on the grounds that describing a cognitive weakness implied that one can never help the child and that he or she was therefore 'word blind'. Our results suggest that an apparent cognitive weakness can be overcome. Alternative strategies can be given and phonological coding deficits, phonemic awareness problems and alphabetical skills can be remediated. In particular, lexical alphabetic skills are improved more easily. More simply expressed, this means that regular written language is more responsive to a phonic approach. Fortunately, 75–80% of English is regular despite its apparent irregularity. Non-lexical phonological spelling is more resistant, i.e. irregular words and more difficult sound patterns (this is something that one would not be surprised at!). In addition, explicit teaching to overcome a deficit, such as phonemic awareness and phonological coding, which provides an alternative approach, e.g. a motor or kinaesthetic coding, is very advantageous. The multisensory techniques such as simultaneous oral spelling, syllable analysis and so on actually focus awareness on the phonemic skills and the kinaesthetic coding may provide an alternative to the weak auditory memory coding that we know dyslexic children have.

Some more specific interpretations include the fact that dyslexic children doing rather better at regular word reading suggests that they are not totally at the logographic stage. They have some lexical or alphabetic skills. If they did not, they would be equally poor at reading regular *and* irregular words.

The syllable analysis results are of interest. Data from these studies indicated that as the number of syllables in a word increased, all children found them more difficult but those with dyslexia were consistently weaker than their non-dyslexic peers, even those who were matched on spelling age. Weak syllable skills may be due to an inability to retain phoneme sequences in short-term memory, problems in forgetting the last few syllables or perhaps problems in rhyme and phonemic awareness. Nevertheless, what is suggested is a very specific technique of tapping out syllables, and teaching syllable types, i.e. Open, Closed, Vowel

Combination, Vowel Digraph syllables (see Thomson and Watkins, 1991), in a very explicit way may overcome this problem to some extent. This research also indicated a kind of 'alphabetic barrier' in reading and spelling which can be overcome at around the 8–9 year attainment age. It is here where children's reading and spelling performance can take off very rapidly, up to attainments of around 11–12 years where there is another 'barrier'. The latter appears to be more due to complex orthography and irregular words. Nevertheless, our experience is that there is a plateau prior to 8-year attainment, a rapid increase and then another plateau at around the 11-year attainment age.

The study on the simultaneous oral spelling used both chronological-age- and spelling-age-matched controls. A recent guide to specific learning difficulties for local authorities, in describing teaching techniques for dyslexic children, said that the teaching methods were 'not necessarily different from the methods used for children with general learning difficulties at the lower end of the continuum'.

Certainly, these results do not support that contention. The idea that dyslexic children require just 'more of the same' has been a very common description in children receiving inappropriate help. The fact that visual inspection does not work for dyslexic children, whereas simultaneous oral spelling (that is, hearing, sounding out, writing or tracing and saying, and looking) does, suggests that these children are a very idiosyncratic group. Remember, *both* techniques were equally good for the matched spelling-age controls. The same experience does not help all children. It is appropriate to mention at this point that the notion of dyslexic children being a very specific and separate group from other children is something to which Professor Miles has devoted a good deal of his writings. This is certainly support of his position as far as teaching methodology is concerned. Why simultaneous oral spelling kinds of approach work is, of course, not totally answered by research such as this. It may be the helping to map phoneme/grapheme links; it may be providing an alternative code as suggested earlier in terms of kinaesthesis; it may be the applying of short-term memory to these above skills; or it may, in fact, help to facilitate lexical access, i.e. help children apply the spelling knowledge they already have about words. A possibility from recent research by Goswami (1993) might be a focus on the intrasyllabic 'onset and rime'. It is hoped to do further work in this area.

The other two studies mentioned above are early stages of development. As far as the Feuerstein Enrichment Programme (Feuerstein and Jensen, 1980) is concerned, this has been undertaken at school by a number of groups and we found no evidence for improvements in the areas described. The phonological skills again seem to confirm the idea of dyslexic children being a separate group because both matched chronological-age and language-age controls were used in this study also. Here, those with dyslexia having more homophonic confusions confirmed the notion that they have particular difficulties in the phonology and phonemic awareness areas.

This chapter has not provided all the answers to what teaching methods are appropriate, but I hope it has given the reader some flavour of the research that has been undertaken at East Court School. As said earlier, these are not reported in detail but references are given. In many cases it is reassuring to have our feelings about the efficacy (or not as the case may be!) of our teaching procedures supported by research findings. Inevitably there are caveats about this research, as one is never exactly sure what particular aspect of the teaching programme is helping children. However, at least some attempt at systematic, thorough observation and research can help us tease out those variables which are important. The importance of practical observation with children, teaching and assessment of them and consequent feedback into theoretical research has always been a very important part of Professor Miles's work and it has been satisfying and right that this topic should be addressed in this chapter.

Chapter 11
Whole school provision for the whole child

STEVE CHINN

Introduction

It is the contention of this chapter that severe specific learning difficulties, or dyslexia, require very carefully and comprehensively designed provision. This chapter considers the educational, social, parental and political factors which affect the design of this provision.

It is manifestly right that all children should have access to as broad a learning experience as is possible. For dyslexic children the access is more than just physical access to the classroom. For these children, access will require that the school has a complete awareness of the nature and ramifications of the difficulties created by dyslexia and the knowledge of how to address them. This suggests that all staff in the school, academic and pastoral, need an understanding of dyslexia and a knowledge of and an ability to use relevant and effective teaching methods.

Some years ago, when I started to teach dyslexic children, I approached an education department at a university to ask if they would be interested in any joint research projects about dyslexia. The more polite part of the reply was to the effect that if I could define dyslexia to their satisfaction, then they would consider research. This need to define before providing still persists in many areas. A precise and universal definition is an admirable goal, but if pursuit of an ideal definition prevents research and provision, then it is the wrong goal. If the pursuit of an ideal definition does not preclude providing for children who have learning difficulties in their educational environment, then it is worth time. I suspect that experiences gained from helping such children can only be supportive of our understanding of dyslexia and thus lead to a better definition.

Definitions do exist; for example, in 1987 the American government convened a conference of leading experts to consider a definition of learning difficulties. The consequence was a long and comprehensive definition which describes the extent of the problem far beyond the original concept of 'word blindness'. The first part is quoted (Kavanagh and Truss, 1988):

> Learning disabilities is a generic term that refers to a heterogeneous group of disorders manifested by significant difficulties in the acquisition of listening, speaking, reading, writing, reasoning, or mathematical abilities or social skills. These disorders are intrinsic to the individual and presumed to be due to central nervous system dysfunction.

I chose this definition because it lists areas of difficulty I have observed in the three specialist schools I have run. Provision has to be prepared to meet all of these needs. This comprehensive definition was predated in its broad outlook by Miles (1983) when he wrote about *The Pattern of Difficulties* (now in second edition, 1993). What the American definition and Miles provide is a starting place for describing the educational needs of the dyslexic child.

The scientist in me accepts the need for definitions, but the teacher in me knows that any definition of children can only be at best a skeleton. Understanding of the individual provides the flesh that identifies that individual. My concern is that, however complete the definition, the individual will challenge its universality. Understanding and provision must acknowledge this.

Educational provision

Of all the environments a dyslexic child may meet, secondary education must provide the most daunting challenge. Almost everything in this environment is a potential source of failure. It follows therefore that adequate provision at secondary level is likely to be extensive.

Returning to the principle (and its consequences) that any child deserves access to an education as close as is possible to that experienced by his 'normal' peers, he will also require special help in basic skills, for example, language, numeracy, writing and study skills. The special help is essential if the child is to make any progress in these basic skills and equally essential if he is to use these skills to assist effective access to the rest of the curriculum.

This can create an organisational problem when provision is whole school. The present National Curriculum puts such a strain on a normal timetable, that there is a real risk of absorbing opportunities for extra time for special provision. Thus the demands of access to the whole curriculum can become self-defeating. (This can also be a problem when provision is made by withdrawal, because the time used for withdrawal will also reduce time to follow the full curriculum.) The point is made here to illustrate the often conflicting demands of quite reasonable principles. Thus whole school provision and access to a broad (rather than the whole) curriculum are possible if a principle is not taken blindly to an extreme. With this set clearly in mind, then educational provision can be considered.

Language

Language provision is the key provision and will almost certainly include reading, spelling, writing, punctuation and probably spoken language. At least one Local Education Authority will not consider issuing a Statement of Special Educational Needs unless there is a deficit of at least 4 years in one skill at age 11. If there is a 4-year deficit in language skills, it seems an obvious consequence that the provision has to be comprehensive.

If at all possible, provision at secondary age should begin at 11 when, whatever the educational arrangements, secondary education begins. At 11 the student is 5 years away from GCSE or Key Stage 4. Our experience is that it takes at least 2 years to address confidence and attitude to learning (while improving basic skills as well). If provision starts at 13 or later, the prognosis is less optimistic. At 13 the work becomes influenced by year 11 (age 16) examinations. There is less time to spare for basics, confidence is likely to be more battered and attitudes against school more hardened. Assuming the child starts at 11, then there is likely to be more long-term success.

Reading is the primary target as it leads to better access to the other subjects. Eclectic approaches seem to be more applicable as each child must be seen as an individual. We are always reviewing new ideas, partly to enable us to have more approaches to offer the students. New technology is providing many exciting new possibilities.

Whilst reading gains usually seem to come along steadily and reliably, spelling gains are a more daunting task. The sheer complexity and irregularity of spelling in the English language makes perfect remediation almost impossible. Parents, and some psychologists, tend to forget that dyslexia is a life-long problem and that some difficulties remain difficult. A more realistic approach may be to look at improvements in the readability of spelling; for example, is it more phonically acceptable/readable or can a computer spellchecker recognise the word? The teacher has always to try and consider the advantages and limitations of each aspect of language teaching, attempting to keep a balance between the often conflicting demands of mainstream and specialist work.

Children's awareness of their own spelling deficits often limits what they write. They use the words they are more confident of spelling correctly (but probably still spell incorrectly). This results in a very limited written vocabulary, which diminishes the quality and quantity of the children's work. One of the early tasks of the teacher is to free children to write, which means encouraging them to use words they cannot spell correctly.

There is a further consideration with the use of words. We have thought for some time now that children tend not to use in essays and free writing the spellings they so arduously learn in spelling lessons. This could suggest that schools blend spelling lessons into main English rather than label such lessons as separate entities. This may well lead to better transfer of skills (a principle of similar use in other skill areas).

The rapid growth of information technology is creating a quiet revolution in dyslexia. Word processors took away most of the stress of editing for both child and teacher. It is no longer a major task to change a spelling, add punctuation or redraft work. Recent developments are exciting and so new that their benefits have not yet been quantified, though initial research suggests that the effects are dramatic. Voice output from computers is making language work on computer multisensory. An upgrade from robotic voice output to digital speech should be available before the end of this year (1994). The consequences of this facility are enormous. A student can see and hear what he has written. He is receiving constant feedback on his writing. Effectively, the computer is acting like a permanent spelling adviser and tutor. Being in contact with these developments is one of the benefits of links with research organisations, in this case the Center for Approved Special Technology (CAST) in Massachusetts.

Among other benefits voice output means a student can type in work, make a visual check on spelling, then make an auditory check. We have yet to see how this improves awareness of spelling patterns. We already suspect that ordinary spellcheckers have a positive effect on awareness of spelling patterns. The child is learning spelling as an incidental skill, which is closer to the way 'normal' children learn to spell. One could speculate that the computer draws attention to the spelling generalisations the child has previously missed.

An additional use of voice output is access to books on disk (as well as audio tape). Production of these disks is greatly eased by use of a text scanner. The computer displays the words on screen and the student can highlight as much or as little as he wishes to hear. It enables the student to read at a level beyond his normal level of independent reading. It also accesses any written material, independently. Thus the computer is a tool used to extend learning, not just to substitute for lack of skills. It is moving to a new phase in the classroom, away from the early 'drill and kill' programmes.

Another use of technological development is the use of ARROW, Lane's (1990) multisensory use of self-voice. ARROW can form an important part of withdrawal provision and can be tutored by ancillaries under teacher supervision. The technique is a good example of work developed for one disability (partial hearing) being transferred to another.

Despite the specialist nature of a main English programme, there is likely to be a need to provide extra input for some students. There are good reasons to structure this input into a workshop format, so that, for example, a child goes into the workshop for one lesson each day for around three weeks to receive an intensive boost of tuition and then return to the normal timetable. Workshops could include one-on-one work in areas such as phonics, handwriting, speech, ARROW, word processors or voice-output computers.

Through all the new technology, the phonics, the multisensory input, the English department has to remember that its final goal is GCSE/Key Stage 4, a mainstream target and as such a target which is prey to policy changes outside its control. The recent reduction in coursework levels for English examinations in year 11 has been a major blow for dyslexic children. We have seen the motivation this option provided and have watched in admiration as year 10 and 11 students draft and redraft work until they feel it matches their aspirations. We can only hope that yet another educational principle is not over-applied, disadvantaging those who least need further barriers.

Finally, the role of the English department is also to support other departments, with advice on a particular student or on accessing work to a group.

Numeracy and mathematics

There is a real comparison between the effect of spelling deficits on writing and the effect of poor knowledge of basic number facts on mathematics. Both reduce confidence and speed of working. Both affect the quality of work the child produces and, ultimately, the quality of work he is offered. T. Miles (Miles and Miles,1992) considers that difficulties in mathematics are frequently found alongside language difficulties.

Management of these difficulties requires the same level of adaptations that language difficulties demand. The child should be allowed access, via these adaptations, to mathematics at a level which is commensurate with his true ability. This may mean that the child is working concurrently within a wide range of levels. For example, his or her basic fact knowledge may be a level 1 while problem-solving skills may be at level 5.

Several factors affect performance in mathematics (Chinn, 1991). An effective programme has to be structured to address and circumvent these so that the student is enabled to progress to levels appropriate to his real ability. The design of the programme raises, among other matters, the cross-curriculum issue of whether to address factors such as poor memory directly by specific programmes or to address them within the body of, say, the mathematics programme.

Consider one area of numeracy, knowledge of times-table facts

(Pritchard et al., 1986). Many dyslexic children have great difficulty in learning these facts, (other than two, ten and five times tables). It is unlikely that longer sessions of rote learning will improve this situation. An alternative approach is to develop strategies which enable the student to quickly work out an answer, so that the facts which are remembered are built upon in a mathematically structured way. The student should learn by mastering procedures which can be extended beyond just the basic deficits. This provides an example of how a broad curriculum, if taught appropriately, addresses subskills such as memory and generalisation.

Other subjects

These can be divided into three categories. The first includes the subjects which build up the curriculum, such as history, science, drama and so forth. The second includes the 'support' topics such as study skills, memory training, keyboard skills and so forth. The third, which overlaps with social skills/interpersonal development, includes careers education, team work and religious/humanitarian topics.

A child needs a broad curriculum for three major reasons. A wide experience of subjects helps develop the child's knowledge base. In addition, each subject brings its own way of looking at information, its own way of solving problems and its own way of learning. Whilst this second reason is important for all children, I would contend that it is especially important for those with dyslexia, because they so often need to have flexibility of thinking in order to circumvent difficulties. Again I would contend that a child who learns study skills, problem-solving skills, observational skills and so on from within the body of several subjects is more likely to transfer those skills to other areas of the curriculum and to life than if they are taught in isolation.

The third reason has an element of risk, but if properly managed, the risk is slight. A broad range of subjects allows the child to find more chances of success. The risk is that it also allows the child to find more areas of failure. In this situation alone lies a strong argument for whole school provision for severely dyslexic children.

Physical education/games

Physical activities are worth a separate mention. Our experience tells us that there will be a full spectrum of ability. A physical education programme (and attitude) has to acknowledge that range. Again the whole school approach allows each child to participate and benefit from new experiences with minimum fear of failure and ridicule. Physical activity can lead to many (sometimes unpredictable) benefits. For example, a boy who became out of breath on a run spoke with clarity for the first time.

Increased strength often leads to greater coordination skills. The demands of teamwork can improve social and interpersonal skills. A new area of success can boost confidence, both for the child him- or herself and for the rest of the school as it shares in his or her achievements.

School size and class size

For the student to have the individual attention he or she needs and for him or her to learn (predominantly) in a group (which we consider preferable) then class size should be small. Small groups allow for inter-actions, mutual support and discussions where students can talk out their ideas. There is less (and probably little chance) for the student to avoid involvement in the lesson, a survival strategy evolved by some children. A group size of eight seems to be right for most programmes.

For the child to be known and understood by all of the people he or she meets at school, the school must be small. These children need to belong and be a valued part of their society. There is a need to learn and practise skills in a secure environment where the child knows he or she is understood. If the school can generate a positive, caring and nurturing ethos then the child has more encouragement to learn. Small is a relative term: 80–100 is probably about as far as small can stretch!

Environment and facilities

As far as is possible, special education should offer the same opportunities as normal education (and possibly better access to those opportunities). The facilities should therefore be comparable with mainstream facilities. Some, for example, word processors and English resources, should be better.

The general environment should also support positive feelings about learning. I recently read a special school prospectus which emphasised the non-school-like environment. I also recall quite clearly the reaction of the students at the specialist school in America where I was visiting headmaster for 18 months. We started on a split site in two sets of church rooms and a small hut. When we moved to a single site with much better facilities, a redundant secondary school, the boys looked at the building and said, 'Ugh, it's a school!'. School buildings were not a motivating influence. There is a great advantage to attitudes to learning in providing well-maintained, attractive buildings and grounds which do not look like a typical school.

Social skills and interpersonal skills

Although Sally Smith wrote about problems with social and interpersonal skills in 1978, there is not much evidence of widespread acknowledgement of this very critical area of need. Recently there have been more research papers on these topics and therefore more awareness. It would have been hard for me not to acknowledge the existence of such difficulties after 12 years' experience of running specialist schools here and in the USA. This need will almost certainly justify a strong pastoral programme, preferably led by a trained counsellor, and acknowledged as an important part of the school's provision.

It is important to state that, if addressed in time, these social and interpersonal problems rarely create behavioural problems of major significance. Guidance and counselling inputs should be, whenever possible, pre-emptive. This is possible in a small school where students are known as individuals by all staff, whether teaching, pastoral and ancillary, all of whom are available to note any changes or unusual behaviours. A good pastoral structure should have several fail-safe systems built in, so that, for example, the child has access to any adult he chooses within the school (and, of course, to independent outside contacts).

Boarding education, although not the choice of many parents, is fairly inevitable if the child is of secondary age. Whole school provision is needed by only a small percentage of the population, which means that a viable specialist school requires a large catchment area, which means boarding. If this situation is inevitable, then good boarding facilities ease the decision.

There are some positive benefits of boarding for a dyslexic student and his family. The work environment is consistent. Parents are removed from a 'policing' role. A consistent 24-hour-a-day whole approach avoids readjustment problems for the student (in our experience dyslexic children do not cope well with change). A particular pastoral programme can be followed more naturally, with more opportunities to modify behaviours and attitudes. There is more chance to involve the student in social and interpersonal interactions. Independence is developed. Sometimes, boarding allows time for readjustment of family interactions, which may have been upset by parental concerns and anxieties and the child's increasing frustrations.

Research and training

Although recognition of dyslexia is near to its 100 years (Miles and Miles, 1990), many aspects are still in their infancy. Also, technology is introducing facets that are so new that we cannot yet measure their effects. Thus there is still much to be learnt. School-based research has to be one of the most productive forms of research. Teachers in whole-school-provision establishments receive constant feedback and evaluations from their students. Even when this is not structured or documented, it occurs and the experiences colour and shape future work.

Teachers also need to be aware of current outside research. Attendance at conferences can help achieve this goal as can access to research journals. Training for teachers is now more widely available, including the pioneering MEd courses at Bangor, the RSA diploma and the new modular university courses. A school which educates dyslexic children has an obligation to appraise new developments and provide ongoing training in order to continue to offer the best provision to its students.

External agencies

Parents of a child with dyslexia (or indeed any handicap) are vulnerable and susceptible to offers of a quick cure. Validation procedures are therefore important. New developments such as tinted glasses are, in time, evaluated by independent research. Schools have had a limited evaluation by the British Dyslexia Association and some whole school providers have been approved by the Department for Education. Some schools have supported a new, independent body (which has the backing of the British Dyslexia Association and the Dyslexia Institute) which offers validation of provision. Although the Department for Education provided a very thorough validation process for whole school provision, this body extends that to all levels of provision. External agencies such as this can only improve the quality of provision.

Schools which offer whole provision are very likely to take students funded by local education authorities. This will almost always result in further validation visits (from local education authority representatives). Social Services, who have a different agenda, visit all boarding schools. Each visit teaches the school something new, and most visits are positive in attitude. Overall, outside agencies are important contributors to the reassurance process a parent needs when seeking a school for their child.

Parents

As the previous section stated, parents are vulnerable. They have often had traumatic experiences of educational provision for their child. Some parents become, understandably, protective of their child and overanxious about any hiccup in the emotional or educational progress of the child. Optimum progress occurs when the school earns the trust of the parent so that the child, school and parent work together with understanding and cooperation. The same applies when a fourth party, the local education authority, is involved.

As with all human beings, there is great variation in parents. Some need to understand and then accept their child's difficulties (Smith, 1978). Some have to learn to adjust their expectations. Some start with a simple request, 'Make my child happy again. I'm not worried if he gets any GCSEs'. As the boy settles and progresses, the request is often upgraded to, 'How many GCSEs will he get? Can he do A level?'. Although ambition is admirable, parents need to remember that academic work will never be easy for dyslexic children.

Expectation can be a powerful influence: positive or negative. A school often has to negotiate, either directly or indirectly, reasonable expectations. Schools have many reasons to encourage good results, but specialist schools have to balance such expectations against their awareness of the extra pressures dyslexic students experience at examination time (and even offer lessons in relaxation techniques).

Contact with parents and accessibility ease tensions between school and parents. It is an important part of school and pupil management to arrange contact and exchange information. This information should cover the pupil's progress, development and programmes and school policies. The school should be accessible to the parent, and the parent should be accessible to the school.

Monitoring and assessment

As has been stated before, there is a need for balance. Each pupil must be monitored, which will mean testing and examinations, but each pupil needs maximum time to learn, so the time allocated to curriculum testing must balance against the time allocated to learning. Standardised testing in basic skill areas is a part of specialist school life. This also must be used in a balanced and appropriate way and must acknowledge the differentiating capacity of the test.

Testing and examinations in the early years also function as opportunities to practise study skills, organise revision time and practise examination techniques. The results of these tests and assessments are a part of the monitoring procedure of any school. An equally important part, and a very effective part in small schools, are the ongoing evaluations of the staff. Each member of staff can contribute a viewpoint based on evaluation in their subject area (and each subject illustrates different facets) and based on their own standpoint and experience. This tends to provide a very comprehensive view of the student.

Conclusion

There will always be a small percentage of the school population whose specific learning difficulties are so severe that they will need whole school provision. The management of that provision has to ensure that it compensates as much as is possible for all the learning and emotional problems of the child. There are many strengths and talents in those who suffer the problems of dyslexia. It is beholden on us to tap into as many of those skills as we can. It is equally beholden on us to minimise the number of young people with specific learning defficulties who suffer the emotional scars of inappropriate education.

Chapter 12
Early help means a better future

JEAN AUGUR

Introduction

In the past it was thought that the earliest that a child could be identified as having a dyslexic profile was at about the age of six. This was because, by six, the child was already giving cause for concern particularly as regards reading, writing and spelling, all very important skills in the school curriculum. With experience, however, and from the findings of research studies, it is now evident that there are many signs well before school age which may suggest such a profile and the consequent difficulties ahead. Parents and preschool carers as well as educators in those early years are among those in the best position to recognise these signs, and to provide appropriate activities to help. Training in some of these activities will help to build firm foundations for later, more formal, training.

What is dyslexia?

Dyslexia is best described as a specific difficulty in learning, in one or more areas of reading, spelling and written language. This may be accompanied by difficulty in number work, short-term memory, sequencing, auditory and/or visual perception and motor skills. It is particularly related to mastering and using written language – alphabetic, numeric and musical notation. In addition, oral language is often affected to some degree.

Dyslexia occurs despite normal teaching and is independent of socioeconomic background or intelligence. It is, however, more easily detected in those with average or above average intelligence. There are some early signs which may suggest a dyslexic profile, however; for example, there may be a family history of similar difficulties, or the child may have walked early but did not crawl, or was a 'bottom shuffler' or 'tummy wriggler'. Sometimes there are persistent difficulties in

Jean Augur died 15 August, 1993. Her chapter was completed by Gerald Hales.

getting dressed efficiently, or putting shoes on the correct feet; dyslexic children are often unduly late in learning to fasten buttons or tie shoelaces. In more general terms, it may be observed that the child has 'good' and 'bad' days, for no apparent reason, or suffers from excessive tripping, bumping into things and falling over. These children frequently enjoy being read to, but show no interest in letters or words themselves, and are often accused of 'not listening' or 'not paying attention'. They may well have difficulty with catching, kicking or throwing a ball; hopping and/or skipping; and clapping a simple rhythm.

Solutions are not always complex or difficult. For example, marking shoes with 'L' and 'R' may not help the child who still cannot distinguish the difference between left and right. Marking them with 'outside' may do the trick, though.

In the areas of speech and language, children in this group are often seen to learn to speak clearly later than expected and frequently produce persistent jumbled phrases, such as 'cobbler's club' for 'toddlers' club', 'tebby-dare' for 'teddy-bear' or 'pence-fost' for 'fence-post'. An early lisp, such as 'duckth' for 'ducks', is not uncommon. They may be observed using substitute words or 'near-misses' (e.g. 'lampshade' for 'lamppost') and they also mislabel – for instance the child may know colours but mislabel them as, say, 'black' for 'brown'.

There will often also be an inability to remember the label for known objects, e.g. table, chair, and persistent word-searching. There is often confusion between directional words, e.g. up/down, in/out. Difficulty learning nursery rhymes is common, as is using rhyming words such as 'cat', 'mat', 'sat'. This child may find difficulty in selecting the 'odd one out', e.g. 'cat', 'mat', 'pig', 'fat', and also with sequences such as (at first) a coloured bead sequence – and later with days of the week or numbers.

There are frequently compensation strengths, however. Children in this group are often seen to be quick 'thinkers' and 'doers' – but not in response to instruction – and they can have an enhanced creativity: they are often good at drawing, with a good sense of colour. You may find an aptitude for constructional or technical toys, e.g. bricks, puzzles, Lego, blocks, remote control for TV and/or video, computer keyboard. Quite often parents and teachers report that the child appears bright but seems 'an enigma'.

Not all dyslexic children experience all of the difficulties listed above. Moreover, it is important to note that many very young children make similar mistakes to dyslexic children, but it is the severity of the trait, the clarity with which it may be observed and the *length of time during which it persists* which give the vital clues to the identification of the dyslexic learner.

Young children are very perceptive about themselves and very often the things which they say can alert adults to certain difficulties, provided that the adult is wise enough to listen and learn. We should all look out for phrases like the following:

I think God's put my brain in upside down

The word is coming

I'm getting close

The word's near the front of my mouth

Is yesterday the day after tomorrow?

Where is the beginning of the book?

Where does the book start?

This book is stupid

Where's the top of the page?

Which way does it go?

I've dropped it again

What's that word again?

In many ways the dyslexic child is at a disadvantage when he enters school. His main strengths are centred in the right hemisphere of the brain. Hence, he is often a random, intuitive, impulsive, sensitive thinker. Unfortunately for him, school is a left-hemisphered environment where he will be expected to read, write, spell, deal with symbols – letters, numbers, musical notation – learn phonics, follow instructions, listen carefully, respond accurately to what he hears and put things in order. The earlier he or she is given activities that will build a sound foundation for learning such skills, the better chance he or she will have. The period between 3 and 7 years is a most important time for learning.

Practical help

There are general activities which can be of great assistance, although not every one will be appropriate to every child, of course. The following is a list of those found to be particularly helpful:

1. Say nursery rhymes together. These seemed to go out of fashion for a while, but fortunately have had a revival. They are not only part of our history and heritage, but they help to encourage rhythm and rhyme at an early age.
2. Finger play.
3. Read poetry to children, especially amusing or nonsense poems. Try making up jingles and limericks together.

4. Mime a particular nursery rhyme or incident and encourage the children to guess the mime. They can then choose something to mime in return.
5. Use drama.
6. Provide pictures to talk about. Help the child to notice the details using prepositions in discussion. 'Is the man in the blue hat *in front of* or *behind* the lady?' 'Is the boy climbing *under* or *over* the gate?" "Is the bus going *up* or *down* the hill?'
7. Hunt the thimble. Encourage the children to verbalise using prepositions again. 'Is the thimble *inside* the pot, *under* the pot, *on* the box etc.?'
8. Play 'Simon Says'.
9. Playground games, such as 'Follow my leader', 'In and out among the bluebells', or 'The ally ally O'.
10. The Hokey-Cokey – action involving parts of the body.
11. Board games, e.g. Snakes and Ladders, Ludo, Bingo etc., to develop turn-taking.
12. Watching television *together*. Television can be a useful form of learning if it is not allowed to be passive. There are many programmes which give scope for further discussion and activities. Older children enjoy factual programmes involving nature study and exploration which can lead on to project work and interesting files.
13. There are some splendid puzzle books in bookshops and stationers. Make use of these – joining dots, mazes, simple picture crosswords are all useful. Mazes can be amazing fun, but be careful to choose the level of difficulty to match the ability of the developing individual.
14. Encourage your children to help in household activities, e.g. laying the table.

Some activities relate especially to listening activities and auditory sequencing:

1. Put various objects in containers – sand, dried peas, pennies, buttons etc. Shake the containers one at a time and ask the child to say what he or she thinks might be inside and to describe the sound. Ask questions, 'Is there one penny in here or more than one?' 'Is the sound hard? Or gentle? Or soft?'
2. Listen to everyday sounds, preferably with eyes closed. What can be heard? The telephone ringing? Hammering? Voices? A clock ticking? Listen to traffic sounds – motor bike, lorry, ambulance, car etc.
3. Tape some everyday sounds, e.g. tap dripping, toilet flushing, phone ringing. Play them to the child and see if he can recognise them. Sound lotto (published by Learning Development Aids, Wisbech, Cambs) and sound stories are very useful and enjoyable activities.

4. Ask a child to close his or her eyes and guess who is speaking.
5. Tap or clap a simple rhythm for the child to repeat. Gradually make the rhythm more difficult. Clap words of one syllable. Then move on to two-syllable words, then more. Say the words as you clap them, i.e. cat, dog, black-board, hol-i-day, tel-e-vi-sion. Later the child is given a word to clap. Can he say how many *beats* the word has? Use the child's name for this activity.
6. I Spy. This game is too difficult for some children if the letter names are used. Therefore take it in stages and play it several ways, e.g.
   (a) Using the *sound*, e.g. I spy with my little eye something beginning with the sound (b).
   (b) Increase the load, e.g. I spy with my little eye something beginning with the same sound as ball.
   (c) Using the same *letter name*, e.g. I spy with my little eye something beginning with the letter B.
   (d) *Using rhyming.* I spy with my little eye something that rhymes with bat.
   (e) *Ending sound.* I spy with my little eye something *ending* with the sound (b).
7. *Sound* a word in individual units, e.g. m-a-n and ask the child to say the whole word 'man'. Increase the number of sounds in the word, e.g. l-a-m-p, tr-u-m-p-e-t. *Do not* over emphasise the sounds!
8 Say pairs of words which rhyme – 'cat', 'bat' do they rhyme? Say pairs of words which do not rhyme – 'cat', 'dog' – do they rhyme? Start off a round with a word and ask each child to say a rhyming word, e.g. 'day' – 'play' – 'may' – 'tray'. The first to break the rhyme must start a new round, e.g. 'pin' – 'tin' – 'thin' – etc.
9. 'Simon Says'. Start with very simple instructions, e.g. 'Simon says, clap your hands'. Gradually make the instructions more difficult, e.g. 'Simon says, touch your ear and your nose'.
10. Say a group of words with a 'stranger' in it, e.g. 'cat', 'dog', 'apple', 'fox'. The child tells you or draws a picture of the stranger. Ask why it is different. This can also be played with rhyming words, e.g. 'cat', 'bat', 'fox', 'hat'. Which word didn't rhyme?
11. I went to market and I bought.... Start with a particular group of things, e.g. fruit or vegetables, because it is easier to remember related things. Later, shop for random things, e.g. a piano, a thimble, table-mats, a coat etc. This game can also be played where each item must begin with a given letter, e.g. peas, potatoes, pancakes etc. Vary the game with different openings, e.g. I packed my case with; In my Christmas stocking I found; On my birthday I had....
12. Songs involving memory and sequencing, e.g. 'Old Macdonald had a farm'; 'The twelve days of Christmas'; 'Ten green bottles'. Songs and rhymes involving days of the week and months of the year are also most useful.

13. *Following instructions*. Start with one or two only, e.g. 'Please pick up the pencil and put it in the box'. Gradually make the sequence longer, e.g. 'Go to the shelf, find the red box, bring it to me'. *Encourage the child to repeat the instruction before carrying it out. His own voice is his best memory aid.*

Other activities encourage visual (looking) activities and visual sequencing. Consider the following:

1. *Snap*. Use pictures only at first, then introduce letters and simple words.
2. Pairs.
3. Pelmanism or memory games.
4. Dominoes require little setting up, but they provide simple help with numbers as well as visual sequencing.
5. Sorting things into colours, shapes and sizes. Sorting pictures, e.g. 'Put all the pictures that start with the same sound as table in one pile, and all the pictures which start with the same sound as dog in another pile'.
6. Happy Families.
7. Look together at a picture. Cover the picture and ask the child questions about it, e.g. 'How many children were in the picture?' 'How many people were wearing hats?' 'Was it winter or summer?'.
8. Provide a tray of objects for the child to look at. After a few seconds cover the tray and ask the child to name all the objects he saw.
9. Provide a tray of objects for the child to look at. Ask the child to close his eyes. Remove one or two objects from the tray. Ask the child to open his eyes and say which objects he thinks were removed.
10. After shapes have been taught, draw three shapes on a card. Show the card to the child, cover it, and then ask him to draw what he saw, or put out the sequence with shapes drawn on cards. Gradually increase the length of the sequence. Keep the shapes nice and simple. You could also use these for snap.
11. Show the child several pictures – three is enough at first – and ask him to arrange them in order to make a story. Encourage him to tell you the story.
12. Bingo – looking only.
13. Draw several related pictures and include a stranger, e.g. apple, pear, book, plum. Ask the child to point to the 'odd one out'.

Other skill development tasks encourage kinaesthetic awareness. These are things such as:

1. Tracing shapes, letters, words, simple pictures etc.

2. Making letters with plasticine, modelling clay or pipe cleaners. Use chalk, paint, thick felt pens to write very large shapes and letters, and make letter shapes with the forefinger in a tray of dry or wet sand.
3. Feeling and naming sandpaper or felt shapes or letters with the eyes closed.
4. Feeling and naming wooden or plastic letters with the eyes closed.
5. Putting various objects or wooden letters in bags and asking the child to name the object or letter.
6. Jigsaw puzzles.
7. Threading a sequence of coloured beads onto a string and asking the child to repeat the sequence several times.

Do not neglect the physical skills such as throwing, catching, kicking balls, skipping, hopping, jumping and balancing. Many children find these activities difficult and will need a great deal of practice.

Research has also shown that where children make an early acquaintance with books and they share this experience with parents, the results are beneficial. It is important to talk about books, using the language of books – pictures, words and letters – to realise that books can be looked at, read and enjoyed over and over again. It is not automatic for a child to know how to hold a book, to know which way it opens, where the story starts, where the top of the page is or in which direction the words flow. All these things often have to be taught. Dyslexic children, in particular, need to have such points drawn to their attention many times over.

When we consider writing, rather than copying letter shapes (which can sometimes create or exacerbate 'anti-writing' movements if not supervised very closely), large writing movements should be encouraged. These can be done as part of music and/or movement lessons, or by using the forefinger with tactile materials such as sand.

When introducing children to 'sounds', sometimes referred to as 'phonics', these should be taught quietly with as little voice emphasis as possible. Rather than saying '(a) is for apple', it is better to say the word first, thereby giving the clue to the sound which the child is required to listen for – hence 'apple (a), bat (b)' etc. Many preschool children know the names of several letters and some can even 'recite' the alphabet in order. Activities using wooden, plastic or tactile letters are all useful and will reinforce the letter shapes, both upper case *ABC* which are easier, and lower case *abc*. Many young children will have difficulty with *b*, *d*, *p*, *g*, *q* but soon outgrow this. The problem persists, however, for dyslexic children.

Parents, and mothers in particular, are often very perceptive about their own children, and may well have had the feeling before formal school starts that 'things were not quite right'. All too often, when they have attempted to express these feelings, they have met with comments such as, 'Don't worry. Don't expect too much. He will catch up'. At worst they may be labelled 'fussy', 'pushy' or 'over anxious'. The parent's comments should always be listened to and their concerns taken seriously.

During regular preschool development checks, a doctor or health visitor may also see children with an uneven developmental profile, indicating weaker areas requiring attention from a speech or language therapist, or they may see an occupational therapist to look at fine motor coordination problems or a paediatric physiotherapist for gross motor problems.

It would be helpful if information from all these sources, plus parents' comments and preschool educators' observations, could be made available to the headteacher when the child enters first school. In too many cases it can take several years for a child to be identified as having a specific learning difficulty/dyslexia, by which time failure and consequent behavioural problems may well be all too apparent. The valuable observations and record keeping of parents and of the early years in education could prevent this sad situation arising.

Part V
Diverse Routes to a Wider Understanding

Chapter 13
Unconventional treatments for dyslexia

C.R. WILSHER

Introduction

The title of this paper is somewhat controversial, because there is much debate as to what should be *the* treatment for dyslexia, let alone what can be considered conventional or unconventional. Therefore it is very important to stress from the beginning that there is no particular merit in being deemed conventional and no slur in being labelled unconventional. After all, the whole history of dyslexia is full of examples of people going against convention. For the purpose of this article, conventional will refer to teaching methods, and unconventional will refer to everything else.

Assessment of methods

All methods of intervention are faced with the same problems when it comes to establishing the proof of their efficacy and benefit (or harm for that matter). Although various methods used to help people with dyslexia may seem to improve their condition, proving it can be a different matter. In modern scientific terms, the proponents of a particular therapy have to prove that its benefits are better than those which could be produced by any other factors (i.e. not the ones being claimed) or for that matter, by chance effects alone. To do this, a scientific study is usually set up in which progress is measured and compared to a control group.

The scientific method now favoured for proving that a treatment is effective, is the randomised, double-blind, placebo-controlled study. This consists of a prospective study in which all the details of how the study is to be performed are committed to a study protocol. When subjects are selected for a study, they are randomly placed in a treatment group or a placebo (dummy treatment) group, and both the subject and the experimenter are unaware of which treatment they are receiving. Although this is a difficult design to follow, a close proximity to it can be gained by comparing one treatment to a similar one, both of which are pursued with equal rigour and enthusiasm, and are assessed by independent 'blind' assessors. The difficulty in operating a scientifically rigorous test of therapies has led to many treatments, both conventional and unconventional being put forward without proper testing. To show that all is not straightforward, I will first take an example from more conventional treatments.

A conventional example

Bradley and Bryant (1983) designed a two-year training system consisting of 40 sessions of one-to-one tuition. There were four groups:

(1) sound categorising ($n=13$);
(2) sound categorising plus handling of plastic letters ($n=13$);
(3) conceptual categorising ($n=26$);
(4) no training ($n=13$).

The children selected for this study were 6 year olds who had sound categorisation problems. There were some limiting factors in interpreting this study. First, although the results were co-varied by age and IQ, they were not co-varied by baseline scores because pre-test scores were not available. When only post-test scores are available, it is usually prudent to employ large groups (approximately 100 subjects) to avoid the chance of unequal distribution of high scorers. Second, it is important to use the most appropriate control group for each hypothesis tested. As Bryant himself points out (Bryant and Goswami, 1987) there was no control group to control for the extra experience which the successful group had with alphabetic letters. For this reason, we are unable to conclude that there was any improvement in reading in these children. Bryant (Bryant and Goswami, 1987) cites many studies similar to that which he performed with Bradley and concludes 'we cannot yet conclude that training in a phonological skill has an effect on reading'. This does not mean that phonological training will not help reading but that the studies so far have not been able to prove it satisfactorily.

An unconventional treatment

Moving to the arena of unconventional treatments, an idea that can seem both plausible and ridiculous at the same time is that people suffering from dyslexia may read better upside-down. Its plausibility may derive from the notion that many dyslexic people reverse letters (i.e. b/d of p/d), and therefore would be better at reading inverted text. The idea is plainly ridiculous, however, because when reading upside-down the child will read d for p instead of p for d (or vice versa) in the upright position (i.e. he can still reverse things when they are upside-down). In any case, the theory does not make physiological sense, because we all view the world upside-down and the brain turns the image up the right way (people wearing inverting prisms adapt to the upside-down world, which soon loses its strangeness (Stratton, 1896; Ewert, 1930)). Ignoring its illogical nature for a moment, however, let us look at the proof which is put forward for this contention.

Larsen and Parlenvi (1984) examined the reading performance of poor readers and controls (good readers). They then presented these subjects with two matching word lists, one upright and one inverted. The results showed that with the text in the upright position the controls were reading almost three times as well as the poor readers (correct words per minute). However, in the inverted condition, the controls were only reading slightly better than the poor readers. The conclusion accompanying these results suggested that poor readers read inverted text better because there is no longer a difference between them and good readers.

The above study does have a control group (a contrasting group that does not have the same diagnostic characteristics as the experimental group) but it does not have an adequate control condition, i.e. an experimental design ensuring that no bias influences the groups differentially. When trying to prove that some change or treatment does affect groups differently, it is important to ensure that there is no a priori (pre-existing) reason for a differential effect. The question in this case was, 'Are these two groups likely to be affected similarly, all things being equal?'. Unfortunately, they cannot be said to have started on an equal footing. In terms of prose reading, the good readers read four and a half times faster than the poor readers (6 seconds compared to 26 seconds to read two sentences of upright text). The poor readers appeared to be at basal, i.e. there was very little room for them to get worse, while, on the other hand, the controls had a great deal to lose. Close examination of the results shows that good readers reduced their reading performance in the inverted condition but poor readers stayed the same. Far from showing that poor readers read better in the inverted condition, the results show that good readers can be transformed into poor readers by inverting the text, and poor readers are at basal in both conditions. To very poor readers, text is a cipher which is just as mystifying whichever way up it is. Important questions to ask in a case like this are: Have the researchers allowed for the possibility of not finding what they set out to find? Has the opposite hypothesis (i.e. that the claimed effect will *not* happen) an even chance of being shown?

A further lesson to be learned from this study is to be wary of results which use, as a means of proof, the change from significant differences between groups at the beginning to a non-significant difference after intervention. It is important to look at the direction of change, and to see whether there have been any changes *within* groups as well as between groups. If the experimental group (poor readers) have not improved their scores as a result of the treatment (a within-group change), it is difficult to conclude that they have progressed, even though they may now be doing as well as the control group. It is also important to construct experimental material which will have the same 'psychological' impact in both conditions. Reading inverted text is clearly a novel task and does not present the threat posed to poor readers by upright text, which has often been associated with failure. It would be important to utilise another novel task to see if the change from upright to inverted text is purely a function of motivation, a reduction in anxiety, or due to Hawthorne effects (Roethlisberger and Dickson, 1939) etc., as a result of presenting novel stimuli.

Tinted glasses

There have been reports in the national media (*Sunday Times*, 22 December 1985; BBC Television News, 31 March 1987) of a new treatment which involves the wearing of tinted glasses. Proponents of this treatment maintain that visual dyslexia is due to 'scotopic sensitivity syndrome' in which white light from the page causes perceptual disturbances. Irlen (1983) maintains that dyslexic subjects improved their reading after being prescribed tinted glasses by the Irlen Institute in the USA. This claim was based on observations and self reports of 37 learning-disabled students, aged 18–49 years, after wearing the glasses for one month. Apparently, the subjects' reading period before frustration was increased from 15 minutes to 2 hours, and *one* subject increased his rate of reading from 63 to 117 words per minute. No other data were reported, no statistical analyses were carried out and no account was taken of motivation, attention and Hawthorne effects. Such studies would benefit from the use of standard scientific methods such as the employment of control groups (i.e. subjects who receive a placebo treatment) and control procedures, such as random allocation to treatment groups, blind assessment, and so on.

There have been four very small-scale studies which used control groups to study tinted glasses. Robinson and Miles (1987) compared a tinted filter with a clear filter and a randomly selected filter in a small heterogeneous group of children aged 9–16. The results showed that in a small subset of children ($n = 9$) letter identification was improved *but word reading was not*. If this result is robust (i.e. *if* it can be replicated) it is difficult to see how useful this gain would be to 12-year-old children whose difficulty is with prose reading. It must also be remembered that with such a small sample, large amounts of variance and a large number of statistical comparisons such a result may be a chance finding. One attempt (Winter, 1987) at replicating this finding of increased letter identification ability has failed. Winter (1987) selected 15 children (7–11 years old) with scotopic sensitivity who were already wearing Irlen lenses and believed them to help with the resolution of black letters on white pages. He then randomised them to Irlen, plain, grey or no lenses and presented a letter identification task. He found no difference between the four conditions in letter identification performance and the subjective reaction to the lenses was unrelated to performance. Winter also stated that school reading tests did not reveal any beneficial effects.

Richardson (1988), in a similar study, found improvements in word reading but not word matching when using a red filter with a small group (n = 10). There were several puzzling inconsistencies in this study and it is not known if 'order effects' may have contributed to the reported effects. One very interesting inconsistency was that a blue filter was selected equally as frequently as the red filter by children who reported that it helped them to read. However, use of the blue filter led to the highest number of reading errors (more than that for yellow or clear) and over twice as many as that for the red filter. Therefore, the evidence from reading tests contradicted the subjective report of the children (Winter, 1987; Richardson, 1988). O'Connor and Sofo (1988) studied six groups of reading-disabled children, four scotopic and two non-scotopic, with clear, selected and random coloured filters, used for one week. Although the number of subjects in each group was small (approximately 15) statistical analysis revealed very highly significant positive effects. The full results of this study were not available at this time so it is not possible to analyse this study fully. As with the previous studies, independent replication in a larger group of children is urgently required.

There is some doubt as to whether there is any theoretical basis for this notion of visual interference from the white page. A great deal of research work has been performed to determine whether dyslexia is due to a visual deficit or a linguistic deficit. The vast majority of this work supports the contention that dyslexic subjects fail to process linguistic material correctly, although they do in fact manage to process non-linguistic material very well (Vellutino, 1979). The examination of two typical studies will show how people with dyslexia only have difficulty with alphabetic sequential material.

The problem of alphabetic material

Vellutino et al. (1972, 1975) asked dyslexic and good readers to copy three-, four- and five-letter words, scrambled words, numbers and geometric designs. A second presentation of the verbal stimuli required the subjects to pronounce each of the words and spell them out in the correct order. Both studies found that dyslexic subjects performed as well as good readers in copying and recalling geometric designs, but performed poorly in naming verbal material only. The geometric designs were black lines on a white sheet of paper.

Ellis and Miles (1978) compared dyslexic subjects and controls on their ability to process verbal information (letter pairs) or non-verbal highly reversible nonsense figures (all presented as black lines on white background). Even though the nonsense figures were presented in rotation, and reversed, the dyslexic subjects had no difficulty in discriminating between the figures. However, when dyslexic subjects had to discriminate between letter pairs on the basis of the names of the letters, their performance was considerably inferior to that of controls. This would seem to demonstrate that people with dyslexia have no difficulty with visual perception, but do have difficulty with naming. Many other studies have failed to find that people with dyslexia have difficulty in dealing with non-verbal visual material. In addition, it has often been reported that many show prowess at technical drawing and some become professional draughtsmen, architects, artists, photographers, etc. This would hardly be the case if they had difficulty in dealing with black lines on white backgrounds.

The use of drugs

The use of antihistamines to treat dyslexia was pioneered by Levinson (1980) in the USA. His theory is that people with dyslexia suffer from a cerebellar–vestibular disorder that results in their feeling motion-sick, and causes difficulty in processing text, which seems to move. A review of this work (e.g. Masland, 1984) shows that there is no substance to this theory. In fact, there are patients with such severe vestibular disorders that they find it extremely difficult to maintain balance but yet suffer no problem with their reading. In addition, a study of subjects with developmental dyslexia (Brown et al., 1983) shows that they have no more of these vestibular problems than controls.

Unfortunately, these methodological shortcomings do not seem to diminish the enthusiasm of Levinson and his followers. Levinson's method of assessment of the efficacy of his treatment ('Each individual was treated with one or more of a series of such antimotion sickness drugs as cyclizine (Marezine), meclozine (Antivert), dimenhydrinate (Dramamine), diphenhydramine (Benadryl), methylphenidate (Ritalin), etc.' (Levinson, 1980, p. 236) is to solicit reports from the children and their parents, and also to assess them on a device designed to test the speed of fusion of moving pictures of elephants. He does not involve control groups because he believes it is unethical to withhold treatment. However, Levinson's own measures failed to be affected by the treatment ('the expected ability to objectively record and quantitatively measure these responses via . . . blurring speeds did not materialise') (p. 252). In these studies only the subjective impression of the child or the parents supports the claim that 88% of dyslexic subjects 'were found to demonstrate some clinical measure or degree of favourable therapeutic response' (p. 237). It is not known whether the same degree of improvement could be found in placebo groups.

Chiropractors in the USA have recently advertised that they can cure dyslexia and learning disabilities. The basis for the theory and treatment is a book by Ferreri and Wainwright (1984) *Breakthrough for Dyslexia and Learning Disabilities*. The authors theorise that learning disabilities are caused by damage to two specific cranial bones, the sphenoid and the temporal, by what they call 'cloacal reflexes,' and by an ocular muscle imbalance they term 'ocular lock'. Silver (1987) in his review of 'magic cures' for dyslexia concluded that their treatment was

> not based on any known research; that some of it is based on anatomical concepts that are not held by the majority of anatomists; that there is no research done by others that replicates the proposed cures; and, that there are no follow-up research studies to document the claimed results.

The introduction of nootropic drugs, which are purported to improve memory and learning, raises the possibility that they might prove beneficial in developmental dyslexia. The first developed drug in this class is piracetam (2-oxo(pyrrolidin-1-yl) acetamide, Nootropil) which is a cyclic derivative of γ-aminobutyric acid (GABA). The exact mechanism of action of piracetam is unknown and discussed in Giurgea and Salama (1977), and Nicholson (1990). The drug is licensed in the UK for the treatment of cortical myoclonus, and presently contra-indicated for use in children. This means that it is currently not available for the treatment of developmental dyslexia in the UK.

Five double-blind controlled studies in normal adults have used tests of verbal learning and memory; in these published studies piracetam was superior to placebo in verbal function (Dimond and Brouwers, 1976; Mindus, 1976; Wedl and Suchenwirth, 1977; Wilsher, Atkins and Manfield, 1979; Hyde, 1980). Dimond and Brouwers (1976) argued that improvements were seen chiefly in the abilities associated with left-hemisphere function. They studied normal university students before and after 14 days of piracetam in a double-blind crossover protocol, applying measures that they had previously investigated in a 'divided visual field' study of different hemisphere abilities (Dimond and Beaumont, 1973). Those measures revealed a significant drug-related increase in left hemispheric function whilst leaving bilateral tasks unaffected. The neurophysiological studies in children (Conners et al., 1984, 1986, 1987) are also of interest, in that the studies examining lateralised differences of power in the EEG are compatible with an enhancement of left-hemisphere activity and therefore tend to support the notion that piracetam facilitates the brain's analysis of linguistically relevant information.

The initial clinical study in dyslexia (Wilsher, Atkins and Manfield, 1979), involving 16 male dyslexic adolescents and 14 normal student volunteers in a 3-week double-blind trial of 4.8 g piracetam or placebo per day, found that dyslexic (and normal) children treated with piracetam showed a decrease in the number of trials required to reach criteria in a rote verbal learning task, whereas after placebo both groups showed insignificant minor changes.

Another early study by Simeon, Waters and Resnick (1980) studied 14 'learning-disordered' boys in a 4-week double-blind crossover study of 4.8 g/day; they found a significant improvement in *global* evaluation of efficacy(a group with equal IQs), but did not find any changes in learning or cognitive tasks. The lack of clinical effect may have been due to population heterogeneity, small numbers in each group, crossover effects or the short duration of treatment. This same team reanalysed their results in light of their EEG findings (Volavka et al., 1981; Simeon et al., 1983). They found that piracetam caused reductions in left-hemisphere delta power, and that this was related to improvement on neuropsychological measures of verbal sequential performance.

Following these initial studies several short-term (6–12 weeks) studies and two long-term (20–36 weeks) studies were performed. An early short-term study was that of Kunneke and Malan (1979) who found a drug-related improvement in school examinations, digit span and visual perception in epileptic children with learning problems. A multicentred study was carried out by DiIanni et al. (1985). The overall results of this short-term (12-week) investigation indicated a significant improvement in reading speed, and claimed an improvement in digit span seen only in those with low digit-span scores at baseline. Individual groups of investigators from this project also described their results independently. Rudel and Helfgott (1984) and Helfgott et al., (1984) reported a marked improvement on the Wide Range Achievement Test of reading and the same team (Helfgott et al., 1986) separately reported significant changes in verbal memory and delayed recall as a result of piracetam treatment in the same children. Chase et al. (1984) and Tallal et al. (1984, 1985) described significant effects of piracetam upon reading speed, writing accuracy, and a combined measure obtained by multiplying speed and accuracy scores to give 'effective reading accuracy' and speed and comprehension scores to give 'effective reading comprehension'. Van Hout and Giurgea (1990) published a 12-week double-blind study on 36 dyslexic boys, finding piracetam-related improvements in text reading, word reading and spelling, verbal learning and the Stroop naming of colours. Recently a short-term (10-week) study of different subgroups of dyslexic subjects found no difference between piracetam and placebo (Ackerman et al., 1991). Ackerman considered the negative finding to be inconclusive because of the short duration of treatment, small numbers of subjects (dropping to six subjects in one condition) and the use of a new reading test (GORT-R) which they found most unsatisfactory.

The need for longer-term trials was met by a large multicentred study by Wilsher et al. (1987) and a large single-centre study by Levi and Sechi (1987). In the Wilsher et al. (1987) study 225 dyslexic children were recruited in a 36-week double-blind trial of 3.3 g/day piracetam. Children of below average intelligence, or with abnormal findings on audiological, ophthalmological, neurological, psychiatric and physical examinations, were excluded from the trial. The children were of average IQ (Full-scale IQ, WISC-R = 104.3) and an average of 3.4 school grades (US; equivalent to UK school years) behind expected reading age on the Gray Oral Reading Test (Gray, 1963). This five-centre study was completed by 200 children and intensively monitored by an independent group. Primary efficacy measures were: the Gray Oral Reading Test – a prose reading test with a total passage score which combines speed and accuracy, and a comprehension checklist; the Gilmore Oral Reading Test (Gilmore and Gilmore, 1968) – a prose reading test yielding rate, accuracy and standardised comprehension score; and the WRAT-R (Wide Range Achievement Test – Revised) reading sub-test (Jastak and Wilkinson, 1984) – a single-word reading test that yields a score of the number of words correctly read.

Analysis of baseline scores in this study revealed that, although the demographic profile of the piracetam treatment group was similar to that of the placebo group, some reading test scores were slightly lower. One site was found to have significant differences between treatment groups at baseline, and when the data were analysed without that centre this eliminated the significant baseline differences for the whole group. Consequently, the results of the study were reported both with and without these data. In addition, co-variance analysis was performed, co-varying change by baseline score. Significant effects common to both analyses were found on the Gray Oral total passage score and the Gilmore Oral comprehension score, but not on the other reading tests. Significant effects were also found in the more homogeneous sample (with equal baselines) on the Gray Oral comprehension score and the WRAT-R reading score (details of these results are reported in Wilsher et al. (1987)). This study does contain some 'internal replication' because three of the five study centres produced significant drug-related findings within their own patient samples.

Conners and Reader (1987) found that dyslexic children treated with piracetam made more progress than those taking placebo on the Gray Oral Reading Test passage score and the Gilmore Oral Reading Test accuracy (form D only) and comprehension scores (both scores). They concluded that their results suggest that 'the gain made by children who received piracetam is greater than the academic gain made by LD children who participated in other controlled treatment outcome studies'. The second team (Chase and Tallal, 1987) found significant drug-related improvements in the Gray Oral Reading Test passage score, the improvement in the piracetam group being 58% compared to 33% in the placebo group. There were also significant improvements in reading comprehension at 36 weeks (Gilmore Oral), the piracetam group making a 22% gain compared with 7% in the placebo group. The single-word reading test (WRAT-R) showed significant results favouring piracetam at 24 and 36 weeks, culminating in a 12% improvement in the treated group compared with 6% on placebo.

Finally, Helfgott et al. (1987) reported the clinical results of their part of the 36-week study. Their results showed a significant improvement in single-word reading (WRAT-R) at 12 weeks, but by 24 weeks this diminished to only a trend. On the Gray Oral Reading Test passage score the piracetam group improved significantly more than the placebo group at 12 and 24 weeks; however, by 36 weeks, although the piracetam group had made more progress than the placebo group, this was no longer statistically significant. In contrast, the effect of piracetam on reading comprehension appeared to be very durable: there were very significant drug-induced improvements in both the Gray Oral and the Gilmore Oral reading comprehension scores at 36 weeks.

In the large single-centre trial Levi and Sechi (1987) conducted a double-blind study of 127 learning-disabled children, aged 7½ to 12½, treated with piracetam 3.2 g/day for 20 weeks. All the children were of average IQ, had no psychiatric or medical problems, but were at least 2 years behind in one of the following tests: silent reading comprehension, oral reading accuracy, oral reading speed and writing accuracy. The results of the study showed a complete lack of action of piracetam on tests of spatial ability or tests of concentration (attention). However, piracetam did significantly improve the recall of an oral story, the ability to solve anagrams, and prose reading accuracy on a standardised reading test. Despite a marked ceiling effect, silent reading comprehension was significantly improved in the piracetam group but there was no significant difference between treatment groups (no measure of oral reading comprehension was used). The blind evaluation of whether the children had benefited from treatment showed that 54% of treated children had really improved compared to 22% on placebo ($p = 0.001$). In a special subgroup ($n = 38$) of children with very poor written language ability, piracetam significantly improved reading accuracy and writing accuracy.

The safety aspects of any drug treatment administered to children must be of primary concern. Piracetam has been in use for 23 years and is on sale in 86 countries, mainly for memory and learning problems in the elderly. However, in the last decade there have been a large number of controlled trials in children, and these have all been remarkable for their low level of reported adverse effects. Two large-scale multicentre studies (DiIanni et al., 1985; Wilsher et al., 1987) monitored safety intensively and found a similar incidence of adverse in the placebo group (combined $n = 237$) to that among the drug group ($n = 245$). The long-term study of 36 weeks ($n = 225$) revealed that more children on piracetam suffered from 'nervousness' ($n = 3$) compared to none in the placebo group. Emotional lability, skin rash and allergic dermatitis were also reported very occasionally. The use of any treatment should be closely monitored to look for undesirable effects and long-term effects can never be ruled out.

Conclusion

The main conclusion from reviewing various 'treatments' for dyslexia is *caveat emptor* (buyer beware). There are many proposed cures and very few of them have adequate studies to back up their claims. It is very important that properly conducted studies of both conventional and unconventional treatments be conducted so that we can separate the 'wheat from the chaff'. Alternative or unconventional treatments are often very attractive and seem to offer all the advantages without any drawbacks. This may well be because they are new and have not been tested properly to establish their safety and efficacy. It should be noted that all forms of treatment have their negative effects and rather than ignoring these it is important to quantify them and compare them to a control group. Conventional teaching may provide improvements in reading performance (although this has yet to be proven categorically – Gittleman, 1983) but it is important to measure the negative effects which could range from tiredness and irritability to bed wetting and social isolation. Without probing for this information, collating it and comparing it to a control group not so treated, we cannot dismiss them out of hand.

We should keep an open mind towards new and unconventional treatments while wielding a very healthy scepticism about their claims and closely scrutinising the information.

Chapter 14
The human aspects of dyslexia

GERALD HALES

Introduction

During many years, research in the field of dyslexia has covered a very wide field of investigation, and many causes, methodologies and treatment have been postulated. From the earliest days this has encompassed physiological attributes: in 1861 Broca suggested the causative aspect of lesions in the left hemisphere, and Déjerine coupled word blindness with a lesion in the angular gyrus (Déjerine, 1892).

More recently, some workers have examined social and interpersonal factors, suggesting that many of the causative elements relate to poor interpersonal relations in the family structure (Ravenette, 1985). Although few people have attempted to argue that this type of personal and perceptual element is a mainstream cause of dyslexia, nevertheless emotional factors are recognised as an important component. In 1974, a report of the British Royal Society for the Rehabilitation of the Disabled stated that:

> A substantial number of individual workers who have given evidence to us have referred to cases in which the emotional repercussions of dyslexia have begun to manifest themselves before the age of seven.
>
> (Kershaw, 1974)

Slowly, over recent years, an increasing number of workers have begun to suggest that the emotional and personal element is more important than we might have thought. In 1967, Akins stated that 'the majority of children with severe reading retardation also suffer from emotional disturbance' (Akins, 1967), and 20 years later Manzo suggests that 15–20% of problems in the areas of reading and learning have their foundations in emotional difficulties (Manzo, 1987).

So we see that it is not sufficient to approach dyslexia in a mechanistic manner. Those investigations which effectively regard the dyslexic individual as a 'learning machine' (or, even worse, a *broken* learning machine!) are no longer sufficient for the complete understanding of the problem. However, how to consider, quantify and use non-performance aspects is a serious question. In 1985, Williams and Miles used the Rorschach projective technique, and found that dyslexic children produced distinctive and characteristic Rorschach records (Williams and Miles, 1985).

The personality factor study

In order to obtain some definitive information about some personal aspects of the personal functioning of dyslexic people, a group was studied using objective measurement, using the Cattell Sixteen Personality Factor Questionnaire (Cattell, Eber and Tatsuoka, 1970), together with its variants for different ages of children. Three hundred dyslexic subjects took part in the investigation, of whom 74.7% were male and

Table 14.1 Distribution of subjects

Age range (years)	Total number Subjects	Male	Female
6–8	48	29 (60.4%)	19 (39.6%)
8–12	128	99 (77.3%)	29 (22.7%)
12–18	92	74 (80.4%)	18 (19.6%)
18+	32	22 (68.8%)	10 (31.3%)
Totals	300	224 (74.7%)	76 (25.3%)

25.3% were female. The distribution of subjects is seen in Table 14.1.

All assessment information was available, including reading and spelling test scores. IQ was established by use of either the Wechsler Intelligence Scale for Children, Revised (WISC-R) (Wechsler, 1978) or the Wechsler Adult Intelligence Scale (WAIS) (Wechsler, 1981). These tests have a mean of 100 and a standard deviation of 15. For the experimental group, the figures are presented in Table 14.2.

The analyses of the data were carried out in three ways: (1) by ageband; (2) by sex; and (3) by intelligence.

Table 14.2 Characteristics of IQ scores

	Overall mean IQ score	Standard deviation
Verbal IQ	103.62	14.15
Performance IQ	104.67	14.34
Full-scale IQ	103.42	15.14

Analysis by age

The first school years (6–8)

For the youngest children the highest score is on ergic tension. In addition, the score on super-ego strength is low, and from this combination we can see that the younger children are tense and frustrated. They do not have much of a feeling of obligation to conform to the value system of the adult world, and even at this young age they are already affected by their experience of something puzzling which they cannot name, they do not understand, but which makes them feel inferior in some way to their friends.

The middle school years (8–12)

Here the children have a notably low score for self-sentiment integration. This is the sort of child who finds it difficult to be self-controlled and is not conscientious or ambitious to do well. Children with a pattern like this are also not particularly motivated to control their own expressions of emotion, and may show outbursts of temper for apparently minor stimuli. Porter and Cattell (1975) call this pattern 'essentially an untutored, unreflective emotionality and a narcissistic rejection of cultural demands'; they also claim that this picture includes a major aspect of anxious insecurity, and when the second-order factors were calculated for this group, the score for anxiety appeared as the highest.

The children in this middle-school band also show score patterns which represent the person who prefers working alone and finds it more difficult to join in with others; they may also have a likelihood of liking things rather than people. A child with these types of predilections will find the classroom context particularly difficult and may also have problems in relating to peers; for many dyslexic children repeated opportunities to participate (generally regarded as a good and desirable thing) can easily become repeated chances to appear inadequate.

The secondary school years (12–18)

Here the pattern of results shows us a group of children who prefer to do things on their own and keep in the background. They believe they have fewer friends (which affects them, and their relationships, whether it is actually true or not) and they show a higher score on measures of independence.

The adult years (18+)

There is less deviation from the norm in the adults, but there is a substantially higher score on the measure of dominance (see Figure 14.1).

This is not necessarily a negative finding, for such people have a higher degree of assertiveness and independent-mindedness. However, research by Cattell, Eber and Tatsuoka (1970) also suggests that they will be more solemn, unconventional and rebellious. Of course, school and (to a slightly lesser extent) college and university environments are very supportive: a good deal of organisational and survival aspects are taken off the individual's shoulders – although we may not appreciate it at the time. However, as the move is made away from these relatively supportive contexts, and as dyslexic people move into the less comfortable context of adult work and life, it may be that a certain degree of assertiveness and possibly even stubbornness are essential in order to cope with the otherwise negative aspects of being dyslexic.

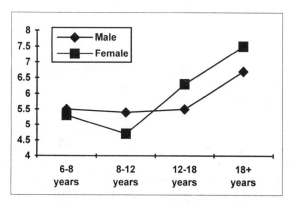

Figure 14.1 Dominance as a function of age and sex

Analysis by sex

The subjects all started off with a high level of tension (Figure 14.2). For both sexes, this falls as childhood passes, but tends to rise again into adult life. The rise is noticeably higher for the females than the males.

In the measure of Independence (Figure 14.3) we see that the male picture is of a steady rise during school days, with a return almost to the original position by adult life. The females, however, although showing the same relative pattern, start with a higher level of independence, which starts to fall earlier, although it finishes at almost the same point as for males.

On the measure of emotional stability we see once again a change of relative position (Figure 14.4). Here the overall level of emotional stability falls during the middle school years and then rises again. It is, however, interesting to note that by adulthood the positions are almost exactly inverted, so the young girls are more emotionally stable than the young

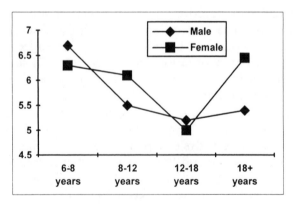

Figure 14.2 Tension as a function of age and sex

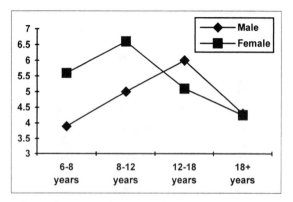

Figure 14.3 Independence as a function of age and sex

boys, but the women are less so than the men. The lowest point on this measure is obtained by the girls in the 8–12 age range, and this is supported by the scores for the factor measuring apprehension and insecurity (Figure 14.5). Here the score for the girls in the middle age range rises dramatically from below the level for the boys, and although it falls again as they become older, it never regains its original level. People with this pattern also feel that they are not accepted and believe they are not free to participate.

We may see part of this as being the function of the different rates of maturity between the boys and girls, with the effect being that the girls begin to realise the implications of the position they are in because of their difficulties earlier than do the boys. However, children with these types of results also tend to be very sensitive to the approval or disapproval of other people – and this is a particularly important aspect when we consider the opportunities a dyslexic person has for other people disapproving of what he or she does! Particularly in education,

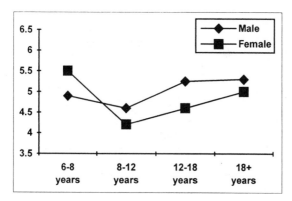

Figure 14.4 Emotional stability as a function of age and sex

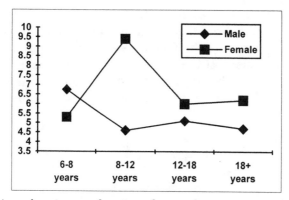

Figure 14.5 Apprehension as a function of age and sex

this means that the dyslexic child may well be far more upset by the criticism they receive than other children might be – and, crucially, more upset than teachers realise or believe to be the case.

The next factor to be measured was concerned with enthusiasm, optimism and self-confidence (Figure 14.6). We find here a marked drop for all children in the middle school age-band, although it then recovers. This pattern does indicate that dyslexic children, and particularly female dyslexic children, pass through a pessimistic patch during the 8–12 year stage of their lives. This is significant because the middle school years encompass the period during which decisions are being made about their secondary education, which possibly include examinations, testing or assessment procedures. These matters are decisions that will affect the rest of their lives and yet they are being made, and the individual is being assessed, at a time when they are at their most depressed in certain ways. This is an aspect that must be borne in mind by schools, parents and teachers.

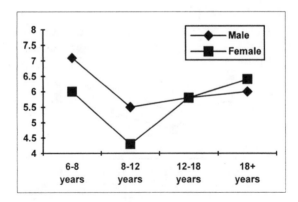

Figure 14.6 Self-confidence as a function of age and sex

Among the adults in the study, the most significant results were on the measure of super-ego strength (Figure 14.7). Here the pattern changes considerably from that which has pertained during childhood; during the younger years the females were consistently higher, but in the adult group this position has reversed. The female adults have a tendency not to be so bound by rules as the men, and this also means that they are less likely to suffer from somatic upset because of stress.

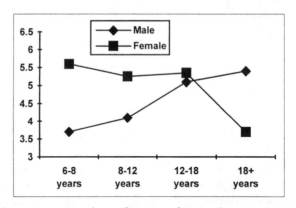

Figure 14.7 Super-ego strength as a function of age and sex

Analysis by IQ

For the purposes of this analysis three groups were identified:

- the high IQ group – IQ scores above 115 (one standard deviation above the mean)
- the middle IQ group – IQ scores between 85 and 115 (–1 to +1 standard deviations from the mean)
- the low IQ group – IQ scores below 85 (one standard deviation below the mean).

The overall trend here is for IQ level and anxiety scores to be inversely related, so generally the dyslexic people with lower IQ figures were more anxious and those with higher IQ figures were less anxious (Figure 14.8). However, although at most ages the high IQ group was less anxious and the low IQ group more so, this did not hold true for the youngest subjects, where the relationship is reversed. This is also true for scores relating to apprehension, where the more intelligent younger children are more worried and troubled, and the less intelligent more placid and untroubled.

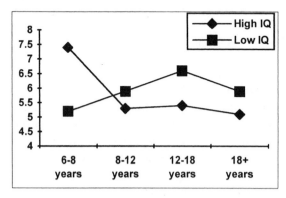

Figure 14.8 Anxiety as a function of age and IQ

In addition to this general link between anxiety and IQ level, in the youngest age group (6–8 years), there was also a direct relationship between two other scores and IQ. These were the measures of excitability and tension (Figure 14.9). The pattern here shows a greater level of emotional placidity among the less intelligent, and the more intelligent children being more excitable. The factor scores in this age range led us to expect that there will be tendency among the higher intelligence group to exhibit distress on less provocation – in other words, it takes less extravagant difficulties to produce negative patterns of experience and behaviour. This is frequently a component of what is often called 'hyperactivity', and may be part of the elements which create the situation where the less intelligence dyslexic child is less readily noticed in the classroom because he is less of a 'nuisance'.

In the middle school age range (8–12) we see a direct relationship between two factors and IQ level. These were the measures of restraint and detachment (Figure 14.10). This pattern indicates that the more intelligent children in this age band are more detached and able to act individualistically; they are also likely to be be more intellectually fastidious. The relationship between these scores and the IQ scores suggests that the less intelligent children may well be more critical, but also more rigid. However, there is evidence that children with lower

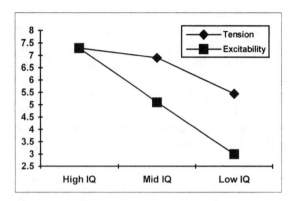

Figure 14.9 Tension and excitability as a function of IQ for the 6- to 8-year-old sample

detachment scores (which in this case means the less intelligent dyslexic children) are more disturbed by criticism (Cattell and Stice, 1960). This is a relevant aspect when we consider the amount of criticism a dyslexic person is likely to meet, especially before the condition is diagnosed and no-one knows why the behaviour or performance is unusual.

Among the older children (12–18 years) the strongest link is between IQ scores and the measure of dominance (Figure 14.11). This indicates that dyslexic teenagers with high IQ scores are much more assertive and self-assured, but also more independent-minded and unconventional. This is balanced by the pattern found for those with low IQ scores, which indicates that they are more tender-minded and dependent, and more apprehensive and insecure.

Second-order factors are calculated from the same data as primary factors, and once again the inverse relationship between IQ and anxiety is seen. Additionally, we see something of the same pattern with neuroticism, although the difference is less than with the teenagers.

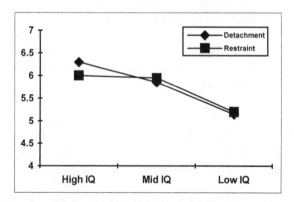

Figure 14.10 Detachment and restraint as a function of IQ for the 8- to 12-year-old sample

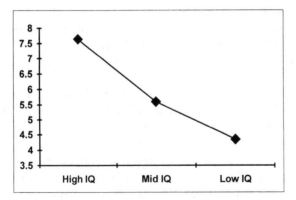

Figure 14.11 Dominance as a function of IQ for the 12- to 18-year-old sample

Discussion

There was no expectation that there would be a highly idiosyncratic 'dyslexic personality' emerging from this research, any more than there is a 'blind personality' or a 'deaf personality'. Each individual carries his or her own pattern of interface with the world, and this includes the component of any difficulties or disabilities, as well as strengths and abilities. However, the results do indicate some insights into the relationship between the personal experience and the development of the dyslexic individual and problems of participation in the learning process, especially during childhood.

The substantial inverse relationship between IQ and anxiety is not necessarily a situation which would be expected by many practitioners in the field. Nevertheless, it has been established here using both primary and second-order data. There is still a residual belief in some quarters that only 'intelligent' people can be dyslexic, yet the results of this study suggest that those who are less intelligent may, in reality, suffer more.

Whatever the level of intelligence, the dyslexic person effectively 'diverts' some of his ability into use of coping strategies, whether these are formal strategies he has been taught or informal ones he has worked out for himself. However, although this may enable the individual to cope in day-to-day situations with his peers, it will also mean that he is less likely to achieve at the level commensurate with his real potential. This means that the less able may perform at a level which casts doubt on their entire intellectual ability to achieve anything and the more able (because even at the reduced level they are still as good as many of their peers) may find people denying that they have a problem at all! In both cases, the effort put into coping with the problem can actually create some of the conditions that lead other people not to offer sufficient support or help. This can also develop into a situation in which many handicapped people find themselves, whereby there arises effectively a double handicap, where the individual is handicapped once by the disability and a second time by the effects on his educational experience of being disabled. This has been expanded upon elsewhere (Hales, 1987).

The results presented here might indicate, however, that this could be (at least to some extent) learned behaviour on the part of the more intelligent, for there is a relative difference in the results for the youngest children, where the more intelligent are more anxious than later turns out to be the case. One relevant suggestion is that in some ways the more intelligent find a slightly more sympathetic world, because their innate potential may be seen and recognised, whereas those with less ability are regarded as failing solely because of low intelligence, with less (or no) regard being paid to their difficulties of dyslexia.

It is quite vital that we realise that these anxieties and fears:

- start very young, and
- are very real.

The first person to realise that there may be a problem is very often the dyslexic child himself. Yet a small child who realises that there is a difficulty is most unlikely to mention his worries to anyone. The risk in approaching a teacher or parent and asking a question which amounts to 'Is there something odd about me?' is that they might say 'yes'! So the child runs the risk of regressing into himself, hiding his fears and commencing a retreat from reality, as may be seen from the following example, taken from a Case Study.

> John was nine years old when his parents decided that they needed to know why he was not progressing at school. A full diagnostic assessment was carried out, and dyslexia was established. John's mother, a teacher, explained to him in a suitable fashion the details of the problem: John listened carefully, and then asked,
>   'Do you mean I've got something?'
>   His mother thought that this was by no means a bad description for a small boy, and so she answered in the affirmative. John replied,
>   'That's OK then. If I've got something I can cope. *I thought I was going round the bend.*'

There is little question that the primary requirement of people with dyslexia is training that will enable them, as far as possible, to acquire and use as many of the literacy skills that life requires as they can. Thus, there are perfectly good reasons why the practical and mechanistic questions must be addressed first. However, it is extremely easy for professionals to make the assumption that dyslexic people see the difficulty largely, or even entirely, in these terms. That this is by no means always true can be seen in an extract from an account written by a dyslexic adolescent boy in 1987. He said

> I was sent to a school . . . all geered up for dyslexics and to my amasement I found I as no idiot but top of the form in my first term. I was very happy there . . . *they made me into a person again.*

(Stirling, 1987)

Conclusion

This research was designed to establish parameters relating to personality in people who are dyslexic. One of the points which the results make clear is that it is quite crucial that we take note of the position in which the dyslexic individual finds himself as a person. Particularly as children develop, they pass through various stages of learning both social and interpersonal skills; this is not effortless, and for many children it can be traumatic and worrying. If we add to this the uncertainties and disorientations that rise when dyslexia is present, the effects on the individual can be profound.

The information presented in this chapter enhances our knowledge of the pressures and tensions faced by the dyslexic individual, especially during his educational experience. It is relevant to our practice as professionals, too: there is good reason for including some measure of personality factors in our assessment procedures. We cannot – we must not – separate an individual's dyslexia from other aspects of his existence as a person, and some assessment of the effects on personal structures is, and should be, a part of our service to the dyslexic person. Not only does this add to our accumulated understanding of the handicap of dyslexia, but it enables us better to be able to treat, assist and help as *whole individuals* those who are the object of all our endeavours.

Chapter 15
Musical problems? Reflections and suggestions

MARGARET HUBICKI

Introduction

Music is a word whose many meanings relate both to the *sound* of music and to the *names* and *symbols* given to represent it and which form musical notation. It is important to focus upon a clear distinction between these two aspects of music because of their fundamental differences.

The sound of music is abstract. Its powers of communication are there for anyone of any age or ability. No knowledge whatsoever is needed for responding to it – whether that response is one of love, indifference, anger or even hate! This response is a natural one and is involuntary. However, if we wish to talk about music, read it or write it down we must have knowledge – that is, information for bridging the gap between the *abstract* sound of music itself and the *facts* of musical theory and its notation.

This information includes both words and names which refer to the pitch and the lengths of sounds, and symbols which represent pitch, lengths of sounds, phrase marks and interpretation signs. For those who are dyslexic and have a particular difficulty with words and symbols it is here that trouble can arise.

Words can be confusing because so many of them have various meanings and references within music itself – quite apart from the different meanings they have in everyday life. Uncertainty of meaning is the cause of many muddles and frustrations which block understanding. Symbols present a problem because only black or white is used to represent all musical sounds – whether of pitch or length.

It always has to be remembered that for a dyslexic learner the potential confusion within words and/or the uniformity of blackness or whiteness of symbols is able to create a bewilderment that is defeating and depressing enough to discourage even a willing student from learning – even one who has a natural instinct and feeling for music. A learner must be encouraged to find words to connect the abstract sounds with the verbal and written representations – which are so often implied rather than expressed clearly.

Where to begin

The best introduction to music is at a child's earliest age. To hear the sound of singing in such contexts as nursery songs and folk songs is an initial experience of tremendous importance in helping to develop an awareness and response to music.

Gradually the listener learns to join in and imitate what is heard – perhaps clapping or waving arms and getting the sensations of being involved with music. For many people the remembrance of that singing and movement remains as a valuable yardstick of musical and rhythmic experience: the great thing is to have fun.

When the child is old enough we should encourage listening to the sounds all around and about. Can we see what has made any of these sounds? For example, a bird singing high up on a tree or a dog barking low down on the ground. We can suggest that the listener makes hand movements to show the direction of the sound he has heard (e.g. bird 'high up' or dog 'low down') as well as pointing to its direction: 'high up' or 'low down'. Maybe a picture can be drawn; then look at the picture and point in the direction 'up' or 'down' as the sound is made. Drawings or pictures of anything which makes a sound can be of use. Encourage the listener to imagine the sound and point in its direction. When children are older it can be fun to draw pictures of anything whose sound is known and then make that sound.

Until this moment the listener has been given the chance to give a name to sounds he or she has heard and encouraged to draw pictures of them. Also, without knowing it, he or she has been laying a foundation for reading music, i.e.

- *notice* a symbol
- *name* it
- *make* it.

We have established familiarity with sounds and personal names for them and the drawings. They can be seen and felt on the page and are nothing to be afraid of.

Where problems lie

Later, when the sounds are musical ones, they may be talked about. This is where problems can begin because musical sounds are given names which are *other people's* name-labels and symbols. Unlike the personal drawing-symbol of, say, a bird, other people's names and symbols indicate nothing. For someone who is dyslexic this can be the beginning of disaster, for they find themselves being expected to understand and remember other people's names and symbols which simply don't add up. So it may be difficult to understand how a sound is called what it is or 'what that symbol is supposed to be telling' me. If it is difficult to remember the name of the sound or follow relationships, there begins the feeling that a door is starting to close, a trap of misunderstanding growing into fear. His muddles can give the impression of his being dim and stupid when, in fact, his natural response to music-making may be anything but that. If any of us is made to feel a fool, we naturally lose confidence.

What lies at the root of the matter needs some understanding on the part of parent or teacher. The human brain is divided into two main hemispheres, and each one has its chief characteristics (see Table 15.1). If sounds don't easily connect up with the words, symbols etc. relating to them, then the learner can have trouble and needs understanding, encouragement, time and space to make the necessary join.

Table 15.1 Characteristics of hemispheres in the human brain

Left side (factual side)	Right side (creative side)
Deals with Facts	Is involved with Art
Words	Music
Symbols	Drama
Logic	Emotions
Sequencing etc.	Creativity etc.

Others must be sensitive towards the possibility of a blockage between these two areas. When a difficulty arises, based on such a likely cause, imaginative help is necessary towards finding ways round the problems. So often there can be more than one way for information to make sense. If one attempt doesn't seem to work, keep on trying to find another. As and when that happens, it creates the happy situation that both sides are exploring things together and it is exciting – an extension in fact of those early days, mentioned previously, when the young listener was encouraged to give his or her name for a sound he or she heard, imitated and drew. This approach will prove to be of continual assistance for all aspects of learning and will be well worth cultivating.

Some words which cause 'blockages'

Words which can cause blockages include 'high' and 'low', 'left' and 'right'. Part of the difficulty lies in their uses for so many different purposes very far removed from musical ones. In daily life we talk about a 'high wall' or a 'low chair'. These are concrete objects whose existence we can touch and feel.

High and low

In music we say a 'high sound' or a 'low sound'. We are using these same words to describe the intangible qualities of sound – untouchable and unseeable. It isn't the differences of sound which are the problem; the problem lies in these words 'high' and 'low', familiar enough in daily life, being used in relationship to music. The learner may find it impossible to make any connection between the musical sound he hears and the name 'high' or 'low' which we give to it and so, unhappily, flounders about.

Musical uses of the words 'high' or 'low' include reference to pitch of sounds, location on an instrument, and notation on a page of written music or the staff. For encouraging a sense of spatial awareness and the use of these words for that purpose, an extension of the suggestions given for a very young child can be of use as follows:

1. Keep very quiet.
2. Listen to sounds all around.
3. Invite learner to select one, and
4. Move his hand in the direction he hears the sound coming from.
5. Give his name for that direction. For example, 'ceiling' as he points upwards or 'floor' as he points downwards.

From the learner's response to doing this we discover his own words for our words. For the time being use the learner's own words whenever referring to a 'high' sound or to a 'low' sound. Confidence will have been gained through the use of meaningful-to-him names for the sensation of hand movements in these different directions. At a later stage, when some security has been gained, the more usual terms 'high' or 'low' can always be substituted for the learner's names.

Concerning notation

We often say 'look high up on the page' or 'low down on the page'. The learner may be confused: the page looks flat!

A help for this problem is the use of a large piece of paper or cardboard about the size of a piece of music. Guide the learner's hand to feel all around it getting a complete tactile awareness of its shape and space. Also provide some little stickers to place on this page, for example, two little stars or two little dots. Place a little star on each top corner of the page and a little dot on each low corner of the page (see Figure 15.1). Holding the page upright, guide the learner's hand to feel up towards each star in the direction that we mean by 'high up'. Ask for the name for that upward sense of movement to the star for reference if needed – both as a feeling and as a name. Then guide the hand downward towards each dot in the direction we mean by 'low down'. Again ask for the name for that downward sense of movement to the dot ('low down') – yet again both as a feeling and as a name.

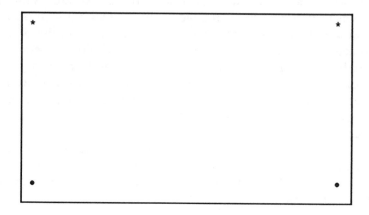

Figure 15.1 Illustration to a board with stars and dots to assist familiarity with 'high' and 'low' and 'left' and 'right' on the page

Awareness of the hand's sensations of these movements and following them with the eye gives a valuable multisensory recognition of direction. There is a growing coordination of hand and eye relating to what the ear hears as 'high' or 'low'.

It is useful to apply this exercise to the 'feel' and 'look' of different pieces of music. This encourages a sense of 'direction-awareness' to a page of music as a whole. Suggest that the learner also applies this to each set of staff-lines to get their 'sense-feel' of 'up or down'. Done peacefully without the pressure of any problems to do with performance on an instrument or vocally this becomes a valuable experience and a habit to cultivate.

Left and right

These are two more of the words which can cause difficulties especially to those people who cannot remember which word refers to what direction! Musical examples include such uses as these:

The key-signature is always on the left side of the staff.

Try this fingering for your right hand.

Use the left pedal for these chords.

One pupil suffering from this problem overcame it in a logical and simple way. The thumb on his right hand shows the direction of his 'left side'. The little finger on this same hand shows the direction of his 'right side'. Whenever he needs to refer to either of these directions he says 'thumb side' or 'little finger side' and it works like a charm. Some learners prefer to use a personal item for their 'memory-aid' such as a watch which they always wear on the same hand. Whatever is chosen needs to be an item which is continuously used and completely familiar.

This solution to a problem by a pupil is a good example of the value of encouraging a learner *to help himself.* We constantly need to put ourselves in the position of those who are bewildered or afraid in order to assist *them* to find *their* way which leads from confusion to clarity.

This direction for left to right can be practised on the board (Figure 15.1). Encourage the learner to move the hand across the board either from the little star (or the dot) on the left side over to the little star (or the dot) on the right side. Use his or her name for this movement/direction as they make it. For anything to do with these two directions 'up or down' and 'left or right' this board is a useful memory-aid. It could be handy to make a small pocket-size one to take about, to cultivate the habit of coordinating the visual look and tactile feel of these directions as an essential part of reading music.

Musical notation

As was mentioned earlier, only black and white symbols are used to represent all musical sounds. For anyone with a short-term memory it can be very difficult to recall what they mean, especially as each symbol only *implies* information. This 'implied information' falls into two categories of symbols: those which represent *time* (time symbols follow one another across the page from left to right) and *pitch* (pitch symbols are placed one above or below another – the eye sees them as 'high' or 'low').

Time symbols represent various lengths of time. These include symbols which imply two different aspects. One is the length of *sound* and this is shown by notes, e.g. semibreve (o), minim (d), crotchet (♩) etc. The other is the length of *silence*, which is shown by rests, e.g. semibreve, minim, crotchet etc. Other time symbols such as dots and ties imply additions to lengths of notes or rests. Much understanding and imaginative help may be needed for a learner to grasp the 'feel' of what these additional symbols tell.

Each time symbol relates to a regular beat at a given speed. This beat is comparable to the pulse which exists in all of us. Those who do not feel a very secure sense of inner beat need special practice to develop it. Encourage listening to the tick of a clock, then imitate its regular 'tick'. Play with mechanical toys which make a regular, repeating sound and clap that. Invite the learner to walk, march or dance. Anything of this kind which stimulates an awareness of beat is helpful. Saying words and clapping them is also useful. For some people French time names 'Taa' etc. are excellent; for others, to have to remember additional unknown words would be a hazard. The same purpose can be served by choosing a familiar word like 'cat'.

1. Say 'cat'. Invite learner to say 'cat'.
2. Clap and say 'cat'. Invite learner to imitate this.
3. Suggest that learner draws a cat.
4. Ask learner to point to his picture, say 'cat' and clap once.

Choose other one-clap words or names such as John, Ann, Jean, James – or names of friends. Follow the same four steps mentioned above. Then add a little stem to each name showing it as a one-clap name, e.g.

| | | | |
John   Ann   Jean   James

Now point to each stem and say the name belonging to it. This can then be tried with two-clap names (Mary), three-clap names (Jonathan) and four-clap names (Arabella).

This idea, based on early days of experiences of 'sound, name and picture', can develop indefinitely. Make up short phrases such as 'have a glass of milk'. Invite learner to walk, march or skip as he says and claps the words. Any ideas along these lines can be fun and provide a most valuable sensation awareness of a basic beat to which a rhythmic pattern can be added.

Musical notation uses short black lines for grouping beats together. These black lines | are called bar-lines. Here are two bar-lines either side of two crotchet beats: | ♩ ♩ | The distance between the bar-lines is called a bar. Encourage the learner to give his name for 'bar-line' and 'bar'.

Time signatures

This is the name given to the numbers, one above the other, which are placed at the beginning of a piece or section of a piece. The *top* figure tells how many beats in a bar. The *lower* figure tells the length of each beat reckoned from a semibreve. This concept has much in common with mathematical fractions and can cause confusion.

Pitch symbols

Musical pitch is represented by a staff of alternate black lines and white spaces which stand one above the other. Each black line or white space belongs to a sound whose name is one of the first seven letters of the alphabet used in music A, B, C, D, E, F or G. This order of names repeats higher or lower.

A dyslexic learner may be faced with several problems. For example:

1. These seven letters may present difficulties when reading words.
2. Their order and repetition could be confusing.
3. Remembering which line or space belongs to which letter-name.

To help identify letter-names, their order and position on the staff, colour has been proven by research and practical experience to be very useful. The present writer used the following colours for material which she devised ('Colour Staff')

Orange	for G
Violet	for F
Blue	for E
Yellow	for D
Red	for C
Indigo	for B
Green	for A

The choice of colours is personal and does not have to be those as shown here. A learner could make his own choice provided that its order remains consistent. Right away a point has to be stressed that the learner is *not* expected to associate any particular colour with the sound of pitch. That would be an added difficulty. Colour, if used, should be thought of simply as an aid for recognition of pattern or identifying detail.

For anyone who finds the use of A B C D E F G for naming sounds a real hurdle it would be possible to think of substitute name-symbols. For instance seven familiar objects grouped in families – such as is seen in Figure 15.2.

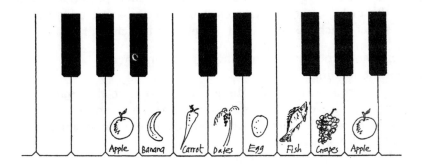

Figure 15.2 Familiar object symbols which can be used to represent notes

Of course the learner could choose any familiar objects and draw them as his memory-aid. The pictures could even be stuck onto the keyboard. Similarly, the symbols may be drawn on a staff with an appropriate clef (for example, as in Figure 15.3).

Figure 15.3 Placing on the staff the familiar objects representing notes

In the effort of trying to remember the details, some learners find it a helpful memory-aid to write the names of the lines and spaces at both left and right ends of a staff to remind them that the whole of a line from left to right side belongs to the same name. The use of Tonic-Solfa is invaluable for a great number of learners – but it is not for everyone. The Orff (Orff-Schulwerk, *Music for Children*, published by Schott) and Kodaly (Vadjoda, 1974) teaching material can also be very useful. Some, but not all, people find mnemonics helpful for remembering the lines or spaces of a staff. For example: 'All Cows Eat Grass' for the spaces of the bass staff. But recalling the *right* words could present difficulties!

Limitation of space makes it impossible to discuss all the symbols of musical notation and musical theory, but the approach behind the help which a learner requires for understanding such patterns as scales, keys, the order of key signatures, harmony etc. is based on just the same secret which has been used throughout this chapter, i.e.

- Begin at the beginning (nothing to go wrong there).
- Assume nothing.
- Be prepared to encourage the learner to listen to the sound of each pattern. Guide them to observe and name, for themselves the visible and tactile details of its construction as, for example, in a major scale:
  - the order of note-names;
  - the order of tones and semitones;
  - what their differences are;
  - the sequences it contains.

To hear the sound of a pattern played first makes it easier to grasp what symbols represent it. With encouragement and help, 'building' musical theory can become an exciting exploration.

Sight reading

Sight reading is looking at a piece of music and then playing it straight away. For anyone who finds this difficult it is well worth checking over the following points:

1. Choose music well within a learner's playing capacity.
2. If a learner finds it hard to sustain focus, break the piece into small sections of suitable length.
3. Encourage the learner just to sit quietly and let his or her eyes glance over the music with no fear of having to play anything.
4. Check that all the symbols (pitch, time and dynamics) are
   (a) familiar;
   (b) really understood.
5. Invite the learner to touch each printed symbol with the hand as it is named. This will include:
   (a) *Staff lines and spaces.* Encourage the learner to move the hand across the page on each line or space: left to right. Give the name of each one at the same time.
   (b) *Clef*
       (i) Name it.
       (ii) Trace its shape using finger.
       (iii) Name the line on which it is placed.
       (iv) Trace that named line across the page from left to right.
   (c) *Key-signatures*
       (i) Name each accidental in the key signature
       (ii) Ask the learner what key that suggests. Make sure there is knowledge that these accidentals are implied throughout the music being looked at.
       (iii) Notice and name any accidentals which do not belong to this key.
   (d) *Time signatures*
       Invite the learner to say what:
       (i) the top figure indicates: 'number of beats in a bar';
       (ii) the lower figure indicates: 'kind of notes each beat is'.
       Check to make sure that this information is really clear.
   (e) *Pitch and time symbols*
       Check that the learner is clear about each one while looking at the music without playing anything – particularly the length of each symbol.

(f) *Speed*

   If the piece gives a speed instruction demonstrate the sound of it
   or invite the learner to demonstrate it. Suggest that the learner
   claps this speed for each beat while the eyes follow the music on
   the page.

6. The musical line: the illustration in Figure 15.4 suggests a helpful
   way of 'feeling' a phrase in order to play its shape.

   (a) Invite learners to put their fingers on each symbol as they say its
       letter-name.
   (b) Looking from *x* to *x* and feeling each symbol to tell you if 'it goes
       up or down'?
   (c) Look and feel from *y* to *y*. Ask if it goes up or down.
   (d) If that is difficult avoid making an issue of it. Simply guide the
       hand to feel each direction and ask for the name for that 'feel'.
   (e) Encourage the learner to wave his or her hands in the air and
       'draw' the shape that has been felt and seen. This is a valuable
       help towards performance. Looking at the shape of line before
       trying to play is a useful habit to develop.

Figure 15.4 A helpful way of 'feeling' the musical line. The process is explained in
the text

All the ideas suggested here have infinite possibilities for extension
and are applicable to any music for any instrument. Their basic principle is aimed at coordinating eye, information and hand response in
preparation for actual performance. Growing security can develop
through preparing the feel of beat, clear understanding of rhythm patterns and the awareness of key: not just naming the accidentals but
being conscious of their 'geography' on an instrument or voice.

Sight-reading performance

1. Take time to look through the music.
2. Aim to play straight through from first to last note.
3. If something goes wrong:
   (a) try not to stop;
   (b) be prepared to leave out a beat or two;
   (c) pick up afresh.

4. The great point is to concentrate on the feel of a flowing line from beginning to end:
   (a) ignore mistakes;
   (b) keep going;
   (c) be like a grasshopper! Leap over difficulties.

This is not intended to encourage mistakes! But how to cope if they occur. The great point to concentrate on is shaping the musical line so that it reaches the last bar.

Points to remember

1. Speak slowly when giving new information.
2. Only offer one fact – or step in an argument – at a time.
3. Check up on what lies at the root of a problem.
4. Be prepared either
   (a) to help a learner find his way to tackle this problem; or
   (b) be open to a new way to discuss it.
5. Symbols with more than one name need care. For example, should we call it the G clef or the treble clef? Always try to explain the reason for the difference, then choose one name and keep to it.
6. Key, note etc. are words with more than one meaning. It is well worth while keeping a list of these.
7. Be alert towards any desperate struggle a learner may have towards trying to remember what was never really understood in the first place.
8. Be prepared to give endless chances to retrace any unclear or forgotten step.
9. Someone with a short-term memory needs much patience – both on the learner's side and on the side of those helping.
10. For those who like making things there are fascinating materials on the market with which a learner can make 'memory-aids' to help recall different aspects of musical theory. These can give visual and tactile information in innumerable ways. The learner can move them about and feel all kinds of musical patterns and sequences which are hard to remember.
11. Try to create an atmosphere in which the learner feels free to ask questions.
12. Encouragement is required all the time – not by lowering standards but by bolstering up what the learner can do and allowing that to develop.
13. Avoid dampening enthusiasm by needless criticism.
14. Never hesitate to state the obvious.
15. Allow that mistakes can sometimes lead to creative new information.

16. There may be occasions when a learner lacks the right words for expressing difficulties. They may need your help for telling what they want to say. For this we require sensitive willingness to follow after a learner in the dark places of uncertainty.

17. [These five sections are re-printed from *Music and Dyslexia* with kind permission of the British Dyslexia Association.]

 (a) *Physical problems*
   (i) Problems with scanning – the learner may have difficulty with finding the place in a piece of music. At a more advanced stage there may be a problem with glancing at the conductor and back to the music, finding the beginning of a new line of music, and/or coping with repeat marks. For orchestral or band percussionists the problems can also apply to moving between instruments and finding the relevant line of music on their various music stands.
   (ii) Inability to sustain concentration – things may suddenly appear blurred and muddled.
   (iii) Exhaustion and/or frustration – this may arise because dyslexics usually need to spend more time that non-dyslexics on deciphering the notation; they may need to practise for longer, perhaps only to achieve the same or worse results.

 (b) *Choice of instrument*
   It is impossible to recommend one particular instrument which will suit all dyslexic musicians. Much will depend, as always, on the individuals' physique and preference, the specific difficulties they have in relation to music, and their determination. Many dyslexic musicians have found the piano to be difficult, and if this is the case it might be worth trying an instrument which reads only from a single line of music. Conversely, many successful dyslexic pianists are very skilled at improvisation, so it may mean finding a teacher who can develop these skills rather than changing the instrument. Always be prepared to make a change if the instrument turns out to be the wrong choice, and preferably before it becomes a source of anxiety or distress.

 (c) *Large print music*
   Some musicians with dyslexia find it helpful to use large print music or to enlarge music produced in standard sized print. A limited amount of large-print music is produced commercially for musicians with partial sight and information about this can be obtained from the National Music and Disability Information Service.* It is also possible to make enlarged copies of music produced in standard print by using a photocopier with an

---

*National Music and Disability Information Service, Foxhole, Dartington, Totnes, Devon TQ9 6EB.

enlarging facility. Regarding copyright permission, the Music Publishers' Association have stated that there are no objections to musicians purchasing music and subsequently having it enlarged for their own convenience, provided multiple copies are not made and, of course, they are not sold.

(d) *Marking and highlighting music*

Colours may help to give a visual clue to reading music notation, either using coloured notes or preferably marking certain lines of the stave in colour to give a point of reference. Highlighter pens may also be useful for emphasising accidentals, changes in time and/or key signatures, repeats, D.S. or D.C. signs, etc. The Music Publishers' Association has given permission for individuals with dyslexia to photocopy their own music in order to insert their own marks or highlights. This may be particularly useful where individuals are playing with a band or ensemble and wish to mark their own parts without spoiling the set.

(e) It should be remembered that the majority of the difficulties mentioned here relate to the reading of musical notation and that there are many forms of music, including jazz, folk, reggae and popular music of all kinds and from various cultures, where such reading is of less importance. It is important for dyslexic musicians to be given the opportunity to enjoy whatever kind of music they choose without being disadvantaged by their dyslexia. There are known to be many talented musicians with dyslexia whose talent for improvisation and musical memory would be envied by anyone 'tied' to the printed page!

Finale

The theme running throughout these pages is focused upon *awareness* of what is implied behind potentially locked doors of words or symbols in order that their meanings can come alive and, like the sound of music itself, be self-explanatory. Examples have illustrated some ways and means to do this – plus the ever-needed requirement: flexibility of outlook.

Warmest thanks are due to two professional musicians – the singer Annemarie Sand and the composer Nigel Clarke who were students of mine at the Royal Academy of Music. Both of them are dyslexic. Most generously they have wished to share some of their difficulties and experiences so that these could be woven into this text and become of use to others – including parents and teachers – offering insight into the musical difficulties which a dyslexic learner has. Because there is more than one way to learn, their plea is that whenever necessary, support and help may be given to a dyslexic learner so that he can 'build his tools for coping with the rules' in a way that makes sense to him.

These two musicians handle their difficulties in such a way that they are of inspiring encouragement to others not to give up. In Nigel's words 'The Mystery of Music must live – and not become lost in the mysteries of making it'.

References and bibliography

Aaron, P.G. (1989). *Dyslexia and Hyperlexia*. Boston, MA: Kluwer.

Aaron, P.G. (1993). Is there a visual dyslexia? *Annals of Dyslexia*, 43, 110–124.

Aaron, P.G. and Joshi, M.R. (1992). *Reading Problems: Consultation and Remediation*. New York: The Guilford Press.

Aaron, P.G. and Phillips, S. (1986). A decade of research with dyslexic college students: a summary of findings. *Annals of Dyslexia*, 36, 44–66.

Aaron, P.G., Franz, S. and Manges, A. (1990). Dissociation between pronunciation and comprehension in reading disabilities. *Reading and Writing: An Interdisciplinary Journal*, 3, 1–22.

Aasved, H. (1987). Ophthalmological status of school children with dyslexia. *Eye*, 1, 61–68.

Ackerman, P. T., Dykman, R. A., Holloway, C., Paal, N.P. and Gocio, M.Y. (1991). A trial of piracetam in two subgroups of students with dyslexia enrolled in summer tutoring. *Journal of Learning Disabilities*, 24(9), 542–549.

Akins, K. (1967). A psychotherapeutic approach to reading retardation. *Canadian Psychiatric Association Journal*, 12, 497–503.

Akshoomoff, N.A., Courchesne, E., Press, G.A. and Iragui, V. (1992). Contribution of the cerebellum to neuropsychological functioning: evidence from a case of cerebellar degeneration. *Neuropsychologia*, 30, 315–328.

Alessi, G. (1988). Diagnosis diagnosed: a systemic reaction. *Professional School Psychology*, 3(2), 145–151.

Alexander, D., Gray, D.B. and Lyon, G.R. (1993). Conclusions and future directions. In Lyong, G.R., Gray, D.C. Kavanagh, J.F. and Krasnegor, N.A. (Eds), *Better Understanding Learning Disabilities*. Baltimore: Paul H. Brookes.

Allington, R. and Fleming, J. (1978). The misreading of high-frequency words. *Journal of Special Education*, 12, 417–421.

Alpern, M. (1981). Color blind vision. *Trends in Neurosciences*, 4, 131–135.

Alston, J. and Taylor, J. (1987). *Handwriting: Theory, Research and Practice*. London: Routledge.

Ames, T. (1980). *Macmillan Diagnostic Reading Pack* Basingstoke: Macmillan Education.

Anastasi, A. (1988). *Psychological Testing*, 6th edn. London: Collier Macmillan.

Ansara, A., Geschwind, N., Galaburda, A., Albert, M. and Gartrell, N. (Eds) (1981). *Sex Differences In Dyslexia*. Towson, MD: The Orton Dyslexia Society.

Aubrey, C., Eaves, J., Hicks, C. and Newton, M.J. (1982). *The Aston Portfolio*. Wisbech: Learning Development Aids.

Augur, J. (1985). Guidelines for teachers, parents and learners. In Snowling, M. (Ed.). *Children's Written Language Difficulties*. Windsor: NFER-Nelson.

Augur, J. and Briggs, S. (1992). *The Hickey Multisensory Language Course*, 2nd edn. London: Whurr.

Baddeley, A.D., Ellis, N.C., Miles, T.R. and Lewis, V. (1982). Developmental and acquired dyslexia: a comparison. *Cognition*, 11, 185–199.

Baddeley, A.D., Logie, R.H. and Ellis, N.C. (1988) Characteristics of developmental dyslexia. *Cognition*, 29, 197–228.

Baddeley, A.D., Thomson, N. and Buchanan, M. (1975). Word length and the structure of short term memory. *Journal of Verbal Learning and Verbal Behaviour*, 14, 575–589.

Badian, N.A. (1984). Reading disability in an epidemiological context: incidence and environmental correlates. *Journal of Learning Disabilities*, 17, 129–136.

Beck, I.L. and Carpenter, P.A. (1986). Cognitive approaches to understanding reading: implications for instructional practice. *American Psychologist*, 41, 1098–1105.

Beech, J.R. (1989). The componential approach to learning reading skills. In Colley, A.M. and Beech, J.R. (Eds), *Acquisition and Performance of Cognitive Skills*, pp. 113–136. Chichester: Wiley.

Benton, A. L. (1962). Dyslexia in relation to form perception and directional sense. In Money, J. (Ed.), *Reading Disability*. Baltimore: Johns Hopkins Press.

Berscheid, E. and Walster, E. (1972). Beauty and the best. *Psychology Today*, 5, 10.

Birnbaum, M.H. (1984). Nearpoint visual stress: a physiological model. *Journal of the American Optometric Association*, 55, 825–835.

Bishop, D. (1985). Spelling ability in congenital dysarthria: evidence against articulatory coding in translating between graphemes and phonemes. *Cognitive Neuropsychology*, 2, 229–251.

Bishop, D.V.M. (1990). Handedness and developmental disorder. *Clinics in Developmental Medicine*, No. 110. Oxford: Mac Keith Press (Blackwell Scientific Publications).

Boder, E. (1973). Developmental dyslexia: a diagnostic approach based on three atypical reading-spelling patterns. *Developmental Medicine and Child Neurology*, 15, 663–687.

Bookbinder, G. (1976). *Salford Sentence Reading Test*. London: Hodder and Stoughton.

Boynton, R.M. (1979). *Human Color Vision*. New York: Holt, Rinehart and Winston.

Bradley, L. (1980). *Assessing Reading Difficulties*. London: Macmillan Educational.

Bradley, L. (1989). Specific learning disability: prediction-intervention-progress. Paper presented to the Rodin Remediation Academy International Conference on Dyslexia, University College of North Wales, September 1989.

Bradley, L. and Bryant, P. E. (1983). Categorizing sounds and learning to read – a causal connection. *Nature*, 301, 419–421.

Brannon, J. and Williams, M. (1988). Developmental vs sensory deficit effects on perceptual processing in the reading disabled. *Perception and Psychophysics*, 44, 437–444.

Breitmeyer, B. (1989). A visually based deficit in specific reading disability. *The Irish Journal of Psychology*, 10, 534–541.

Breitmeyer, B. and Ganz, I. (1976). Implications of sustained and transient channels for theories of visual pattern masking, saccadic suppression and information processing. *Psychological Review*, 83, 1–36.

Brimer, M.A. and Dunn, L.M. (1970). *English Picture Vocabulary Tests*. Bristol: Educational Evaluation Enterprises.

Brimer, M.A. and Gross, H. (1972). *Wide-span Reading Test*. Windsor: NFER-Nelson.

Brown, B., Haegerstrom-Portnoy, G., Yingling, C.D., Herron, J., Galin, D. and Marcus, M. (1983). Dyslexic children have normal vestibular responses to rotation. *Archives of Neurology*, 40, 370–373.

Brown, J.I., Bennett, M.J. and Hanna, G. (1981). *The Nelson Denny Reading Test.* Chicago, IL: The Riverside Publishing Co.

Bruck, M. and Waters, G. (1988). An analysis of spelling errors of children who differ in their reading and spelling skills. *Applied Psycholinguistics*, 9, 77–92.

Bryant, P.E. and Bradley, L. (1980). Why children sometimes write words which they do not read. In Frith, U. (Ed.), *Cognitive Processes in Spelling.* London: Academic Press.

Bryant, P.E. and Bradley, L. (1985). *Children's Reading Problems.* Oxford: Blackwell.

Bryant, P.E. and Goswami, U. (1987). Phonological awareness and learning to read. In Beech, J.R. and Colley, A.M. (Eds), *Cognitive Approaches to Reading.* New York: Wiley.

Burt, C. (1917). *The Distribution and Relations of Educational Abilities.* London: King.

Butcher, H.J. (1968). *Human Intelligence: Its Nature and Assessment.* London: Methuen.

Cantwell, D.P. and Baker, L. (1992). Association between attention deficit-hyperactivity disorder and learning disorders. In Shaywitz, S.E. and Shaywitz, B.A. (Eds), *Attention Deficit Disorder Comes of Age.* Austin, TX: Pro-Ed.

Carpenter, P.A. and Just, M.A. (1975). Sentence comprehension: a psycholinguistic processing model of verification. *Psychological Review*, 82, 45–73.

Carr, T., Brown, T., Vavrus, L. and Evans, M. (1990). Cognitive skill maps and cognitive skill profiles: componential analysis of individual differences in children's reading efficiency. In Carr, T.H. and Levy, B.A. (Eds), *Reading and its Development.* New York: Academic Press.

Carr, T.H. and Levy, B.A. (Eds) (1990). *Reading and its Development: Component Skills Approaches.* New York: Academic Press.

Carroll, J., Davies, P. and Richman, B. (1971). *Word Frequency Book.* New York: Houghton Mifflin.

Carroll, J.B. (1993). *Human Cognitive Abilities.* Cambridge: Cambridge University Press.

Carver, C. (1970). *Word Recognition Test.* London: U.L.P. Ltd.

Cataldo, S. and Ellis, N.C. (1988). Spelling, reading and phonological skills in interactive development. *Journal of Research in Reading*, 11(2), 86–109.

Cataldo, S. and Ellis, N.C. (1989). Learning to spell, learning to read. In Pumphrey, P.D. and Elliott, C.D. (Eds), *Children's Difficulties in Reading, Writing and Spelling: Challenges and Responses.* Basingstoke: Falmer Press.

Cattell, R. B. and Stice, G. F. (1960). *The Dimensions of Groups and Their Relations to the Behaviour of Members.* Champaign, IL: Institute for Personality and Ability Testing.

Cattell, R. B., Eber, H. W. and Tatsuoka, M. M. (1970). *Handbook for the Sixteen Personality Factor Questionnaire.* Champaign, IL: Institute for Personality and Ability Testing.

Catts, H.W. (1989). Phonological processing deficits and reading disabilities. In Kamhi, A.G. and Catts, H.W. (Eds), *Reading Difficulties: A Developmental Language Perspective.* Boston: Little Brown and Co.

Chall, J. (1967). *Learning to Read: The Great Debate.* New York: McGraw-Hill.

Chapman, J.W, Lambourne, R, and Silva, P.A. (1990). Some antecedents of academic self-concept: a longitudinal study. *British Journal of Educational Psychology*, 60, 142–152.

Chase, C.H., Schmitt, R.L., Russell, G. and Tallal, P. (1984). A new chemotherapeutic investigation: piracetam effects on dyslexia. *Annals of Dyslexia*, 34, 29–48.

Chase, C.H. and Tallal, P. (1987). Piracetam and dyslexia: a thirty-six week double blind clinical trial. In Bakker, D., Wilsher, C. Dbruyne, H. and Bertin, N. (Eds), *Child Health and Developmen*, Vol. 5. *Dyslexia and Learning Disorders*. Basel: Karger.

Chiarenza, G.A. (1987). Effect of piracetam on sensory-motor and cognitive processes. Neurophysiological analysis. In Bakker, D., Wilsher, C. Dbruyne, H. and Bertin, N. (Eds), *Child Health and Development*, Vol. 5. *Dyslexia and Learning Disorders*. Basel: Karger.

Chinn, S. J. (1991). Factors to consider when designing a test protocol in mathematics for dyslexics. In Snowling, M. and Thomson, M (Eds), *Dyslexia: Integrating Theory and Practice*. London: Whurr.

Chomsky, C. (1977). Approaching reading through invented spelling. In Resnick, L.B. and Weaver, P.A. (Eds), *The Theory and Practice of Early Reading*. Vol. 2. Hillsdale, NJ: Erlbaum.

Clark, H.H. and Chase, W.G. (1972). On the process of comparing sentences against pictures. *Cognitive Psychology*, 3, 472–517.

Clark, M.M. (1970). *Reading Difficulties in Schools*. Harmondsworth: Penguin.

Cohen, J. (1977). *Statistical Power for the Behavioural Sciences*. New York: Academic Press.

Coltheart, M., Patterson, K. and Marshall, J.C. (Eds) (1980). *Deep Dyslexia*. London: Routledge and Kegan Paul.

Conners, C.K. and Reader, M. (1987). The effects of piracetam on reading achievement and visual event-related potentials in dyslexic children. In Bakker, D. Wilsher, C., Dbruyne, H. and Bertin, N. (Eds), *Child Health and Development*, Vol 5. *Dyslexia and Learning Disorders*. Basel: Karger..

Conners, C.K., Blouin, A.G., Winglee, M., Lougee, L., O'Donnell, D. and Smith, A. (1984). Piracetam and event-related potentials in dyslexic children. *Psychopharmacology Bulletin*, 20, 667–673.

Conners, C.K., Blouin, A., Winglee, M., Lougee, L., O'Donnell, D. and Smith, A. (1986). Piracetam and event-related potentials in dyslexic males. *International Journal of Psychophysiology*, 4, 19–27.

Conners, C.K., Reader, M., Caldwell, J., Clymer, R., Reiss, A., Adesman, A., Caldwell, L., Mayer, L. and Berg, M. (1987). The effects of piracetam upon visual event-related potentials in dyslexic children. *Psychophysiology*, 24 (5), 513–521.

Cook, J. and Cook, R. (1988). *Reading Progress Chart, Experimental Edition*. Chichester: Lyminster Publications.

Cotterell, G. (1970). Teaching the dyslexic. In Franklin, A. and Naidoo, S. (Eds), *The Assessment and Teaching of the Dyslexic Child*. London: Invalid Children's Aid Association.

Cotton, M.M. and Evans, K.M. (1990). An evaluation of the Irlen lenses as a treatment for specific reading disorders. *Australian Journal of Psychology*, 42, 1–12

Critchley, M. (1970). *The Dyslexic Child*. London: William Heinemann Medical Books.

Dain, S.J. (1984). Some current issues in the mechanisms of color vision. *Australian Journal of Optometry*, 67, 60–65.

Daniels, J.C. and Dyack, H. (1956). *Progress in Reading*. Nottingham: University of Nottingham Institute of Education.

Decety, J., Sjoholm, H., Ryding, E., Sternberg, G. and Ingvar, D.H. (1990). The cerebellum participates in mental activity: tomographic measures of regional cerebral blood flow. *Brain Research*, **535**, 313–317.

DeFries, J.D. (1991). Genetics and dyslexia: an overview. In Snowling, M. and Thompson, M. (Eds), *Dyslexia: Integrating Theory and Practice*. London: Whurr.

DeFries, J., Fulker, D. and LaBuda, C. (1987). Evidence for a genetic aetiology in reading disability of twins. *Nature*, **329**, 537–539.

Déjerine, J. (1892). Contribution à l'étude anatomo-pathologique et clinique des différentes variétés de cécite verbale. *Memoires du Société de Biologie*, **27** (February).

DiIanni, M., Wilsher, C.R., Blank, M.S., Conners, C.K., Chase, C.H., Funkenstein, H., Helfgott, E., Holmes, J.M., Lougee, L., Maletta, G.J., Milewski, J., Pirozzolo, F.J., Rudel, R.G. and Tallal, P. (1985). The effects of piracetam in children with dyslexia. *Journal of Clinical Psychopharmacology*, **5**, 272–278.

Dimond, S.J. and Beaumont, J.G. (1973). Hemisphere function and paired associate learning. *British Journal of Psychology*, **65**, 275–278.

Dimond, S.J. and Brouwers, E.Y.M. (1976). Increase in the power of human memory in normal man through the use of drugs. *Psychopharmacology*, **49**, 307–309.

Dinklage, K.T. (1971). Inability to learn a foreign language. In Blaine, G.B. Jr and McArthur, C.C. (Eds), *Emotional Problems of the Student*, 2nd edn. New York: Appleton-Century-Crofts.

Dobbins, D.A. (1986). An empirical classification of children with reading difficulties. *Education and Child Psychology*, **3**(2), 70–79.

Dobbins, D.A. (1988). An exclusionary approach to the identification of pupils with unexplained underachievement in reading. In Hales, G. (Ed.), *Meeting Points in Dyslexia – Proceedings of the First International Conference of the British Dyslexia Association*. Reading: British Dyslexia Association.

Dobbins, D.A. and Tafa, E. (1991). The 'stability' of identification of underachieving readers over different measures of intelligence and reading. *British Journal of Educational Psychology*, **61**, 155–163.

Dockrell, J. and McShane, J. (1993). *Children's Learning Difficulties: A Cognitive Approach*. Oxford: Blackwell.

Done, D.J. and Miles, T.R. (1978) Learning, memory and dyslexia. In Gruneberg, M.M., Morris, P.E. and Sykes, R.N. (Eds), *Practical Aspects of Memory*. London: Academic Press.

Dow, R. S. and Moruzzi, G. (1958). *The Physiology and Pathology of the Cerebellum*. Minneapolis: University of Minnesota Press.

Downing, J. (1973). *Comparative Reading: Cross National Studies of Behaviour and Processes in Reading and Writing*. New York: Macmillan.

Downing, J. and Leong, C.K. (1982). *Psychology of Reading*. New York: Macmillan.

Duane, D.D. (1991). Neurobiological issues in dyslexia. In Snowling, M. and Thomson, M. (Eds), *Dyslexia: Integrating Theory and Practice*. London: Whurr.

Duane, D.D. (1993a). Alertness: vigilance and wakefulness in developmental disorders of reading and attention. *Annals of the New York Academy of Sciences*, **682**, 333–334.

Duane, D.D. (1993b). Later life affective, cognitive and neurologic manifestations of developmental right hemisphere syndromes. First William Cruickshank Memorial Lectureship, International Academy for Research in Learning Disabilities, 8 October, Harvard Club, Boston, MA.

Duane, D.D. and Berman, M. (1992). Daytime somnolence by pupillometry in developmental disorders. *Sleep Research*, **21**,102.

Duane, D.D., Brennan, M.E., Clark, M. and Gottlob, L. (1993). Familial occurrence of attention deficit, reading, mood and sleep disorder in ADHD with and without reading disorder. *Annals of Neurology,* 34, 249–250.

Duane, D.D., Clark, M., Brennan, M.E. and Bryan, T. (1994). Later life neuropsychiatric concomitants of developmental right hemisphere dysfunction. *Neurology* 44 (suppl. 1), in press.

Duffy, F.H., Denckla, M.B., Bartels, P.H. and Sandini, G. (1980). Dyslexia: regional differences in brain electrical activity by topographic mapping. *Annals of Neurology,* 7, 412–420.

Duffy, F.H., Denckla, M.B., McAnulty, G. and Holmes, J.A. (1988). Neurophysiological studies in dyslexia. In Plum, F. (Ed.), *Language, Communication and the Brain.* New York: Raven Press.

Dunlop, D.B. and Dunlop, P. (1976). A new orthoptic technique in learning disability due to visual dyslexia. In Moore, S., Mein, J. and Stockbridge, L. (Eds), *Orthoptics: Past, Present, Future.* New York: Stratton Intercontinental Book Corp.

Dunn, L.M., Dunn, L.M., Whetton, C. and Pintilie, D. (1982). *British Picture Vocabulary Test.* Windsor: NFER-Nelson.

Eccles, J. C. (1989). *Evolution of the Brain: Creation of the Self.* London: Routledge.

Edwards, A.L. (1953). *Edwards Personal Preference Schedule.* Chicago, IL: Science Research Associates.

Ehri, L.C. (1983). A critique of five studies related to letter-name knowledge and learning to read. In Gentile, L.M., Kamil, M.L. and Blanchard, J. (Eds), *Reading Research Revisited,* pp. 143–153 Columbus, OH: Charles Merrill.

Ehri, L.C. and Wilce, L.S. (1987). Does learning to spell help beginners learn to read words? *Reading Research Quarterly,* 22, 47–65.

Elkonin, D.B. (1973). U.S.S.R. In Downing, J. (Ed), *Comparative Reading.* New York: Macmillan.

Elliott, C.D. (1990a). *Differential Ability Scales: Introductory and Technical Handbook.* New York: Harcourt Brace Jovanovitch. Inc., The Psychological Corporation.

Elliott, C.D. (1990b). The definition and identification of specific learning difficulties. In Pumfrey, P.D. and Elliott, C.D. (Eds), *Children's Difficulties in Reading, Spelling and. Writing.* Basingstoke: Falmer Press.

Elliott, C.D., Murray, D.J. and Pearson, L.S. (1979, 1983). *The British Ability Scales.* Windsor: NFER-Nelson

Ellis, N.C. (1981a). Information processing views of developmental dyslexia I–IV. *Dyslexia Review,* 4(1), 10–21; 4(2), 5–17.

Ellis, N.C. (1981b). Visual and name coding in dyslexic children. *Psychological Research,* 43, 201–218.

Ellis, N.C. (1990). Reading, phonological processing and STM: interactive tributaries of development. *Journal of Research in Reading,* 13(2), 107–122.

Ellis, N.C. (1994). Two small longitudinal studies of reading and spelling development. To appear in Grimm, H. and Skowronek, H. (Eds), *Language Acquisition Problems and Reading Disorders: Aspects of Diagnosis and Intervention.* New York: de Gruyter.

Ellis, N.C. and Cataldo, S. (1990). The role of spelling in learning to read. *Language and Education,* 4, 1–28.

Ellis, N.C. and Large, B. (1987). The development of reading: as you seek so shall you find. *British Journal of Psychology,* 78, 1–28.

Ellis, N.C. and Large, B. (1988). The early stages of reading: a longitudinal study. *Applied Cognitive Psychology,* 2, 47–76.

Ellis, N.C. and Miles, T.R. (1977). Dyslexia as a limitation in the ability to process information. *Bulletin of the Orton Society* (now *Annals of Dyslexia*), 27, 72–81.

Ellis, N.C. and Miles, T. (1978). Visual information processing in dyslexic children. In Gruneberg, M., Morris, P. and Sykes, R. (Eds), *Practical Aspects of Memory*. London: Academic Press.

Ellis, N.C. and Miles, T.R. (1981). A lexical encoding deficiency I: experimental evidence. In Pavlidis, G. Th and Miles, T.R. (Eds), *Dyslexia Research and its Applications to Education*, pp. 177–215. New York: Wiley.

Engelmann, S. (1992). *War Against Schools' Academic Child Abuse*. Portland, OR: Halcyon House.

Engelmann, S. and Carnine, D. (1982). *Theory of Instruction:. Principles and Applications*. New York: Irvington.

Ewert, P.H. (1930). A study of the effect of inverted retinal stimulation upon spatially co-ordinated behaviour. *Genetic Psychology Monographs*. 7, 177.

Farrall, C. (1993). *The Effects of Feuerstein's Instrumental Enrichment on Dyslexics*. Report for East Court School, Ramsgate.

Farrall, C., Thomson, M. and Watkins, E.J. (1994). Paper presented at the British Dyslexia Association Conference 1994.

Fawcett, A.J. and Nicolson, R.I. (1994a). Motor skill and dyslexia. *Journal of Motor Behaviour*, in press.

Fawcett, A.J. and Nicolson, R.I. (1994b). Phonological skill and dyslexia. *Reading and Writing*, in press.

Fawcett, A.J. and Nicolson, R.I. (1994c). Naming speed and dyslexia. *Journal of Learning Disabilities*, in press.

Fawcett, A.J., Pickering, S. and Nicolson, R.I. (1992). Development of the DEST test for the early screening for dyslexia. In Wright, S.F. and Groner, R. (Eds), *Facets of Dyslexia and its Remediation*. Amsterdam: North Holland/Elsevier.

Ferreri, C.A. and Wainwright, R.B. (1984). *Breakthrough for Dyslexia and Learning Disabilities*, p. 504. Pompano Beach: Exposition Press of Florida.

Feuerstein, R. and Jensen, M.R. (1980). The Instrumental Enrichment Programme: theoretical basis, goals and instruments. *Educational Forum*, May, 404–423.

Filipek, P.A., Kennedy, D.N., Caviness, V.S., Klein, S. and Rapin, I. (1987). In vivo MRI-based volumetric brain analysis in subjects with verbal auditory agnosia. *Annals of Neurology*, 22, 410–411.

Flesch, R. (1955). *Why Johnny Can't Read and What You Can Do about It*. New York: Harper and Brothers.

Flowers, D.L., Wood, F.B. and Naylor, C.E. (1991). Regional cerebral blood flow correlates of language processes in reading disability. *Archives of Neurology*, 48, 637–643.

France, N. (1979). *Profile of Mathematical Skills*. Windsor: NFER-Nelson.

Frederiksen, J.R. (1982). A componential theory of reading skills and their interactions. In Sternberg, R.J. (Ed.), *Advances in the Psychology of Intelligence*, Vol. 1, pp. 125–180. Hillsdale, NJ: Erlbaum.

Frederiksen, J.R. and Warren, B.M. (1987). A cognitive framework for developing expertise in reading. In Glaser, R. (Ed.), *Advances in Instructional Psychology*, Vol. 3, pp. 1–39. Hillsdale, NJ: Erlbaum.

Frederiksen, J.R., Warren, B.M. and Rosebery, A.S. (1985a). A componential approach to training reading skills: Part 1. Perceptual units training. *Cognition and Instruction*, 2, 91–130.

Frederiksen, J.R., Warren, B.M. and Rosebery, A.S. (1985b). A componential approach to training reading skills: Part 2. Decoding and use of context. *Cognition and Instruction*, **2**, 271–338.

Frith, U. (1981). Experimental approaches to developmental dyslexia: an introduction. *Psychological Research*, **43**, 97–110.

Frith, U. (1985). Beneath the surface of developmental dyslexia. In Marshall, J., Patterson, K. and Coltheart M. (Eds), *Surface Dyslexia in Adults and Children*. London: Routledge and Kegan Paul.

Frith, U. (1992). Cognitive development and cognitive deficit. *The Psychologist: Bulletin of the British Psychological Society*, **5**(1), 13–19.

Frith, U. and Snowling, M. (1983). Reading for meaning and reading for sound in autistic and dyslexic children. *British Journal of Developmental Psychology*, **1**, 320–342.

Frostig, M. (1964). *Developmental Test of Visual Perception*. California: Consulting Psychologists Press.

Gaddes, N. (1976). Prevalence and the need for the definition of learning disabilities. In Knights, R. and Bakker, D. (Eds), *The Neuropsychology of Learning Disorders*. Baltimore: University Park Press.

Galaburda, A.M. (1990). The testosterone hypothesis: assessment since Geschwind and Behan. *Annals of Dyslexia*, **30**, 18–38.

Galaburda, A.M. (Ed.) (1993) *Dyslexia and Development: Neurobiological Aspects of Extra-Ordinary Brains*. Cambridge, MA: Harvard University Press.

Galaburda, A.M. and Kemper, T.L. (1979). Cytoarchitectonic abnormalities in developmental dyslexia: a case study. *Annals of Neurology*, **6**, 94–100.

Galaburda, A.M., Rosen, G.D. and Sherman, G.F. (1989). The neural origin of developmental dyslexia: implications for medicine, neurology and cognition. In Galaburda, A.M. (Ed.), *From Reading to Neurons*, pp. 377–388. Cambridge, MA: MIT Press.

Galaburda, A.M., Sherman, G.F., Rosen, G.D., Aboitiz, F. and Geschwind, N. (1985). Developmental dyslexia: four consecutive patients with cortical anomalies. *Annals of Neurology*, **18**, 222–233.

Galaburda, A.M., Corsiglia, J., Rosen, G.D. and Sherman, G.F. (1987). Planum temporale asymmetry: reappraisal since Geschwind and Levitsky. *Neuropsychologia*, **28**(3), 314–318

Gardner, H. (1983). *Frames of Mind*. New York: Basic Books.

Gathercole, S.E. and Baddeley, A.D. (1990). Phonological memory deficits in language disordered children: is there a causal connection? *Journal of Memory and Language*, **29**, 336–360.

Gentry, J.R. (1982). Analysis of developmental spelling in GNYS AT WORK. *The Reading Teacher*, **36**, 192–200.

Georgeson, M. (1985). On seeing temporal gaps between gratings: a criterion problem for the measurement of visible persistence. *Vision Research*, **25**, 1729–1733.

Geschwind, N. (1982). Why Orton was right. *Annals of Dyslexia*, **32**, 13–30.

Geschwind, N. and Galaburda, A.M. (1985). Cerebral lateralization: biological mechanisms, association, and pathology. *Archives of Neurology*, **42**, 428–462, 521–556, 634–654.

Gesell, A., Halverson, H.M., Thompson, H., Ilg, F.L., Costner, B.M., Ames, L.B., and Armatruda, C.S. (1940). *The First Five Years of Life: A Guide to the Study of the Preschool Child*. New York: Harper and Row.

Gibson, E. and Levin, H. (1975). *The Psychology of Reading*. Cambridge, MA.: MIT Press.

Gibson, E.J. and Guinet, L. (1971). Perception of inflections in brief visual presentation of words. *Journal of Verbal Learning and Verbal Behavior*, 10, 182–189.

Gilger, J.W., Pennington, B.F. and DeFries, J.C. (1992). A twin study of the etiology of comorbidity: attention-deficit hyperactivity disorder and dyslexia. *Journal of the American Academy of Child and Adolescent Psychiatry*, 31, 343–348.

Gillingham, A. and Stillman, B.W. (1979). *Remedial Training for Children with Specific Disability in Reading, Spelling and Penmanship*. Cambridge, MA: Educators Publishing Service.

Gilmore, V.J. and Gilmore, C.E. (1968). *Gilmore Oral Reading Test*. New York: Harcourt Brace Jovanovich

Gittleman, R. (1983) Treatment of reading disorders. In Rutter, M. (Ed.), *Developmental Neuropsychiatry*. New York: Guilford Press.

Giurgea, C. and Salama, M. (1977). Nootropic drugs. *Programmes of Neuropsychopharmacology*, 1, 235–247.

Goswami, U. (1993). Orthographic analogies and reading development. *The Psychologist*, 6, 312–316.

Gough. P. and Tunmer, W. (1986). Decoding, reading, and reading disability. *Remedial and Special Education*, 7, 6–10.

Gray, W.S. (1963). *Gray Oral Reading Test*. Austin, TX: Pro-Ed.

Guilford, J.P. (1967). *The Nature of Human Intelligence*. New York: McGraw-Hill.

Guilford, J.P. (1981). *Fundamental Statistics in Psychology and Education*. London: McGraw-Hill.

Hagman, J.O., Wood, F.B., Buchsbaum, M.S., Tallal, P., Flowers, L. and Katz, W. (1992). Cerebral brain metabolism in adult dyslexic subjects assessed with positron emission tomography during performance of an auditory task. *Archives of Neurology*, 49, 734–739.

Hales, G. W. (1987). The educational experience of disabled people: irresistible force or immovable object? Paper presented to the Conference Education as Challenge and Emancipation, The Open University.

Hales, G.W, (Ed.) (1990). Meeting points in dyslexia. *Proceedings of the First International Conference of the British Dyslexia Association*. Reading: British Dyslexia Association.

Halpern, D.F. (1992). *Sex Differences In Cognitive Abilities*, 2nd edn. Hove: Lawrence Erlbaum Associates.

Hannell, G., Gole, G.A., Dibden, S.N., Rooney, K.F., Pidgeon, K.J. and McGlinchey, N.D.A. (1989). Reading improvement with tinted lenses: a report of two cases. *Clinical and Experimental Optometry*, 72, 170–176.

Hanson R.A., (1975). Consistency and stability of home environment measures related to I.Q. *Child Development*, 46, 17–24.

Harris, A.J. (1974). *Harris Tests of Lateral Dominance* Windsor: NFER-Nelson.

Harrison, B. (1988). The Harrison–Winter reading and spelling programs. *Australian Journal of Remedial Education*, 20, 1.

Haslum, M.N. (1989). Predictors of dyslexia. *Irish Journal of Psychology*, 10, 622–630.

Healy, J. (1982). The enigma of hyperlexia. *Reading Research Quarterly*, 17, 319–338.

Helfgott, E., Rudel, R.G. and Kairam, R. (1986). The effects of piracetam on short and long term verbal retrieval in dyslexic boys. *International Journal of Psychophysiology*, 4(1), 53–61.

Helfgott, E., Rudel, R.G., Koplewicz, H. and Krieger, J. (1987). The effect of piracetam on reading test performance of dyslexic children. In Bakker, D. Wilsher, C.

Dbruyne, H. and Bertin, N. (Eds), *Child Health and Development*, Vol 5. *Dyslexia and Learning Disorders*. Basel: Karger.

Helfgott, E. Rudel, R.G. and Krieger, J. (1984). Effect of piracetam on the single word and prose reading of dyslexic children. *Psychopharmacology Bulletin*, 20, 688–690.

Helveston, E.M., Weber, J.C., Miller, K., Robertson, K., Hohberger, G., Estes, R., Ellis, F.D., Pick, N. and Helveston, B.H. (1985). Visual function and academic performance. *American Journal of Opthalmology*, 99, 346–355.

Henderson, E.H. (1980). Developmental concepts of words. In Henderson, E.H. and Beers, J.W. (Eds), *Developmental and Cognitive Aspects of Learning to Spell: A Reflection of Word Knowledge*. Newark, DE: International Reading Association.

Henderson, E.H. and Beers J.W. (Eds) (1980). *Developmental and Cognitive Aspects of Learning to Spell: A Reflection of Word Knowledge*. Newark, DE: International Reading Association.

Hickey, K. (1977). *Dyslexia: A Language Training Course for Teachers and Learners.*

Hinshelwood, J. (1917). *Congenital Word-blindness*. London: H.K. Lewis.

Hornsby, B. (1984). *Overcoming Dyslexia*. London: Martin Dunitz.

Hornsby, B. and Miles T. (1980). The effects of a dyslexia-centred teaching programme. *British Journal of Educational Psychology*, 50, 236–242.

Hornsby B. and Shear F. (1974). *Alpha to Omega*. London: Heinemann.

Howell, E. and Stanley, G. (1988). Colour and learning disability. *Clinical and Experimental Optometry*, 71, 66–71.

Hudson, L. (1971). Intelligence, race and the selection of data. *Race*, 12.

Hunt, E., Lunneborg, C. and Lewis, J. (1975). What does it mean to be high verbal? *Cognitive Psychology*, 7, 194–227.

Hyde, J.R.G. (1980). The effect of an acute dose of piracetam on human performance. Unpublished doctoral dissertation, University of London School of Pharmacy.

Hynd, G.W., Hern, K.L., Novey, E.S., Eliopulos, D., Marshall, R., Gonzalez, J.J. and Voeller, K.K.S. (1993). Attention deficit-hyperactivity disorder and asymmetry of the caudate nucleus. *Journal of Child Neurology*, 8, 339–347.

Hynd, G.W., Semrud, M., Lorys, A.R. and Novey, E.S. (1990). Brain morphology in developmental dyslexia and attention deficit disorder/hyperactivity. *Archives of Neurology*, 47, 919–926.

Ingram, T.T.S. (1971). Specific learning difficulties in childhood: a medical point of view. *British Journal of Educational Psychology*, 41(1), 6–13.

Irlen, H. (1983). Successful treatment of learning disabilities. Paper presented at the 91st Annual Convention of the American Psychological Association at Anaheim, California, August.

Ito, M. (1984). *The Cerebellum and Neural Control*. New York: Raven Press

Ito, M. (1990). A new physiological concept on cerebellum. *Revue Neurologique (Paris)*, 146, 564–569.

Ivry, R. B. and Keele, S. W. (1989). Timing functions of the cerebellum. *J. Cognitive Neuroscience*, 1, 136–152.

Jackson, M.D. and McClelland, J.L. (1979). Processing determinants of reading speed. *Journal of Experimental Psychology*, 108(2), 151–181.

Jarman, C. (1988). 12 rules for good handwriting. *Handwriting Review*, 7, 8.

Jastak. J.F. (1992). *Jastak Assessment Systems Catalogue 1992–3*. Wilmington, DE: Jastak Associates.

Jastak, J.F. and Jastak, S. (1979). *Meanings and Measures of Mental Tests* (Manual: Jastak Cluster Analysis). Wilmington, DE: Jastak Associates.

Jastak, J.F. and Wilkinson, S. (1984). *Wide Range Achievement Test – Revised.* Wilmington, DE: Jastak Associates.

Jensen, A.R. (1970). Hierarchical theories of mental ability. In Dockrell, W.B. (Ed.), *On Intelligence: The Toronto Symposium on Intelligence, 1969.* London: Methuen.

Jöreskog, K.G. and Sörbom, D. (1984). *LISREL VI: Analysis of linear structural relationships by the method of maximum likelihood.* Chicago: Scientific Software.

Jorm, A. F. (1983). Specific reading retardation and working memory: a review. *British Journal of Psychology*, 74, 311–342.

Jorm, A.F., Share, D.L., McLean, R. and Matthews, D. (1986). Cognitive factors at school entry predictive of specific reading retardation and general reading backwardness: a research note. *Journal of Child Psychology and Psychiatry and Allied Disciplines*, 27, 45–54.

Joshi, R.M. and Aaron, P.G. (1991). Developmental reading and spelling disabilities: are these dissociable? In Joshi, R.M. (Ed.), *Written Language Disorders.* Boston, MA: Kluwer Academic.

Juel, C., Griffith, P.L. and Gough, P.B. (1986). The acquisition of literacy: a longitudinal study of children in first and second grade. *Journal of Educational Psychology*, 78, 243–255.

Kagan, J. (1971). *Understanding Children.* New York : Harcourt Brace Jovanovich.

Karlsen, B., Madden, R. and Gardner, E. (1984). *Stanford Diagnostic Reading Test.* New York: Harcourt, Brace, Jovanovich.

Kaufman, A.S. (1979). *Intelligent Testing with the WISC-R.* New York: Wiley.

Kavale, K. (1988). The long-term consequences of learning disabilities. In Wang, M.C., Reynolds, M.C. and Walberg, H.J. (Eds), *Handbook of Special Education: Mildly Handicapped Conditions*, Vol 2, pp. 305–331. New York: Pergamon.

Kavanagh, J. K. and Truss, T. J. (Eds) (1988). *Learning Disabilities: Proceedings of the National Conference.* Parkton, MD: York Press.

Kershaw, J. (1974). *People with Dyslexia.* London: British Council for the Rehabilitation of the Disabled.

Kunneke, P.S. and Malan, G.M. (1979). A controlled clinical trial on the effects of piracetam in epileptic children. *British Journal of Clinical Practice, 33,* 266–271.

Lahita, R.G. (1988). Systemic lupus erythematosus: learning disability in the male offspring of female patients and relationship to laterality. *Psychoneuroendocrinology*, 13, 385–396.

Lane, C. (1992). Now listen hear. *Special Children, 54,* 12–14.

Larsen, S. and Parlenvi, P. (1984). Patterns of inverted reading and subgroups in dyslexia. *Annals of Dyslexia, 34,* 195–203.

Legein, Ch. P. and Bouma, H. (1981). Visual recognition experiment in dyslexia. In Pavlidis, G. Th. and Miles, T.R. (Eds), *Dyslexia Research and its Applications to Education.* New York: Wiley.

Lehmkuhle, S., Garzia, R.P., Turner, L., Hash, T. and Baro, J.A. (1993). A defective visual pathway in children with reading disability. *New England Journal of Medicine, 328,* 989–996.

Leiner, H. C., Leiner, A. L. and Dow, R. S. (1989). Reappraising the cerebellum: what does the hindbrain contribute to the forebrain? *Behavioural Neuroscience,* 103, 998–1008.

Leiner, H. C., Leiner, A. L. and Dow, R. S. (1991). The human cerebro-cerebellar system: its computing, cognitive and language skills. *Behavioural Brain Research*, 44, 113–128.

Lennerstrand, G. and Ygge, J. (1992). Dyslexia: ophthalmological aspects 1991. *Acta Ophthalmologica*, 70, 3–13.

Leonard, C.M., Voeller, K.K.S., Lombardino, L.J., Morris, M.K., Alexander, A.W., Andersen, H.G. et al (1993). Anomalous cerebral morphology in dyslexia revealed with MR imaging. *Archives of Neurology*, 50, 461–469.

Leong, C.K. (1987). *Children with Specific Reading Disabilities*. Lisse: Swets & Zeitlinger.

Leong, C.K. (1988). A componential approach to understanding reading and its difficulties in preadolescent readers. *Annals of Dyslexia*, 38, 95–119.

Leong, C.K. (1989a). The effects of morphological structure on reading proficiency. A developmental study. *Reading and Writing: An Interdisciplinary Journal*, 1, 357–379.

Leong, C.K. (1989b). Productive knowledge of derivational rules in poor readers. *Annals of Dyslexia*, 39, 94–115.

Leong, C.K. (1991a). From phonemic awareness to phonological processing to language access in children developing reading proficiency. In Sawyer, D.J. and Fox, B.J. (Eds), *Phonological Awareness in Reading: The Evolution of Current Perspectives*, pp. 217–254. New York: Springer-Verlag.

Leong, C.K. (1991b). Modelling reading as a cognitive and linguistic skill. In Mulcahy, R. Short, R.H. and Andrews, J. (Eds), *Enhancing Learning and Thinking*, pp. 161–173. New York: Praeger.

Leong, C.K. (1992a). Cognitive componential modelling of reading in ten- to twelve-year-old readers. *Reading and Writing: An Interdisciplinary Journal*, 4, 327–364.

Leong, C.K. (Ed.) (1992b). Reading and spelling with text-to-speech computer systems [Special issue]. *Reading and Writing: An Interdisciplinary Journal*, 4, 95–229.

Leong, C.K. and Lock, S. (1989). The use of microcomputer technology in a modular approach to reading and reading difficulties. *Reading and Writing: An Interdisciplinary Journal*, 1, 245–255.

Leong, C.K. and Parkinson. M.E. (1992). Sensitivity to orthotactic rules in visual word recognition by below average readers. *Reading and Writing: An Interdisciplinary Journal*, 4, 1–17.

Leong, C.K., Simmons, D.R. and Izatt-Gambell, M.-A. (1990). The effect of systematic training in elaboration on word meaning and prose comprehension in poor readers. *Annals of Dyslexia*, 40, 192–215.

Levi, G. and Sechi, E. (1987). A study of piracetam in the pharmacological treatment of learning disabilities. In Bakker, D., Wilsher, C., Dbruyne, H. and Bertin, N. (Eds), *Child Health and Development*, Vol 5. *Dyslexia and Learning Disorders*. Basel: Karger.

Levinson, H.N. (1980). *A Solution to the Riddle Dyslexia*. New York: Springer-Verlag.

Levy, B. A. and Carr, T.H. (1990). Component process analysis: conclusions and challenges. In Carr, T.H. and Levy, B.A. (Eds), *Reading and its Development: Component Skills Approaches*. New York: Academic Press.

Levy, P. and Goldstein, H. (1984). *Tests in Education – a Book of Critical Reviews*, London: Academic Press.

Lewkowicz, N.K. (1980). Phonemic awareness training: what it is and how to teach it. *Journal of Educational Psychology*, 72, 686–700.

Liberman, I.Y. and Shankweiler, D. (1979). Speech, the alphabet, and teaching to read. In Resnick, L.B. and Weaver, P.A. (Eds), *Theory and Practice of Early Reading.* Hillsdale, NJ: Erlbaum.

Livingstone, M. S. and Hubel, D. H. (1983). Anatomy and physiology of a colour system in the primate visual cortex. *Journal of Neuroscience,* 3, 309–356.

Livingstone, M. S. and Hubel, D. H. (1987). Psychophysical evidence for separate channels for the perception of form, color, movement and depth. *Journal of Neuroscience,* 7, 3416–3468.

Livingstone, M. S., Rosen, G.D., Drislane, F.W. and Galaburda, A.M. (1991). Physiological and anatomical evidence for a magnocellular defect in developmental dyslexia. *Proceedings of the National Academy of Sciences USA,* 88, 7943–7947.

Lovegrove, W. (1986). Spatial frequency processing in dyslexic and normal readers. In Stein, J.F. (Ed.), *Vision and Visual Dyslexia.* London: Macmillan, 1991.

Lovegrove, W. and Slaghuis, W. (1989). How reliably are visual differences found in dyslexics? *Irish Journal of Psychology,* 10, 542–550.

Lovegrove, W.J., Garzia, R. P. and Nicholson, S. B. (1990). Experimental evidence of a transient system deficit in specific reading disability. *Journal of the American Optometric Association,* 61, 137–146.

Lovegrove,W.J., Heddle, M. and Slaghuis,W. (1980). Reading disability: spatial frequency specific deficits in visual information store. *Neuropsychologia,* 18, 111–115.

Lovegrove, W., Martin, F. and Slaghuis, W. (1986). A theoretical and experimental case for a visual deficit in specific reading disability. *Cognitive Neuropsychology,* 3, 225–267.

Lovegrove, W.J., Bowling, A., Badcock, D. and Blackwood, M. (1980a). Specific reading disability: differences in contrast sensitivity as a function of spatial frequency. *Science,* 210, 439–440.

Lovegrove, W.J., Martin, F., Bowling, A., Blackwood, M., Badcock, D. and Paxton, S. (1980b). Contrast sensitivity functions and specific reading disability. *Neuropsychologia,* 20, 309–315.

Lubs, H. A., Duara, R., Levin, B., Jallad, B., Lubs, M., Rabin, M., Kusch, A. and Gross-Glenn, K. (1991). Dyslexia subtypes: genetics, behaviour and brain imaging. In Duane, D.D. and Gray, D.B. (Eds), *The Reading Brain: The Biological Basis of Dyslexia.* Parkton, MD: York Press.

McCall, R.B., Appelbaum, M.I. and Hogarty, P.S. (1973). Developmental changes in mental performance. *Monographs of the Society for Research in Child Development,* 38(3), 1–83.

McCall, R.B., Hogarty, P.S. and Hurlburt N. (1972). Transitions in infant sensorimotor development and the prediction of childhood I.Q. *American Psychologist,* 27, 728–748.

McClelland, J.L. (1992). Toward a theory of information processing in graded, random, interactive networks. In Meyer, D.E. and Kornblum, S. (Eds), *Attention and Performance X~V: Synergies in in experimental psychology, artificial intelligence and cognitive neuroscience – A Silver Jubilee Volume.* Cambridge, MA: MIT Press.

McGuire, T.R. and Hirsch, J. (1977). General intelligence and heritability. In Uzgiris, I.C. and Weizmann, M.F. (Eds), *The Structuring of Experience.* New York: Plenum.

McKeown, M.G. and Curtis, M.E. (Eds) (1987). *The Nature of Vocabulary Acquisition.* Hillsdale, NJ: Erlbaum.

Manzo, A. V. (1987). Psychologically-induced dyslexia and learning disabilities. *Reading Teacher,* 40, 408–413.

Marshall, J.C. (1984). Rational taxonomy of developmental dyslexias. In Malatesha, R.N. and Whitaker, H.A. (Eds), *Dyslexia: A Global Issue*. The Hague: Martinus Nijhoff.

Marshall, J.C. and Newcombe, F. (1973). Patterns of paralexia. *Journal of Psycholinguistic Research*, **2**, 179–199.

Martin, F. and Lovegrove, W. (1984). The effects of field size and luminance on contrast sensitivity differences between specifically reading disabled and normal children. *Neuropsychologica*, **22**, 73–77.

Masland, R.L. (1984). Book Review. *Newsletter of New York Branch of the Orton Dyslexia* (November), pp. 5–6.

May, J., Williams, M. and Dunlap, W. (1987). Temporal order judgements in good and poor readers. *Neuropsychologia*, **26**, 917–924.

Miles, E. (1992). *The Bangor Dyslexia Teaching System*, 2nd edn. London: Whurr.

Miles, T.R. (1957). On defining intelligence. *British Journal of Educational Psychology*, **27**, 153–165.

Miles, T.R. (1961). Two cases of developmental aphasia. *Journal of Child Psychology and Psychiatry*, **2**, 48–70.

Miles, T.R. (1970). *On Helping the Dyslexic Child*. London: Methuen.

Miles, T.R. (1978). *Understanding Dyslexia*. Aylesbury: Hodder and Stoughton.

Miles, T.R. (1982). *The Bangor Dyslexia Test*. Wisbech: Learning Development Aids.

Miles, T. R. (1983). *Dyslexia: The Pattern of Difficulties*. Oxford: Blackwell.

Miles, T.R. (1986). On the persistence of dyslexic difficulties into adulthood. In Pavlidis, G.Th. (Eds), *Dyslexia: Its Neuropsychology and Treatment*, pp. 149–163. New York: John Wiley.

Miles, T.R. (1991). On determining the prevalence of dyslexia. In Snowling, M. and Thomson, M. (Eds), *Dyslexia: Integrating Theory and Practice*, pp. 144–153. London: Whurr.

Miles, T.R. (1993). *Dyslexia: The Pattern of Difficulties*, 2nd edn. London: Whurr.

Miles, T.R. (1994) A proposed taxonomy and some consequences. In Fawcett, A.J. and Nicolson, R.I. (Eds), *Skills and Their Development in Children with Dyslexia*. Hemel Hempstead: Harvester Wheatsheaf.

Miles, T.R. and Ellis, N.C. (1981). A lexical encoding deficiency. II. In Pavlidis, G.Th. and Miles, T.R. (Eds), *Dyslexia Research and its Applications to Education*. Chichester: Wiley.

Miles, T.R. and Haslum, M.N. (1986). Dyslexia: anomaly or normal variation? *Annals of Dyslexia*, **36**, 103–117.

Miles, T.R. and Miles, E. (1975). *More Help for the Dyslexic Child*. London: Methuen.

Miles, T.R. and Miles, E. (1990). *Dyslexia: A Hundred Years On*. Milton Keynes: Open University Press.

Miles, T.R. and Miles, E. (Eds) (1992). *Dyslexia and Mathematics*. London: Routledge.

Miles, T.R. and Wheeler T.J. (1977). Responses of dyslexic and nondyslexic subjects to tachistoscopically presented digits. *IRCS Medical Science*, **5**, 149.

Miles, T.R., Wheeler, T.J. and Haslum, M.N. (1993). Picking out dyslexics in a population of 10-year-olds. Paper delivered at the Hornsby International Conference, London.

Miller, G.A. and Gildea, P.M. (1987). How children learn words. *Scientific American*, **257**, 94–99.

Mindus, P., Cronholm, B., Levander, S.E. and Schalling, D. (1976). Piracetam-induced improvement of mental performance: a controlled study on normally aging individuals. *Acta Psychiatrica Scandinavia*, 54, 150–160.

Mitchell, D.C. (1982). *The Process of Reading*. New York: Wiley.

Moir, A. and Jessel, D. (1989). *Brain Sex*. London: Mandarin/Octopus.

Moray House (1981). *Edinburgh Reading Tests, Stages 3 and 4*. London: Hodder and Stoughton.

Morgan, W.P. (1896). A case of congenital wordblindness. *British Medical Journal*, 2, 1378.

Morris, D. (1983). Concept of word and phoneme awareness in the beginning reader. *Research in the Teaching of English*, 17 (4), 359–373.

Moseley, D.V. (1988). Dominance, reading and spelling, *Bulletin d'Audiophonologie, Annales Scientiques de l'Université Franche-Comte*, 4, 43–64.

Neale, M.D. (1989). *Neale Analysis of Reading Ability*. Windsor: NFER-Nelson.

Newman, S.P., Wadsworth, J. F., Archer, R. and Hockly, R. (1985). Ocular dominance, reading, and spelling ability in schoolchildren. *British Journal of Ophthalmology*, 69, 228–232.

Nicolson, C.D. (1990). Pharmacology of nootropics and metabolically active compounds in relation to their use in dementia. *Psychopharmacology*, 101, 147–159.

Nicolson, R.I. (1992). The cognitive operations multimedia battery. Internal report LRG 92/17, University of Sheffield.

Nicolson, R.I. and Fawcett, A.J. (1990). Automaticity: a new framework for dyslexia research? *Cognition*, 35, 159–182.

Nicolson, R.I and Fawcett, A.J. (1992). Toward the origins of dyslexia. In Kruschke, J.K. (Ed.), *Proceedings of the Fourteenth Annual Conference of the Cognitive Science Society*. Hillsdale, NJ: Erlbaum.

Nicolson, R.I and Fawcett, A.J. (1993a). Reaction times and dyslexia. *Quarterly Journal of Experimental Psychology*, 47, in press.

Nicolson, R.I. and Fawcett, A.J. (1993b). Developmental dyslexia: A learning perspective. *Cognition*.

Nowakowski, R.S. (1988). Development of the hippocampal formation in mutant mice. *Drug Development Research*, 15, 315–336.

O'Connor, P.D. and Sofo, F. (1988). Dyslexia and tinted lenses. A response to Gordon Stanley. *Australian Journal of Remedial Education*, 20(1), 10–12.

O'Connor, P.D., Sofo, F., Kendall, L. and Olsen, G. (1990). Reading disabilities and colored filters. *Journal of Learning Disabilties*, 23, 597–603.

Oakhill, J. and Garnham, A. (1988). *Becoming a Skilled Reader*. Oxford: Blackwell.

Oldfield, R.C. (1971). The assessment and analysis of handedness: The Edinburgh inventory. *Neuropsychologia*, 9, 97–113.

Orton, S.T. (1937). *Reading, Writing and Speech Problems in Children*. New York: Norton.

Palincsar, A.S. and Brown, A.L. (1984). Reciprocal teaching of comprehension-fostering and comprehension-monitoring activities. *Cognition and Instruction*, 1, 117–175.

Palmer, J., McCleod, C., Hunt, E. and Davidson, J. (1985). Information processing correlates of reading. *Journal of Memory and Language*, 24, 59–88.

Patterson, K. (1981). Neuropsychological approaches to the study of reading. *British Journal of Psychology*, 72, 151–174.

Patterson, K.E., Marshall, J.C. and Coltheart, M. (Eds) (1985). *Surface Dyslexia*. London: Erlbaum.

Pennington, B.F. (1991a). *Diagnosing Learning Disorders: A Neuropsychological Framework*. Hove: Lawrence Erlbaum Associates.

Pennington, B.F. (ed.) (1991b). *Reading Disabilities: Genetic and Neurological Influences.* Dordrecht: Kluwer

Pennington, B.F. and Smith, S.D. (1988). Genetic influences on learning disabilities: an update. *Journal of Consulting and Clinical Psychology,* 56, 817–826.

Pennington, B.F., Smith, S.D., Kimberling, W.J., Green, P.A. and Haith, N.M. (1987). Left-handedness and immune disorders in familial dyslexics. *Archives of Neurology,* 44, 634–639.

Perfetti, C. (1985). *Reading Ability.* New York: Oxford University Press.

Phillips, S., Taylor, B. and Aaron, P.G. (1985). Developmental dyslexia: Subtypes or substages? Paper presented at the Annual Convention, Indiana Psychological Association, Indianapolis, IN.

Pirenne, M.H. (1962) *Visual Acuity.* In Dawson, H. (Ed.), *The Eye,* Vol. 2. *The Visual Process.* New York: Academic Press.

Polanyi, M. (1951). *Personal Knowledge.* London: Routledge.

Popper, K.R. (1945). Against the sociology of knowledge (Chapter 23 of *The Open Society And Its Enemies*). Reprinted in Miller, D. (Ed.), *A Pocket Popper.* Glasgow: Collins (Fontana), 1983.

Porter, R. B. and Cattell, R. B. (1975). *Handbook for the Children's Personality Questionnaire.* Champaign, IL: Institute for Personality and Ability Testing.

Posner, M.I. (1993). Seeing the mind. *Science,* 262, 673–674.

Pritchard, R. A, Miles, T. R., Chinn, S. J. and Taggart, A. T. (1989). Dyslexia and knowledge of number facts. *Links,* 14(3), 17–20.

Pumfrey, P.D. (1985). *Reading: Tests and Assessment Techniques,* 2nd edn. Sevenoaks: Hodder and Stoughton.

Pumfrey P. D. (1990). Testing and teaching pupils with reading difficulties. In Elliott, C. and Pumfrey, P. (Eds), *Children's Difficulties in Reading, Spelling and Writing.* London: Falmer.

Pumfrey, P.D. and Reason, R. (1991). *Specific Learning Difficulties (Dyslexia): Challenges and Responses.* Windsor: NFER-Nelson.

Rack, J. (1994). Dyslexia: the phonological deficit hypothesis. In Fawcett, A.J. and Nicolson, R.I. (Eds), *Skills and Their Development in Children with Dyslexia.* Hemel Hempstead: Harvester Wheatsheaf.

Rack, J.P., Hulme, C. and Snowling, M.J. (1993). Learning to read: a theoretical synthesis. In Reese, H. (Ed.), *Advances in Child Development and Behavior.* Vol. 24, pp. 99–132. London: Academic Press.

Ramsey, F.P. (1931). The foundations of mathematics (Quoted in Popper, K.R. *The Open Society and its Enemies,* Chapter 11). Reprinted in Miller, D. (Ed.), *A Pocket Popper.* Glasgow: Collins (Fontana), 1983.

Rasch, G. (1960/1980). *Probabilistic Models for Some Intelligence and Attainment Tests.* Chicago, IL: University of Chicago Press.

Raven, J.C. (1958). *Standard Progressive Matrices.* London: H.K. Lewis.

Raven, J.C. (1981–1988). *Progressive Matrices and Vocabulary Scales: 1979 British Standardization and 1988 Revision.* London: H.K. Lewis or Windsor: NFER-Nelson.

Ravenette, A.T. (1961). An empirical approach to the assessment of reading retardation. *British Journal of Educational Psychology,* 31, 96–102.

Ravenette, A. T. (1985). *Specific Reading Difficulties: Appearance and Reality.* London: Newham Education Authority.

Read, C. (1971). Preschool children's knowledge of English phonology. *Harvard Educational Review,* 41, 1–34.

Read, C. (1975). *Children's Categorisations of Speech Sounds in English.* Urbana, IL: National Council of Teachers of English.

Read, C. (1986). *Children's Creative Spelling*. London: Routledge and Kegan Paul.

Richards, I.L. (1985). *Dyslexia:* A Study of Developmental and Maturational Factors Associated with a Specific Cognitive Profile. Unpublished PhD thesis, University of Aston in Birmingham.

Richardson, A. (1988). The effects of a specific red filter on dyslexia. *The British Psychological Society Abstracts*, p. 56.

Ridgway, J. (1987). *A Review of Mathematics Tests*. Windsor: NFER-Nelson.

Robinson, G. and Miles, J. (1987). The use of coloured overlays to improve visual processing – a preliminary survey. *The Exceptional Child*, 34, 65–70.

Robinson, G.L.W. and Conway, R.N.F. (1990). The effects of Irlen colored lenses on student's specific reading skills and their perception of ability: a 12-month validity study. *Journal of Learning Disabilities*, 10, 589–596.

Roethlisberger, F.J. and Dickson, W.J. (1939). *Management and the Worker*. Cambridge, MA: Harvard University Press.

Rohl, M. and Tunmer, W. (1988). Phonemic segmentation skill and spelling acquisition. *Applied Psycholinguistics*, 9, 335–350.

Rosenberger, P.B. (1990). Morphological cerebral asymmetries in dyslexia. In Pavlidis, G.Th. (Ed.), *Perspectives on Dyslexia*, Vol. I. Chichester: Wiley.

Rosner, J. and Simon, D.P. (1971). The auditory analysis test: an initial report. *Journal of Learning Disabilities*, 4, 384–392.

Rourke, B.P. and Fuerst, D.E. (1991). *Learning Disabilities and Psychosocial Functioning: A Neuropsychological Perspective*. Hove: Lawrence Erlbaum Associates.

Rudel, R.G. (1985). The definition of dyslexia: language and motor deficits. In Duffy, F.H. and Geschwind, N. (Eds), *Dyslexia: A Neuroscientific Approach to Clinical Evaluation*. Boston: Little Brown.

Rudel, R.G. and Helfgott, E. (1984). Effect of piracetam on verbal memory of dyslexic boys. *Journal of American Academy of Child Psychiatry*, 23, 695–699.

Rumelhart, D.E. and McClelland, J.L. (Eds) (1986). *Parallel Distributed Processing: Explorations in The Microstructure of Cognition*, Vol. 1, *Foundations*. Cambridge, MA: MIT Press.

Rumsey, J.M., Dorwart, R., Vermess, M., Denckla, M.B., Kruesei, M.J.P. and Rapoport, J. (1986). Magnetic resonance imaging of brain anatomy in severe developmental dyslexia. *Archives of Neurology*, 43, 1045–1046.

Runyon, K. (1991). The effect of extra time on reading comprehension scores for university students with and without learning disabilities. *Journal of Learning Disabilities*, 24, 104–108.

Rust, J., Golombok, S. and Trickey G. (1993). *WORD – Wechsler Objective Reading Dimensions*. London: Harcourt Brace Jovanovich.

Rutter, M. (1974). Emotional disorder in educational underachievement. *Archives of Diseases in Childhood*, 49, 249–256.

Rutter, M., Maughan, B., Mortimore, P. and Ouston, J. (1979). *Fifteen Thousand Hours: Secondary Schools and Their Effects on Children*. London: Open Books.

Rutter, M., Tizard, J. and Whitmore, K. (1970). *Education, Health and Behaviour*. London: Longman.

Rutter, M., Tizard, J., Yule, W., Graham, P. and Whitmore, K. (1976). Research report: Isle of Wight studies, 1964–1974. *Psychological Medicine*, 6, 313–332.

Sartain, H. (1976). Instruction of disabled learners: A reading perspective. *Journal of Learning Disabilities*, 9, 489–497.

Scheiman, M. Blaskey, P. and Ciner, E.B. (1990). Vision characteristics of individuals identified as Irlen filter candidates. *Journal of the American Optometric Association*, 61, 600–605.

Schonell, F.J. and Schonell, F.E. (1942–1955). *Schonell Reading Tests*. London: Oliver and Boyd.

Scottish Council for Research in Education (1976). *The Burt Word Reading Test*. London: Hodder and Stoughton.

Seymour, P.H.K. (1987). Developmental dyslexia: a cognitive experimental analysis. In Coltheart, M., Sartori, G. and Job, R. (Eds), *The Cognitive Neuropsychology of Language*. Basingstoke: Lawrence Erlbaum Associates.

Shaywitz, B.A., Shaywitz, S.E., Fletcher, J.M. and Escobar, M.D. (1990). Prevalence of reading disability in boys and girls. Results of the Connecticut Longitudinal Study. *Journal of the American Medical Association*, 264, 998–1002.

Shaywitz, S.E., Escobar, M.D., Shaywitz, B.A., Fletcher, J.M. and Makuch, R. (1992). Evidence that dyslexia may represent the lower tail of a normal distribution of reading ability. *New England Journal of Medicine*, 326, 143–150.

Sherman, G.F., Rosen, G.D. and Galaburda, A.M. (1989). Neuroanatomical findings in developmental dyslexia. In Von Euler, C., Lundberg, I. and Lennerstrand, G. (Eds), *Brain and Reading* (Wenner-Gren International Symposium Series). London: Macmillan.

Sigel, I.E. (1963). How intelligence tests limit understanding of intelligence. *Merrill-Palmer Quarterly*, 9(1), 39–56.

Silver, L.B. (1987). The 'Magic Cure': A Review of the current controversial approaches for treating learning disabilities. *Journal of Learning Disabilities*, 20(8), 498.

Silver, L.B. (1993). The controversial therapies for treating learning disabilities. *Child and Adolescent Psychiatric Clinics of North America*, 2, 339–350.

Simeon, J., Waters, B. and Resnick, M. (1980). Effects of piracetam in children with learning disorders. *Psychopharmacology Bulletin*, 16, 65–66.

Simeon, J.G., Volavka, J., Trites, R., Waters, B., Webster, I., Ferguson, H.B. and Simeon, S. (1983). Electroencephalographic correlates in children with learning disorders treated with piracetam. *Psychopharmacology Bulletin*, 19, 716–720.

Smith, A.T., Early, F. and Grogan, S.C. (1986). Flicker masking and developmental dyslexia. *Perception*, 15, 473–482.

Smith, F. (1973). Alphabetic writing - a language compromise? In Smith, F. (Ed.), *Psycholinguistics and Reading*. New York: Holt Rinehart and Winston.

Smith, S. (1978). *No Easy Answers*. Washington, DC: DHEW Publication.

Smith, S.D., Kimberling, W.J., Pennington, B.F. and Lubs, H.A. (1983). Specific reading disability: identification of an inherited form through linkage analysis. *Science*, 219, 1345–1347.

Smith, S.D., Pennington, B.F., Kimberling, W.J. and Ing, P.S. (1990). Familial dyslexia: use of genetic linkage data to define subtypes. *Journal of the American Academy of Child and Adolescent Psychiatry*, 29, 204–213.

Snowling, M. (1981). Phonemic deficits in developmental dyslexia. *Psychological Research*, 43, 219–234.

Snowling, M. (Ed.) (1990). *Children's Written Language Difficulties*. Windsor: NFER-Nelson.

Snowling, M. and Perin, D. (1983). The development of phoneme segmentation skills in young children. In Sloboda, J. (Ed.), *The Acquisition of Symbolic Skills*. London: Plenum.

Snowling, M. and Thomson, M. (1991). *Dyslexia: Integrating Theory and Practice*. London: Whurr.

Snowling, M. J., Stackhouse, J. and Rack, J. (1985). Phonological dyslexia and dysgraphia: developmental aspects. *Cognitive Neuropsychology*, 3, 309–339.

Snowling, M.J., Goulandris, N., Bowlby, M. and Howell, P. (1986). Segmentation and speech perception in relation to reading skill: a developmental analysis. *Journal of Experimental Child Psychology*, 41, 487–507.

Solman, R.T. and May, J.G. (1990). Spatial localization discrepancies: a visual deficit in reading. *American Journal of Psychology*, 103, 243–263.

Solman, R.T., Cho, H-S. and Dain, S.J. (1991). Colour-mediated grouping effects in good and disabled readers. *Ophthalmic and Physiological Optics*, 11, 320–327.

Spache, G. D. (1976). *Investigating the Issues of Reading Disabilities.* Boston: Allyn and Bacon.

Spalding, R.B. and Spalding, W.T. (1986). *The Writing Road to Read.* New York: Morrow.

Spearman, C.E. (1927). *The Abilities of Man.* New York: Macmillan.

Spring, C. and Capps, C. (1974). Encoding speed, rehearsal and probed recall of dyslexic boys. *Journal of Educational Psychology*, 66, 780–786.

Stanley, G. (1991). Glare, scotopic sensitivity and colour therapy. In Stein, J.F. (Ed.), *Dyslexia.* London: Macmillan.

Stanley, G., Howell, E. and Marks, M. (1988). Eye dominance and reading disability. International Congress of Psychology, August , Sydney.

Stanley, G.V. (1977). Visual information processing and specific reading disability (dyslexia). In Day, R.H. and Stanley, G.V. (Eds), *Studies in Perception.* Nedlands: University of Western Australia Press.

Stanovich, K. (1986). Matthew effects in reading: some consequences of individual differences in the acquisition of literacy. *Reading Research Quarterly*, 21, 360–407.

Stanovich, K.E. (1988). The right and wrong places to look for the cognitive locus of reading disability. *Annals of Dyslexia*, 38, 154–177.

Stanovich, K.E. (1991). The theoretical and practical consequences of discrepancy definitions of dyslexia. In Snowling, M. and Thomson, M. (Eds), *Dyslexia: Integrating Theory and Practice.* London: Whurr.

Stanovich, K.E. (1993). The construct validity of discrepancy definitions of reading disability. In Lyon, G.R., Gray, D.B., Kavanagh, J.F. and Krasnegor, N.A. (Eds), *Better Understanding Learning Disabilities.* Baltimore: Paul H. Brookes.

Stanovich, K.E. (1994). Two conceptually-rich longitudinal studies: comments on the research of ellis. To appear in Grimm, H. and Skowronek, H. (Eds), *Language Acquisition Problems and Reading Disorders: Aspects of Diagnosis and Intervention.* New York: de Gruyter.

Stanovich, K., Cunningham, A. and Cramer, B. (1984). Assessing phonological awareness in kindergarten children: issues of task comparability. *Journal of Experimental Child Psychology*, 38, 175–190.

Stein, J.F. (1989). Visuospatial perception and reading problems. *Irish Journal of Psychology*, 10, 521–533.

Stein, J.F. and Fowler, M.S. (1984). Ocular motor problems of learning to read. In Gale, A.G. and Johnson, F. (Eds), *Theoretical and Applied Aspects of Eye Movement Research.* Amsterdam: Elsevier.

Stein, J.F., Riddell, P.M. and Fowler, M.S. (1986). The Dunlop test and reading in primary school children. *British Journal of Ophthalmology*, 70, 317–320.

Sternberg, R.J. (1985). *Beyond IQ: A Triarchic Theory of Human Intelligence.* New York: Cambridge University Press.

Stirling, E. G. (1987). *Help for the Dyslexic Adolescent.* Llandudno: St David's College.

Stratton, G.M. (1896). Some preliminary experiments on vision. *Psychological Review*, 3, 611.

The Sunday Times (1985). Glasses hope for dyslexia. 22 December.

Taft, M. (1987). Morphographic processing: The BOSS re-emerges. In Coltheart, M. (Ed.), *Attention and Performance XII: The Psychology of Reading*, pp. 265–279. London: Lawrence Erlbaum Associates.

Tallal, P. (1980). Language and reading: some perceptual requisites. *Bulletin of the Orton Society* (now *Annals of Dyslexia)*, 30, 170–178.

Tallal, P., Miller, S. and Fitch, R.H. (1993). Neurobiological basis of speech: a case for the preeminence of temporal processing. *Annals of the New York Academy of Sciences*, 682, 27–47.

Tallal, P., Chase, C., Schmitt, L. and Russell, G. (1984, 1985) Piracetam effects with dyslexia; results from the San Diego study. In Conners, C.K. (Chair), *Effects of Nootropics on Dyslexia*. Symposium presented at the 13th Annual International Neuropsychological Society Meeting, San Diego, California, USA, 6-9 February 1985 and abstract published in *The INS Bulletin*, November 1984, 73–74.

Terman, L.M. and Merrill, M.A. (1960). *Stanford–Binet Intelligence Scale*. London: Harrap.

Thomson, M.E. (1982). The assessment of children with specific reading difficulties (dyslexia) using the British Ability Scales. *British Journal of Psychology*, 73(4), 61–78.

Thomson, M.E. (1984). *Developmental Dyslexia: Its Nature, Assessment and Remediation*. London: Edward Arnold.

Thomson, M.E. (1988). Preliminary findings concerning the effects of specialised teaching on dyslexic children. *Applied Cognitive Psychology*, 2, 19–33.

Thomson, M.E. (1990a). *Developmental Dyslexia: Its Nature, Assessment and Remediation*, 3rd edn. London: Whurr.

Thomson, M.E. (1990b). Teaching programmes for children with specific learning difficulties: implications for teachers. In Elliott, C. and Pumfrey, P. (Eds), *Children's Difficulties in Reading, Spelling and Writing*. London: Falmer.

Thomson, M.E. (1991). The teaching of spelling using techniques of simultaneous oral spelling and visual inspection. In Snowling, M. and Thomson, M. (Eds), *Dyslexia: Integrating Theory and Practice*. London: Whurr.

Thomson, M.E. and Newton, M. (1982). *Aston Index (Revised)*. Cambridge: Learning Development Aids.

Thomson, M.E. and Watkins, E.J. (1991). *Dyslexia: A Teaching Handbook*. London: Whurr.

Treiman, R. (1993). *Beginning to Spell*. New York: Oxford University Press.

Treiman, R. and Hirsh-Pasek, K. (1985). Are there qualitative differences in reading behaviour between dyslexics and normal readers? *Memory and Cognition*, 13(4), 357–364.

Turner, M. (1993). Testing times (two-part review of tests of literacy). Part 1, *Special Children*, 65, 12–16, April 1993; Part 2, *Special Children*, 66, 12–14, May 1993.

Vadjoda, C. (1974). *The Kodaly Way to Music*. London: Boosey & Hawkes.

van den Bos, K. (1989). Relationship between cognitive development, decoding skill, and reading comprehension in learning-disabled Dutch children. In Aaron, P.G. and Joshi, R.M. (Eds), *Reading and Writing Disorders in Different Orthographic Systems*. Boston, MA: Kluwer Academic.

Van Hout, A. and Giurgea, D. (1990). The effects of piracetam in dyslexia. *Approche Neuropsychologique des Apprentisages chez l'Enfant*, 3, 145–152.

Van Orden, G.C. (1987). A rows is a rose: spelling, sound, and reading. *Memory and Cognition*, 15, 181–198

Vellutino, F.R. (1979). *Dyslexia: Theory and Research*. Cambridge, MA: MIT Press.

Vellutino, F.R., Steger, J.A. and Kandel, G. (1972). Reading disability: an investigation of the perceptual deficit hypothesis. *Cortex*, **8**, 106–118.

Vellutino, F.R., Smith, H., Steger, J.A. and Kamin, M. (1975). Reading disability: age differences and the perceptual deficit hypothesis. *Child Development*, **46**, 487–493.

Vernon, M.D. (1971). *Reading and its Difficulties*. Cambridge: Cambridge University Press.

Vernon, P.E. (1960). *Intelligence and Attainment Tests*. London: University of London Press.

Vernon, P.E. (1977). *Graded Word Spelling Test*. London: Hodder and Stoughton.

Vernon, P.E. (1979). *Graded Arithmetic-Mathematics Test*. London: Hodder and Stoughton.

Vincent, D., Green, L., Francis, J. and Powney, J. (1983). *A Review of Reading Tests*. Windsor: NFER-Nelson.

Volavka, J., Simeon, J., Simeon, S., Cho, D. and Reker, D. (1981). Effect of piracetam on EEG spectra of boys with learning disorders. *Psychopharmacology*, **72**, 185–188.

Warnock, M. (1978). *Special Educational Needs (Report of the Committee of Enquiry into the Education of Handicapped Children and Young People)*. London: HMSO.

Wason, P.C. (1959). The processing of positive and negative information. *Quarterly Journal of Experimental Psychology*, **11**, 92–107.

Wechsler, D. (1976). *Wechsler Intelligence Scale for Children – Revised (WISC-R)*. New York: The Psychological Corporation.

Wechsler, D. (1981). *The Wechsler Adult Intelligence Scale (Revised)*. New York: The Psychological Corporation.

Wechsler, D. (1983). *Wechsler Adult Intelligence Scale*. New York: The Psychological Corporation.

Wechsler, D. (1992). *Wechsler Adult Intelligence Scale for Children – 3rd edn, UK*. Sidcup, Kent: The Psychological Corporation.

Wechsler Individual Achievement Test (1992). New York: The Psychological Corporation.

Wedl, W. and Suchenwirth, R.M.A. (1977). Effects of the GANA derivative piracetam double-blind study in healthy probands. *Nervenarzt*, **48**, 58–60.

Wepman, J.M. (1973). *Auditory Discrimination Test*. Windsor: NFER-Nelson.

West, T.G. (1991). *In the Mind's Eye. Visual Thinkers, Gifted People with Learning Difficulties, Computer Images, and the Ironies of Creativity*. Buffalo, NY: Prometheus Books

Wilkins, A. (1991). Visual discomfort and reading. In Stein, J.F. (Ed.), *Dyslexia*. London: Macmillan.

Williams, A. L. and Miles, T. R. (1985). Rorschach responses of dyslexic children. *Annals of Dyslexia*, **35**, 51–66.

Williams, M.C. and Bologna, N.B. (1985). Perceptual grouping in good and poor readers. *Perception and Psychophysics*, **38**, 367–374.

Williams, M.C. and LeCluyse, K. (1990). Perceptual consequences of a temporal processing deficit in reading disabled children. *Journal of The American Optometric Association*, **61**, 111–121.

Williams, M.C., Brannan, J.R. and Lartigue, E.K. (1987). Visual search in good and poor readers. *Clinical Vision Sciences*, **1**, 367–371.

Wilsher, C.R., Atkins, G. and Manfield, P. (1979). Piracetam as an aid to learning in dyslexia: preliminary report. *Psychopharmacology*, **65**, 107–109

Wilsher, C.R., Bennett, D., Chase, C.H., Conners, C.K., Dilanni, M., Feagans, L., Hanvik, L.J., Helfgott, E., Koplewicz, H., Overby, P., Reader, M.J., Rudel, R.G. and Tallal, P. (1987). Piracetam and dyslexia: effects on reading tests. *Journal of Clinical Psychopharmacology*, 7, 4.

Winter, S. (1987). Irlen Lenses: an appraisal. *Australian Education and Development Psychologist*, 4(2), 1–5.

Wittrock, M.C. and Baker, E.L. (Eds) (1991). *Testing and Cognition*. Englewood Cliffs, NJ: Prentice Hall.

Wolff, P.H., Michel, G. F. and Ovrut, M. (1990). Rate and timing precision of motor coordination in developmental dyslexia. *Developmental Psychology*, 26, 349–359.

Wong, B.Y.L. (1985). Self-questioning instructional research: a review. *Review of Educational Research*, 55, 227–268.

Woodcock, R.W. (1987). *Woodcock Reading Mastering Tests*, revised edn. Circle Pines, MN: American Guidence Service.

World Federation of Neurology (1968). *Report of Research Group on Dyslexia and World Illiteracy*. Dallas, TX.: World Federation of Neurology.

Young, D. (1976). *SPAR (Spelling and Reading) Tests*. London: Hodder and Stoughton.

Young, P. and Tyre, C. (1983). *Dyslexia or Illiteracy*. Milton Keynes: Open University Press.

Yule, W. and Rutter, M. (1976). Epidemiology and social implications of specific reading retardation. In Knight, R.M. and Bakker, D.J. (Eds), *The Neuropsychology of Learning Disorders*. Baltimore: University Park Press.

Yule, W., Rutter, M., Berger, M. and Thompson, J. (1974). Over- and under-achievement in reading: distribution in the general population. *British Journal of Educational Psychology*, 44, 1–12.

Index